THE LIBRARY OF HOLOCAUST TESTIMONIES

Journey through Darkness
Monowitz, Auschwitz, Gross-Rosen, Buchenwald

The Library of Holocaust Testimonies

Editors: Antony Polonsky, Sir Martin Gilbert CBE, Aubrey Newman,
Raphael F. Scharf, Ben Helfgott MBE

Under the auspices of the Yad Vashem Committee of the Board of
Deputies of British Jews and the Centre for Holocaust Studies,
University of Leicester

My Lost World by Sara Rosen
From Dachau to Dunkirk by Fred Pelican
Breathe Deeply, My Son by Henry Wermuth
My Private War by Jacob Gerstenfeld-Maltiel
A Cat Called Adolf by Trude Levi
An End to Childhood by Miriam Akavia
A Child Alone by Martha Blend
The Children Accuse by Maria Hochberg-Marianska and Noe Gruss
I Light a Candle by Gena Turgel
My Heart in a Suitcase by Anne L. Fox
Memoirs from Occupied Warsaw, 1942–1945
by Helena Szereszewska
Have You Seen My Little Sister?
by Janina Fischler-Martinho
Surviving the Nazis, Exile and Siberia by Edith Sekules
Out of the Ghetto by Jack Klajman with Ed Klajman
From Thessaloniki to Auschwitz and Back
by Erika Myriam Kounio Amariglio
Translated by Theresa Sundt
I Was No. 20832 at Auschwitz by Eva Tichauer
Translated by Colette Lévy and Nicki Rensten
My Child is Back! by Ursula Pawel
Wartime Experiences in Lithuania by Rivka Lozansky Bogomolnaya
Translated by Miriam Beckerman
Who Are You, Mr Grymek? by Natan Gross
Translated by William Brand
A Life Sentence of Memories by Issy Hahn, Foreword by Theo Richmond
An Englishman in Auschwitz by Leon Greenman
For Love of Life by Leah Iglinsky-Goodman
No Place to Run: A True Story by Tim Shortridge and
Michael D. Frounfelter
A Little House on Mount Carmel by Alexandre Blumstein
From Berlin to England and Back: Experiences of a Jewish Berliner by Peter Prager
By a Twist of History: The Three Lives of a Polish Jew by Mietek Sieradzki
The Jews of Poznań by Zbigniew Pakula
Lessons in Fear by Henryk Vogler
To Forgive … But Not Forget: Maja's Story by Maja Abramowitch

Journey through Darkness

Monowitz, Auschwitz,
Gross-Rosen, Buchenwald

WILLY BERLER

Preface by SIMON WIESENTHAL

Prepared and annotated by
RUTH FIVAZ-SILBERMANN

Translated from French by MARTINE MITRANI
and ANNETTE CHARAK

VALLENTINE MITCHELL
LONDON • PORTLAND, OR

First published in 2004 in Great Britain by
VALLENTINE MITCHELL
Crown House, 47 Chase Side, Southgate
London N14 5BP

and in the United States of America by
VALLENTINE MITCHELL
c/o ISBS, 920 NE 58th Avenue, Suite 300
Portland, Oregon 97213-3786

Website: www.vmbooks.com

British Library Cataloguing in Publication Data
Berler, Willy
    Journey through darkness: Monowitz, Auschwitz,
    Gross-Rosen, Buchenwald. – (The library of Holocaust testimonies)
    1. Berler, Willy 2. Holocaust, Jewish (1939–1945) – Personal narratives
    3. Jews, Belgian – Biography
    I. Title
    940.5'318'092

    ISBN 0-85303-469-9 (paper)
    ISSN 1363-3759

Library of Congress Cataloging-in-Publication Data
Berler, Willy, 1918–
    [Itinéraire dans les ténèbres. English]
    Journey through darkness: Monowtiz, Auschwitz, Gross-Rosen, Buchenwald/Willy
    Berler; preface by Simon Wiesenthal; translated from the French by Martine Mitrani
    and Annette Charak.
        p. cm. – (The library of Holocaust testimonies)
    Footnotes and appendices by Ruth Fivaz-Silbermann.
    Includes bibliographical references (p.).
    ISBN 0-85303-469-9 (pbk.)
    1. Auschwitz (Concentration camp) 2. Monowitz (Concentration camp)
    3. Gross-Rosen (Concentration camp) 4. Berler, Willy, 1918– 5. Holocaust, Jewish
    (1939–1945) – Belgium – Personal narratives. 6. Buchenwald (Concentration camp)
    I. Fivaz-Silbermann, Ruth. II. Title. III. Series.

    D805.5.A96B4713 2003
    940.53'185–dc22

                                                                    2003057613

Typeset in 11/13pt Palatino by Vallentine Mitchell
Printed and bound in Great Britain by MPG Books Ltd, Bodmin, Cornwall

Ce livre est dédié à ma chère épouse, Ruth, décédée à Bruxelles le 30/09/2003. Pendant nos 56 années de vie commune harmonieuse elle m'a, après les années noires de la guerre, redonné le goût de la vie.

Contents

List of Maps and Illustrations

Between pages 140–141

1. *Hasmoneah*, Czernowitz, 1936–37. Willy is the third from right, on the bottom row.
2. Willy Berler at the Agricultural School, Mikveh Israel, Israel, 1937.
3. The agricultural research buildings at Rajsko.
4. Crematorium IV, Birkenau, in spring 1943, just closed. Picture taken by the SS in 1943.
5. *Kommandant* Arthur Liebehenschel.
6. *Rapportführer* Gerhard Palitzsch.
7. A view of the Buna factories, taken from a documentary film about the liberation of the camp by the Red Army in 1945.
8. Inspection of the building site at Buna by *SS-Reichsführer* Heinrich Himmler, 17–18 July 1942, accompanied by the engineer Max Faust of I.G. Farben and the *Kommandant* of the camp, Rudolf Hess. Picture taken by an unknown SS.
9. Men carrying a tree trunk. Drawing by an ex-prisoner, Mieczyslaw Koscielniak.
10. Carrying corpses to the crematorium. Drawing by Léon Delarbre.
11. Corpses of *musulmen*.
12. Dysentery in the Small Camp: drying the trousers. Drawing by Léon Delarbre.

Acknowledgements

The author sincerely wishes to thank all the following for their kind collaboration and help with testimonies and advice: Rosa Goldstein, Brussels; Odette Abadi, Paris; Fred Weiss, Brussels; Dr Willy Dehon, Brussels; Mr Van Praag, Brussels; J. Ph. Schreiber, Brussels; J.J. Heirwegh, Brussels; Josef Rudel, Israel; Isabella Gabor, Vienna; Professor A. Polonsky, USA; Professor A. Friedman, USA; Anthony Rudolf, London; Rabbi John Rayner, London; and Marion Schreiber, Brussels.

I would also like to thank those individuals and institutions who gave me kind permission to reproduce the illustrations in this book: The State Museum of Auschwitz; Janina Siwek ('Executions at the Black Wall'); Ursula Koscielniak ('Men carrying a tree trunk'); and The Jewish Museum of Deportation and Resistance, Malines.

The Library of Holocaust Testimonies

It is greatly to the credit of Frank Cass that this series of survivors' testimonies is being published in Britain. The need for such a series has long been apparent here, where many survivors made their homes.

Since the end of the war in 1945, the terrible events of the Nazi destruction of European Jewry have cast a pall over our time. Six million Jews were murdered within a short period; the few survivors have had to carry in their memories whatever remains of the knowledge of Jewish life in more than a dozen countries, in several thousand towns, in tens of thousands of villages, and in innumerable families. The precious gift of recollection has been the sole memorial for millions of people whose lives were suddenly and brutally cut off.

For many years, individual survivors have published their testimonies. But many more have been reluctant to do so, often because they could not believe that they would find a publisher for their efforts.

In my own work over the past two decades I have been approached by many survivors who had set down their memories in writing, but who did not know how to have them published. I also realized, as I read many dozens of such accounts, how important each account was, in its own way, in recounting aspects of the story that had not been told before, and adding to our understanding of the wide range of human suffering, struggle and aspiration.

With so many people and so many places involved, including many hundreds of camps, it was inevitable that the historians and students of the Holocaust should find it difficult at times to grasp the scale and range of events. The publication of memoirs is therefore an indispensable part of the extension of knowledge, and of public awareness of the crimes that had been committed against a whole people.

Sir Martin Gilbert
Merton College, Oxford

Preface

Numerous are those among us camp survivors who have, one way or another, been liberated from their nightmares by putting on paper their memories, while others have buried them in the depths of their being, that being the only way to bear the crushing weight.

The story of Willy Berler's 'Way of the Cross' starts with the attack on the 20th Belgian convoy from Mechelen to Auschwitz, an extraordinary act of resistance. His tale then relates the arrival at Monowitz, his fortuitous transfer to the main camp of Auschwitz, and the story of his friend's $100 which would ultimately save both their lives in Buchenwald. It tells of the executions at the Black Wall, which Willy Berler was forced to watch, and the special *kommando* of the SS Hygiene Institute of Rajsko, which has been relatively undocumented. Finally, it describes the death march, and Willy Berler's chance meeting with an SS murderer from his hometown who spoke Yiddish better than he did.

But the narrator does not only describe the horror. His story is also a tale of solidarity and friendship in humanity in a dehumanised universe. Friends, chance, and especially good luck, saved him in that hell, allowing him to survive.

Willy Berler tells his story simply and directly, touching the reader and leaving him moved. The Geneva historian Ruth Fivaz-Silbermann has provided a remarkable document with her footnotes and appendices, putting the tale in its historic context. The commentary confers on this book an almost pedagogical quality, bringing with it a better knowledge and understanding of the Nazi concentration camp universe. This book, with its strong historical foundation, is well worth reading, especially for young people.

I believe that our written testimonies, although they may seem familiar in many details, are important for the future. The more of such testimonies that exist, the less future generations will be able to deny the *Shoah* or portray the Third Reich as harmless.

Simon Wiesenthal

Introduction

Who among us watches from this strange observatory to warn of the
arrival of new torturers? Are their faces really different from ours?

Jean Cayrol, *Nuit et Brouillard* [*Night and Fog*]

In spring 1943, if a young person who arrived in Auschwitz was
reasonably strong and no longer a child he would be fortunate
enough to be sent to the right during selection. He could not
know or understand the unspeakable choice to which he had
just been subjected, and that at that very moment he had
escaped immediate death by cyanide Zyklon B gassing. Having
passed to the right side, he had become an inmate, recorded as
such by the administration of the Auschwitz-Birkenau
complex.

The selection on arrival marked the line between annihilation without commemoration and elimination through work.
The names and exact number of all the Jews who went into the
eight gas chambers will never be known, because the
SS-Reichsführer Himmler had issued orders to destroy on
arrival the precise and well-documented lists of convoys. (The
eight gas chambers were: in the main camp, the *Bunker* basement, and later the crematorium cellar; in Birkenau, two small
farms in the forest, and later the four big death factories.) The
elderly (considered so from the age of about 45), children of 15
or younger, pregnant women or mothers with small children,
babies, the disabled, and all those judged on sight to be 'redun-
dant', immediately disappeared into oblivion. They were not
killed, but destroyed. The act of killing a person implies that he
is considered an equal, maybe even a rival, but at the very least
a human being, while here, humanity was denied even as life

was taken, and they were killed with a gas intended to exterminate lice, bugs, cockroaches.

When a whole community suffers a common fate, the names and memories of its individuals disappear with them.

On entering any camp in the concentration camp complex, inmates fell under the rule of a different logic: not extermination but elimination, which meant elimination through work. They became the duly registered property of the SS administration. Had Germany won the war, these well-documented registration lists would have been kept; these camps were meant to exist as long as 'sub-humans' and 'social misfits' existed. Only the collapse of the Nazi regime led to their dissolution.

As soon as the Jewish inmate received his registration number, he was singled out from others who, like him, were not criminals. He was given a distinctive badge: a Star of David made up of two yellow triangles, or a red triangle superimposed on a yellow one for 'political' Jews. The other non-criminals were political prisoners and Resistance fighters – from Germany, Poland, France and other countries – Russian prisoners of war, gypsies, Jehovah's Witnesses and homosexuals. As an additional form of victimisation, Jews were forbidden to receive parcels, and as late as 1944 they were still subject to internal selections at the infirmary. Nevertheless, all inmates basically shared the same fate. There were less differences horizontally, between the prisoners of different 'colours', than in the vertical hierarchy, from the naïve novice at the lowest level, the *Zugang* [novice], the cannon fodder of the concentration camp machine, to the *Prominenter* [VIP], the high-ranking official, certain of his power and his food rations. Prisoners at the bottom of the ladder were faced with the absolute rule of the SS organisation and of the intervening inmate-officials. Those at the top of the ladder were a little less exposed to it. Benedikt Kautsky commented[1] that the system functioned on the

---

1. Quoted in H. Langbein, *Menschen in Auschwitz* (Wein: Europa-Verlag), p. 101.

principle that he who has will be given more; but from him who has nothing, all will be taken.

Everything is arbitrary in this ideology which rules without mercy, starting with the principle of legitimacy that it claims for itself. However, once adopted as a governing principle, by the Nazi State or inside the concentration camp, and internalised by the SS individual as the ultimate ideal, this ideology becomes frighteningly coherent. It abandons all principles of justice, pity or respect. It is steeped in the Neo-Darwinian ideology of racial superiority, which grants absolute dominance to the 'Aryan', and dooms to enslavement or total extinction the races deemed inferior. The ideology is all the more dangerous as it abolishes all divergent ideas, in particular divine sovereignty, and all moral codes based on respect for life and human integrity, be they Judeo-Christian or secular. The 12 years of Nazi rule succeeded in eliminating or forcing underground any social or political view that did not accord with Nazism. In this lay its totalitarianism.

Survivors' stories are the purest means through which to enter a universe which can now be said to defy all comprehension, being beyond words and imagination. Yet this universe was built by men with a terrifying efficiency, using human means: a political world in which they pursued their own goals and careers.

There is no better portrayal of that universe than the story of one man who was caught in a roundup and lived to tell his story. After this story, one will want to read others. One needs to identify with this journey and with those of others in order to recognise the infinite variety of experiences. Although there were several million martyrs, a reader can identify more easily with the tale of one individual.

'Who survived?', asks Paul Steinberg, another survivor of the house of death:

> The only common denominator between the survivors seems to me to be an unquenchable thirst for life, and the flexibility of a contortionist. I do not believe in the pure, hardened hero who endured all ordeals, without

xvii

compromise, head held high. Not in Auschwitz. If such a man exists, I have not met him, and his halo must make sleep very uncomfortable.[2]

This is true. And yet, what are these compromises he speaks of? For Willy Berler, there was never any compromise with the SS power, never any temptation to put himself above the ordinary prisoner. The only time he is offered a 'promotion', to be a *Vorarbeiter* [foreman], he refuses: to accept means that he would have to punish those men working for him, or receive their punishment himself. The blackmail of this system is intolerable. He could refuse, and as he doesn't see himself as a hero, he does refuse. He does make concessions though, but only to the system of survival within the camp; he learns about 'organising', a necessary condition for surviving on the official food rations which were calculated to ensure the inmate's death within six to twelve weeks.

Love of life is another factor of survival. The 25-year-old man who arrives in Monowitz in April 1943 is psychologically well-balanced, level-headed and in very good physical condition. As time goes by, he learns to be flexible; he is surprised, at first, at this quality in his friend Michel, at both the moral and the physical level. The rest is luck. Each step in this journey through darkness, between destruction and hope, is guided by luck. Willy's luck is similar to that famous $100 bill that Michel takes to Auschwitz, which he manages to keep hidden through all the searches. When they are almost at the end of their journey, luck will meet up with that $100 bill; or rather, it will be luck incarnate for them.

We are about to read an escape story. After 50 years, the tone of the story is neither accusatory, nor tear-jerking. The narrator of this tale has survived, and later read many testimonies and history books, without ever detaching himself emotionally from his past; that would be impossible. As he relives this hell step by step, he is still distressed by it.

---

2.   P. Steinberg, *Chroniques d'ailleurs: Récit* (Paris: Ramsay, 1996), p. 59.

Introduction

Every survivor of the Nazi concentration camps has seen and lived something that other people have not. We need all the testimonies, all the memories, to extract from the abstraction of numbers the complex historical truth. A written testimony is an act of resistance which has not lost its value; after all, wiping out the name and memory of the inmates was conceived as an act of war, and destruction of the Auschwitz archives was planned from the fall of Majdanek in July 1944, for fear that the truth be known outside. Only five per cent of prisoners came back from the camps. To tell their story is their greatest victory against the carefully programmed elimination of their personality, name and future. Let this also serve as a monument to all those who did not come back, so that their memories should not be obliterated.

Willy Berler's unedited story has been corroborated by other sources, and enriched thanks to historical research. It sheds new light on what we already know, and enhances our knowledge of the concentration camps and the *Shoah*.

The authors would like to thank the following, for their help, advice and careful reading: Mr Maxime Steinberg, Brussels; The Centre for Contemporary Jewish Documentation in Paris, in particular its librarian, Ms Sara Halperyn; Mr Ward Adriaens, curator of the Jewish Museum of the Deportation and the Resistance in Mechelen; Mr Giovanni Busino, Lausanne; Mr Damien Mannarino, Paris; Ms Rosa Goldstein, Brussels; Ms Odette Abadi, Paris; Mr Fred Weiss, Brussels; Dr Willy Dehon, Brussels; Mr Paul Van Praag, Brussels; Mr Jean-Philippe Schreiber, Brussels; Mr Jean-Jacques Heirwegh, Brussels; Mr Joseph N. Rudel, Petah Tikva; finally, Mr Pierre Dido for his unconditional support, Ms Isabelle Gabor and Ms Josette Alhadeff, my tireless archivist.

Ruth Fivaz-Silbermann
Geneva
20 April 1998

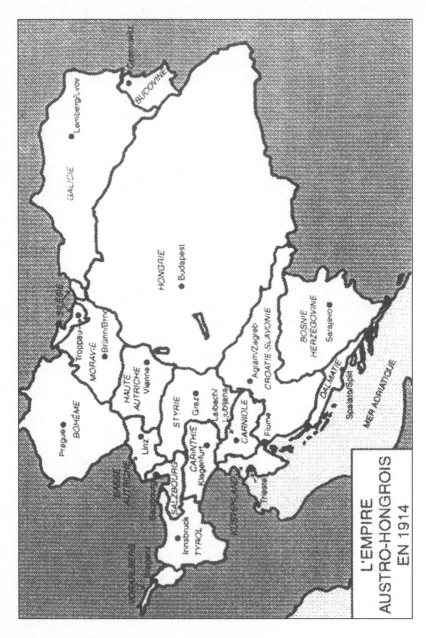

1. The Astro-Hungarian Empire, 1914–1918.

1 A Young Bourgeois Jew from the East

When I came into the world in April 1918 in Bucovina – a province in the far east of the immense Hapsburg Empire, even further east than Galicia – the Great War was still raging. The Austro-Hungarian Empire was declining; it would soon lose the war and break up. At the time of my birth, my father was still at the front, fighting under the Austro-Hungarian flag. We were Jews of the Empire, Austrian citizens. My father had been called up, as had his four brothers. As Jews, we considered our position in the Empire most satisfactory, even enviable. Hadn't Emperor Franz-Joseph granted the Jews of his nations and territories the same rights as all other citizens, such as freedom to practise religion, freedom to settle and trade? It was a blessed period for the Jews, and in return, we were good and loyal citizens. The youngest of my uncles proved his loyalty with his blood, falling in the battle of Isonzo before I was born. In 1916, when Emperor Franz-Joseph died, my father cried, and this was duly reported in the family chronicles.

My family was well established in Czernowitz, the capital of Bucovina. I had a brother six years older than me. My father was a man of the land and a merchant of reasonable means, having gradually purchased his brother's and sister's shares in the land that their father had left them. My mother was a city girl from Tarnopol, a nearby town in Austrian-Polish Galicia. At that time, Jews controlled much of the agriculture and agricultural trade. My father's businesses were prosperous and he exported cattle far beyond the borders of his province and his country. We were clearly part of the middle class, the bourgeoisie.

In 1918, Bucovina had been an Austrian province for 150 years. Its capital, Czernowitz, had grown to become a town of

1

the Empire, in marked contrast to its rural surroundings. The town had a German university, the most easterly German university in Europe. Of its some 100,000 residents, the Jews were in the majority. The rest of its population was comprised of several minorities: some civil servants of the Austrian administration, Germans, Romanians, Ukrainians (who at that time were known as Ruthenians), Poles, gypsies, and some Hungarians. Originally, the Jews had all spoken Yiddish, but as they fell under the Austrian influence and they became more modern, their level of culture rose and some had started speaking German a few generations earlier. My family belonged to that Jewish circle considered 'enlightened', the *maskilim*, and my first language was German.[1]

In this town of diverse cultures, we learned other languages easily, even if only at a basic level. The maid who took care of me was originally from one of the Ruthenian villages around the capital.[2] So, during my early childhood, I learned basic Ruthenian, which was actually Ukrainian. In kindergarten and elementary school I spoke German. In that period, after the Great War when the Empire was breaking up, Bucovina was re-annexed to Romania, and from then on, Bucharest imposed

---

1. On the *Haskala* [Jewish Movement of Lights], see Steven Beller, *Vienna and the Jews 1867–1939: A Cultural History* (Cambridge: Cambridge University Press, 1990). During that period, two linguistic schisms occurred within the Jewish community. Yiddish, the language of the people, was introduced in the sixteenth century by the Ashkenazis when they fled persecution in Germany. But, in the Austro-Hungarian Empire, the well-to-do spoke German. A cultural Yiddish revival started, however, in the twentieth century, with a very active theatre and press, allowing those social classes – which until then had been excluded – to access culture. The second schism, more political, occurred between the supporters of Yiddish as the national language of the Jewish people (namely the Bundists) and those who opted for Hebrew as the revival language (namely the Zionists). However, in the Diaspora, both sides expressed themselves in the local language; here, German. German remained the official language in Bucovina, even after Romanization in 1918 and continued to be legally recognised in addition to Romanian until 1924. It remained, if not the legal, then the *de facto*, language until 1944.
2. In the Austro-Hungarian Empire, the name 'Ruthenian' is reserved for the Subcarpathian Ukrainian population, followers of the Uniate Church, founded in 1596. The Subcarpathian Ukraine was separated from Hungary in 1919 and given to Czechoslovakia; it was then returned to Hungary after the 1938 Munich Agreements. Bucovina, which is southeast of that region, had a large Ruthenian population. This was used as a justification for the re-annexation of northern Bucovina to the Soviet Republic in 1945, at which time the south was returned to Romania.

systematic Romanianization. The name 'Czernowitz' was officially changed to 'Cernauty'. However, this did not stop Austrian structures from continuing to prevail for several years, particularly in schools. German continued to be the main spoken language in the town, and that was not only due to the Jews. There was a sizeable German minority in Bucovina, descendants of the Germans brought there by Empress Marie-Therese in the eighteenth century. Despite Romanian domination, the general atmosphere and character of Czernowitz remained distinctly German.

I went to a series of high schools; each nationality in the town had its own school. I finished my schooling at the Ukrainian Lyceum, where my friend, Gerdi Krauthammer, and I were the only Jews. We were taught in Romanian, with some courses in Ukrainian. I completed high school in 1936, all the exams being in Romanian.

One day in Auschwitz, years later, a political prisoner joined my *kommando*. He was a member of the Iron Guard, arrested and deported by the Germans after the failed fascist *putsch* against the dictator Antonescu.[3] In one of the often-inexplicable turns of deportation, this man mistakenly ended up in Auschwitz. I tried to speak to him in Romanian, but found that I had forgotten that language after the shock and abuse I had experienced on arriving in the camp. Today, I again understand and speak Romanian.

Although brought up with German culture, I was still considered a Romanian citizen of Jewish nationality. While I lived in Czernowitz, I held first Austrian papers, and then a Romanian passport, but I never felt Austrian, or Romanian, for that matter. After 1918, for a while, we considered the Romanians an occupying force! In my youth, I felt a kind of

---

3. The Iron Guard – founded in 1931 by Corneliu Zelea Codreanu – was inspired in a similar fashion to the Italian Fascist Party, and in 1937, it became the third Romanian party. Its leader, Horia Sima, became the council's vice-president in Marshal Antonescu's government. In January 1941, Sima led an attempted *putsch* with the help of the German secret services; but with the help of the *Wehrmacht*, Antonescu managed to bloodily suppress it. Fearing a possible Russian attack, Hitler preferred to support Antonescu's government rather than the legions of the Guards. Many of those involved in the *putsch* were deported to Buchenwald.

personal nationality, a national sense of belonging to the Jewish people, which never really left me. The Jews, like the Hungarians or Ruthenians, were considered an ethnic minority in Romania: a separate nationality. My nation, to be more exact, was that part of the Jewish people living in Romania. This concept was unique to Romania and couldn't be compared with other countries where Jews were full citizens, such as France. Still, even today, I have difficulty conceiving that one could be a French Jew, a Belgian Jew, or an Australian Jew. I am a Jew, and that is a nation; a stateless nation at the time of my youth, but today, a nation with its own Jewish state.

The political conditions of that period contributed significantly to the formation of my Jewish identity. The Jewish ethnic minority in Romania had the same rights as other nationalities: Poles, Hungarians or Ukrainians. However, although those rights were recognised on paper, the Romanian authorities did not always – not to say, rarely – respect them. Each ethnic minority elected its representatives, who sat in the Romanian parliament. They were genuine elections; candidates represented four Jewish parties[4] – two middle-class parties, and one party originating in the *Bund*. The Jewish organizations reflected a wide range of ideologies. *Hashomer Hatzair*[5] was a socialist, leftist organization, and at the other extreme was *Betar*, with 'revisionist'[6] views. My sympathies

---

4. Jewish political life was very active before Romanization, with many political parties: the United Party; the Popular Council; the General Zionists; the Revisionists; *Mizrachi*; the Radical Zionists; the Jewish State Party; the Social Democrats; the International Social Democrats; *Poalei-Zion*; and *Hashomer Hatzair* (see Sternberg, *Zur Geschichte der Juden in Czernowitz* (Tel Aviv: Olamenu, n.d.), p. 33; and M. Reifer, 'Geschichte der Juden in der Bukowina, 1919–1944', in H. Gold (ed.), *Geschichte der Juden in der Bukowina*, 2 Vols (Tel Aviv: Olamenu Publishers, 1958/1962), p. 1.

5. This was a left-wing Zionist movement, revolutionary and collectivist, which focussed on creating Kibbutzim in Palestine. *Hashomer Hatzair* was an important youth movement and was powerful in Czernowitz from 1922.

6. So called because it demanded that the Zionist movement should review its acceptance of Churchill's 1922 White Paper which prohibited Jews from colonising Transjordan, where the British had installed the Hashemite King. Created after 1918, this movement worked tirelessly for the right of the Jewish State to occupy the whole of Palestine; it incarnated, at the extreme right of the political spectrum, a middle-class Zionism – lucid, pessimistic, authoritarian and aggressive. *Betar*

were with the middle class – which was mildly right wing – but I also felt some admiration for Betar's leader, Jabotinsky,[7] who had exceptional charisma. Once, I think it was 1936, he came to give a talk in Czernowitz and arrived late. After waiting over two hours, the crowd received him with a delirious ovation. Not that I feel the comparison is pleasant, nor do I consider it appropriate, but I cannot help thinking that at the same period, the German crowd was hailing Hitler with similar ovations.

The other decisive factors in my youth were student Zionist organizations, in which I was active. For the large Jewish community of Czernowitz, the Zionist ideal had played a very important role from its inception, and I was inculcated with Zionism from a very young age. Almost all young, middle-class Jews belonged to one of the student Zionist organizations.

Student life was very lively in Czernowitz, as was all social and cultural life. Courses in dancing and etiquette were very popular. Quadrille dancing animated lively social evenings and ballrooms. But there were also more serious activities. I still recall with pride how I gathered for myself a library of Zionist works, volume by volume. We also organised interesting mock trials. As many of us were law students, there were prosecutors, lawyers, a judge, experts and a jury. The public voted its verdict. Our favourite subjects for these mock trials were the controversial characters of Joseph Flavius from *La Guerre des Juifs* [The War of the Jews] and *Jud Süss* [Jew Süss] by Leon Feuchtwanger.

The student clubs were formed according to nationalities, and some were similar to German *Burschenschaften*. The students wore decorative uniforms, practised fencing duels,

---

(*Brith Hanoar al Shem Josef Trumpeldor* – named after the Russian founder of the Jewish Legion of Palestine) was founded in Riga in 1923; this was the Revisionist youth movement, which organised itself as a real militia and, in 1939, numbered 100,000 followers in several countries (see E. Barnavi, *Une histoire moderne d'Israël*, 2nd edn (Paris: Flammarion/Champs, 1988), p. 58.

7.   Vladimir (Zeev) Jabotinsky, journalist and man of letters, was born in Odessa in 1880, was educated in Switzerland and in Italy, and fought in the Jewish Legion of Palestine. He admired Garibaldi's romantic nationalism and he fought against the Zionist Labour 'establishment'. He left the Zionist movement in 1939 and in 1935 – together with his Revisionist troops – created the New Zionist Organisation (see Barnavi, *Histoire moderne*, p. 57).

and drank while raucously singing *Gaudeamus* (Latin student songs), etc. There was one German, one Polish, one Ukrainian, one Romanian and four or five Jewish societies. After high school, I became a member of the *Hasmonea*,[8] quite an old organization, which had been founded by Jewish students of Czernowitz on their return from Vienna, the place where the Zionist idea[9] had originated and blossomed. During my high school years, even before I entered university, I was already part of the *Davidia* high school association, which was a preparatory step for the student organizations. There I met a boy a bit younger than myself, who read a lot and was already writing poetry. He was Paul Antschel – the future great poet, Paul Celan – who, soon after the war, declared the final judgment in German: 'Der Tod ist ein Meister aus Deutschland … ' [Death is a Master out of Germany …]. He was to leave *Davidia* soon after for a political association with stronger leftist affiliations.[10]

In 1936, after my final exams, I asked my parents' permission to go to Palestine for a month. I was obsessed with the idea of returning to the land. I didn't want to follow any of the traditional careers that interested the young middle class. I actually thought there were already too many doctors and lawyers in Czernowitz, and there couldn't possibly be enough work for all of them.

I arrived in Palestine during the Arab revolt,[11] and I travelled throughout the country with a backpack, going from one kibbutz to the next. I managed to get hired at the port of

---

8. The *Hasmonea* was created in 1891 by Mayer Ebner as an offshoot of *Kadima*. Ebner was a future Zionist leader from Bucovina. The four Jewish student societies of Bucovina were allowed to continue their activities under the more or less deomo-cratic Romanian rule, until around 1936, when they became forbidden.
9. Theodor Herzl was Viennese, and Vienna was the home of the World Zionist Organisation, originally founded in Basle in 1897 during the First Zionist Congress.
10. Paul Antschel was born in 1920 and died in Paris in 1970. On his youth in Czernowitz, see J. Felstiner, *Paul Celan: Poet, Survivor, Jew* (London: Yale University Press, 1995), pp. 3–21. The verse is taken from the poem 'Todesfuge' (see Paul Celan, *Mohn und Gedächtnis*, Stuttgart: Deutsche Verlags Anstalt, 1952).
11. The years 1936 and 1937 were marked in Palestine by violent Arab uprisings against both the Jewish settlers and the British administration. These riots were called *moraoth*.

Tel Aviv, which was then being built. After working in agriculture and construction, I felt good about life in Palestine, despite my short stay. The country was still under the British Mandate, with only about half a million Jewish residents. One reason for my stay was to find a way to immigrate. Great Britain had very strict quotas on Jewish immigration, authorising only a trickle of immigrants, and I was losing hope. However, I eventually found a little-known way. All I needed was to register as a student at the University of Jerusalem, which had been founded in 1926, or in a professional school. University had no appeal for me. I was determined to find a manual profession. I wanted to return to the land. I then discovered the School for Agriculture in Mikveh Israel near Tel Aviv, which had been founded by the *Alliance Israélite Universelle de Crémieux*,[12] an organisation that supported schools around the Mediterranean.

After this brief exploratory visit, I returned to Romania and announced my decision to my parents: I wanted to be a farmer in Israel. My emigration project may even have come as a relief to them, as Hitler's shadow was already looming over Europe, and I convinced them. Of course, in Czernowitz and elsewhere for that matter, we were still unaware of what was about to happen. But we did know, from centuries of abuse and pogroms, that Hitler's politics were bad news for the Jews. Events in Germany already testified to that.

I went back to Palestine in 1937 to start a full programme of agricultural studies at the Mikveh Israel school. It was hard work. We learned to plough, to cut hay; we learned about fruit cultivation in orange groves, breeding cattle, raising chickens; and we were even introduced to ironworks. The climate was also very trying, much hotter and drier than today, because there were fewer trees. Forestation would change the country's climate in later years. But, as hard as it was, the teaching at

---

12. The *Alliance Israelite Universelle* (Universal Israeli League) was created in 1860 in France by a group of young Republicans and Liberal Jews, with the goal of encouraging instruction of the Jewish populations found around the Mediterranean basin (including Syria and Persia). It founded many elementary and professional schools, one of which was the first farming school in Mikveh Israel in 1870. Adolphe Cremieux became its president in 1864.

Mikveh Israel turned out to be a blessing for me. It hardened me, got me used to manual labour, and taught me physical endurance. Without knowing it, I was preparing myself to survive the slavery of Auschwitz better than many others.

Meanwhile, my parents had been thinking it over, and as my apprenticeship year was coming to an end, they reconsidered my future. Like any self-respecting Jewish middle-class family, they wanted their doctor or engineer. My older brother came to convince me to come home, and I let myself be convinced. I gave in when I was promised that I could study in the European country of my choice and that I could travel. They told me that I could always go back and settle in Palestine later. I then took a decision that would have dire consequences: I returned to Romania.

My father kept his promise, and in 1938, I left for the West. Of course, this was quite a prestigious undertaking for a young Jew from Bucovina who knew only his province and the Jewish settlements in Palestine. As I had not changed my mind, expecting to eventually settle in Palestine, I decided to study in Great Britain, under the protection of the Mandatory Power. After two or three weeks in Paris, I arrived in London, with the idea of becoming a chartered accountant. To be a company auditor seemed an intelligent choice. Unfortunately, the year was already too advanced for me to join, and I couldn't register for courses. I don't remember exactly what my considerations were, but I ultimately decided to study in Belgium. There was at least the financial reason; the Belgian franc was very low, and I realised I could live much better in Belgium on the allowance from my father.

I was still determined to learn a real trade, a useful trade. I registered in the Liège Tannery School, which offered a course in chemistry applied to tannery. It was a two-year course, at the end of which I would get a technical diploma in chemistry, with an option to complete a degree at the University of Lyon and become a Tannery Engineer. I liked the arrangement, and settled in Liège on 1 January 1939. Until May 1940, I led a studious life, working hard at my courses and reading a lot. I had already started recording in little notebooks all my readings and the important events in my life. I immersed myself in French civilization and culture; I devoured French books, including translations of German writers. The year went by delightfully, with me deeply involved in books including *Les Thibault* by Roger Martin du Gard, and *Les Hommes de bonne volonté* by Jules Romains.

Two of my childhood friends came to study with me in Belgium. Fred Weiss and Gerdi Krauthammer had registered at the Textile School in Verviers, 30 kilometres from Liège. During that period in Liège, I also fell in love for the first time. C. was a very pretty girl, and after a while, she moved into my small student flat with me. At the same time, Hitler was lashing out, galvanising crowds into action, trampling the rights of nations by annexing first Austria, and then Sudetenland, and then Bohemia-Moravia, and dispossessing German Jews of their rights, of their belongings, and of their freedom. While the war was brewing, I was in Belgium, leading the quiet life of a student.

The day Hitler invaded Poland, we were enjoying our summer holiday. I was 21 years old. Fred, Gerdi and I were cycling across Belgium, sleeping in youth hostels. On 1 September 1939, the war caught us in Knokke-le-Zoute, an upper middle-class holiday resort. What did we feel? Worry? Definitely. We had met Jews from Germany who had fled Hitler's regime, and we were aware of living in a troubled and, indeed, a dangerous period. But who among us could ever have imagined the magnitude of the calamity that was to befall the Jews? We returned home, with the understanding that if the situation worsened, Gerdi and Fred would join me in Liège.

Before beginning this story, I must mention that, from 1938, I had developed the habit of recording daily in my notebooks the things I did, lived or read. These notebooks are the foundation of my memory. I updated them regularly until 1 April 1943, the day I was arrested. The two terrible years of my deportation, until my liberation from Buchenwald, are therefore missing. It was unthinkable and dangerous to write in the

9

camps; it could have resulted in death.[13] Once repatriated and nursed back to health, my main concern was to piece together the notebooks of 1943, 1944 and 1945, to remember, to note the daily events and atrocities that had gone on while those pages remained blank. Alas, my memory had also been devastated; fear had damaged it badly, as had hunger, violence, exhaustion and disease. It was absolutely essential that I date each of the stages as accurately as possible, while I still remembered. And so, I reconstructed my daily notes, inevitably approximating some dates. Reordering events chronologically allowed me to pass them on. In 1945, however, I didn't know to whom I could pass them on. Today, 50 years later, some of these precious notes have become incomprehensible to me, and I now regret having made them so brief. Part of the horrifying experience is lost to my memory. However, the essential facts remain.

I must also mention something that I feel is essential to properly understanding the following pages. Most readers who have not studied this subject in depth have a uniform notion of the camps, all bathed in the same horror. It is, of course, undeniable that the whole concentration camp universe had common traits, as Solzhenytsin solemnly wrote in *A Day in the Life of Ivan Denisovitch*: hunger, harassing work, lack of hygiene, the terrifying wait for what tomorrow would bring, and the feeling, every night, that another day had gone by.

However, despite those startling similarities, within this concentration camp universe there were enormous differences. First, we need to differentiate between the German *Konzentrationslager* (KZ) and the Soviet Gulag. The Russians did not select, did not gas, and had no defined policy for eliminating certain ethnic groups. However, what I most wish to underline is that there was a world of difference between one KZ and another, and within one camp from one period to another. They cannot all be lumped together. The purpose of German KZ disciplinarian camps (like Sachsenhausen, Dachau and

---

13. See A. Wieviorka, *Déportation et génocide: Entre la mémoire et l'oubli* (Paris: Plou, 1992), p. 192 ff.

Buchenwald) was different from extermination camps (like Treblinka, Majdanek and Auschwitz, and especially Birkenau). There were also smaller annexed camps, the so-called work camps, like Fürstengrube or Jawischowitz, where one died very quickly in the coal mines, the salt mines and the quarries. The disciplinarian camps had no provision for mass extermination (although Sachsenhausen did have one gas chamber), and the political inmates took over their internal control in the early days of the war. Despite many common traits, the differences in conditions of life and death in these two kinds of camps were far greater than those, for example, between a Brazilian *Favela* and the Hotel Ritz in London: consider the contrast between the paved streets of the main camp of Auschwitz, its brick buildings, its bunk beds for one person, and the foul muddy paths of Birkenau, where one sank in a mix of sludge and excrement in almost any season, those uninhabitable barracks, meant to stable *Wehrmacht* horses and their *kojas* [bunks], ten or more women stacked together for the night. I have seen enough horrors in the work camps to last me a lifetime and yet I was still shocked when, 25 years after my liberation, I went to Birkenau. I had never been in Birkenau, although for a year and a half, I was just three kilometres away from it, in the main camp of Auschwitz.

Just as working conditions, abuse and chances of survival varied enormously within the same KZ, depending on the period, so did conditions in Auschwitz vary from one year to the next. When I arrived in Auschwitz in 1943, I couldn't believe or even imagine, when told, the things that had occurred a few months earlier. Finally, I want it to be known that survival in the camps was due to at least 95 per cent chance and luck (the first lucky stroke was not to be gassed on arrival). The other five per cent was a combination of language skills (especially German, some Polish/Russian/Ukrainian, some Yiddish and even some French), age, physical condition, a good mental state, the will to live, and finally, being assigned to a good *kommando*.

11

Probably like all survivors who, at some time, have decided to put down on paper their terrible experiences, I stress that what I have to say, including the most minute details, is to bear witness to the unbearable injustice that was done to us. These are all precise charges against our torturers. I declare my testimony to be the truth, and nothing but the truth, and I take on the oath formulated by Andre Lettich:[14]

> I solemnly swear to tell the truth, and nothing but the truth, and to report in these pages only what I witnessed or what was told to me by those of my companions in misfortune who could be fully trusted. I have systematically dismissed any rumour or fantasy, and I have told only my experiential truth.

---

14. See the Introduction in A. A. D. Lettich, *Trente-quatre mois dans les camps de concentration* (Tours: Imprimerie Union coopérative, 1946), p. 14.

2 Exodus and Mousetrap

The day I became prey to the Nazis was the day the war broke out on the Western Front, the day the Germans invaded Belgium: 10 May 1940.

At 9 a.m. of the morning following that ill-fated day, my friends, Fred and Gerdi, burst into my flat, having sped by bike across the 30 kilometres that separated Verviers from Liège. They tell how they were constantly overtaken by German troops surging behind them while they were pedalling frantically towards the haven of my home. This time, we must face the fact that it is war; the Germans are in Belgium.[1] The strange war – which was also a strange kind of peace – was real. Yet the three of us, wedged together in my tiny abode, almost forget our fears for a moment: wasn't Liège well protected by its massive fortifications, the Eben-Emaël fort?

What a pathetic illusion! Liège would be taken after only two hours of battle. I tell my friends they are welcome to stay in my shack if they wish, but I am leaving. I am often asked what we knew then, in May 1940, about Hitler's intentions, whether we felt threatened in France or in Belgium. For me, the answer is easy. Hitler meant pogroms, *Kristallnacht* [The Night of Broken Glass], and brutal violence against Jews. From 1933, I saw Germans as anti-Semites. It was impossible, therefore, for me to think of remaining even one second longer in an area or country under their occupation. I had to flee. After some

---

1. On 11 May, German parachutists staged a surprise attack and took the bridges over the Albert Canal and, later, the powerful modern fort of Eben-Ebaël, which protected the region around Liège. The 6th German Army, under von Reichenau's command, entered Belgium. Liège fell on 13 May, and all her forts were taken and disarmed soon thereafter.

discussion, the three of us decide to leave together.[2] While battles rage in Liège, Fred Weiss, Gerdi Krauthammer and I escape on bikes, on 12 May at 10 a.m. The only possible route is south, to France. However, the road we need to take continues on the other side of the river Meuse. Just as we reach the river, the Belgian Army is blowing up the last bridges to try and stop the German advance. We have just crossed the bridge when it blows up. On we go, pedalling furiously towards the French border, which we reach on the 13th. We are finally there ... and we cannot cross because Fred's passport has expired. The three of us hold Romanian passports, and he is refused entry into France. What now? The only answer is for Fred to go to a Romanian consulate to renew his papers.

We must therefore return to the heart of Belgium. But our bikes are so damaged that it is impossible for us to continue by bike. Resigned, we take a train to Mons. I climb aboard the train with my friends unaware that one of the most dangerous episodes of my life is about to take place, even more dangerous than my camp experience! In the middle of the countryside, the train stops. Belgian soldiers arrive to check the passengers. I am wearing puffy golf pants (Tintin-style), town shoes and long white socks, looking quintessentially German! What we don't know then, but find out later, is that German soldiers had parachuted down into the area and the Belgians thought that some of them had managed to board the train. Fred, Gerdi and I are sitting in our compartment when the door suddenly opens, and two soldiers, their guns pointed at us, yell at us to raise our hands. One brusque movement ... and they will not hesitate to shoot.

In those early days of exodus and panic, a number of German Jews seeking refuge in France had been arrested by

---

2. On the eve of the German invasion, there were about 70,000 Jews in Belgium, the majority in Antwerp and Brussels and a few thousand in Liège and Charleroi (see M. Steinberg, *La Question juive (1940–1942)* (Brussels: Vie ouvrière, 1983), p. 99). Ninety-three per cent of them did not have Belgium citizenship, most having immigrated in the 1920s and 1930s (40 per cent from Poland and 19 per cent from Austria and Germany; Steinberg, *Question juive*, p. 76). In the early days of the war, there was a mass exodus, mainly to the south of France: only 15– 20,000 would not return to Belgium (see M. Steinberg, 'La *Shoah* en Belgique', *Les Cahiers de la Shoah*, 3 (1996), p. 60).

the Belgian Army and some were killed: everyone was understandably on full alert for spies in Belgium, and the soldiers were extremely nervous.

With the guns still pointed at us, we are asked to show our papers. Our Romanian passports perplex them. Still, they don't arrest us, and although they let us continue our trip, one of their soldiers is posted to watch us. We arrive in Mons, and we want to get off the train, through the door of one of those old-fashioned carriages that give directly onto the platform without a corridor, when a gun is suddenly pointed at our chests. We are expected. They had called to identify us! While the young Belgian officer demands to see our papers, we launch into a flurry of confused explanations: 'I study in Liège, my friends in Verviers ..'.

'Ah, in Verviers? Where?'

'At the Textile School'.

'Is that so? As it happens I was also a student at the Textile School. So tell me, what is the name of the professor of mathematics?'

Fred and Gerdi give his name.

'And the chemistry professor?'

Fred gives his name, too. The young officer's tone softens. We are extraordinarily lucky to have been able to convince him. He lets us go. We could very well have been taken away and executed as spies by the Belgian police, like other German Jews.

We find shelter for the night in the Mons Conservatory. In the middle of the night, the building is shelled. We wake and spend the rest of the night in trenches.

One war and an eternity later, I will discover that during the bombing, a young German–Jewish girl, who was to become my wife, had spent that same night in exactly the same place. Thousands of Jews fleeing Hitler's army have started their exodus to France.[3]

---

3. Of the 64,000 Jews in Belgium before 10 May 1940, 34,442 survived or returned; it is estimated that 25,000 Jews survived hidden in Belgium and 28,518 deportees from Belgium and France died during deportation. In the case of Belgium, these statistics refers to those persons nominally identified as Jewish (M. Steinberg, *Las Traque des Juifs*, 2nd Vol., Brussels: Vie ouvrière, 1986, p. 259).

The following day, on 14 May, while Fred goes to look for the Romanian consulate in Brussels, Gerdi and I go in the opposite direction. We take a train to the French border. Before reaching the border, near Erquelinnes, we notice French tanks coming towards us. It is a moment of intense emotion; the courageous French Army is coming to the rescue of little Belgium! The French are going to teach those German barbarians a lesson! I see tiny Renault tanks advancing, like little ants. I also see a French officer, standing, buttoned up tight in an old dark blue uniform probably dating from 1914. My throat tightens with overwhelming emotion and tears come to my eyes; those Germans, they'll get what they deserve! The passengers of the train start singing the *Marseillaise*. My throat is tight; I feel I am going to cry.

Surprise: in Erquelinnes, a border post a few kilometres from Maubeuge, we unexpectedly meet my girlfriend from Liège. Although she is not Jewish, the German invasion terrifies her, and she has decided to leave with her sister and join the exodus. Naturally, we decide to stay together. Here we are, four young people, two boys and two girls, sitting in a train rolling away, taking us who knows where, as long as it is far from Belgium and even further from the Germans.

Suddenly, the train stops. German *stukas* start bombing the train. We jump out. Passengers run and scatter though the surrounding fields. Indescribable panic ensues. Bombs continue to fall. A group forms beside me; they fall on their knees and pray. The group grows and in its midst, a Catholic priest leads the prayer. It is very moving.

At the same time, a frightened woman, her clothes betraying her middle-class status, runs along the carriages, asking at each window:

'A bottle, don't you have a bottle?'

'What do you want a bottle for?'

'I need to pee ... '

The train goes on. In Paris, where we want to stop, we are not allowed to disembark because the capital refuses to take in refugees from Belgium. Not knowing that the truce would be short – as Paris would fall a month later – we go on to the south and, after three days of travel, find ourselves in the village of Saint-Georges d'Orques, in Hérault. It is a village of wine growers. The locals take in the refugees and give them work in the vineyards. We are put up by Mrs Vidal, who owns a sizeable farm and many vineyards. Her husband and two sons have been drafted. We work there from 20 May to 6 June. It is an eerily euphoric period, because most of the time we are tipsy from the alcohol. And, whenever we can, C. and I sneak out behind the vineyards and make love. Those 15 days pass in a dreamlike haze.

Yet one incredible scene stays engraved in my mind. The day after the king of the Belgians surrendered, on 28 May, the president of the French Cabinet, Paul Reynaud, gives a speech on the radio that will become famous.[4] We are sitting opposite a huge chimney, in Mrs Vidal's large kitchen, workers and helpers, all in all about 30 boys and girls. Our boss is cutting a gigantic loaf of bread with an enormous knife, when we hear Paul Reynaud on the radio dragging the name of Belgium and King Leopold III through the mud. Mrs Vidal, whose two sons and husband were trapped at the front in Maginot, stops cutting the bread and, turning towards our little group, with the knife still in her hand and a menacing look on her face, asks:

---

4. King Leopold III surrendered on 27 May. The French Army was taken by surprise in the Ardennes by an attack carried out with Guderian tanks, and lost the battle in the north. The Allied forces were trapped in the Dunkirk fold and the British recalled their scout unit. The question still remains as to Reynaud's intentions when he decided, in his speech of 28 May, to make the 'traitor king' take the blame for the humiliating situation of the Allied forces. He must have expected that his words would turn the French against the Belgian refugees:

> France can no longer rely on the Belgian Army. Since 4 a.m., the French and the British Armies have been fighting alone against the enemy in the north...the Belgian Army [was defending our front] in the north. It is this same Belgian Army that has suddenly surrendered unconditionally in open country, by order of the king...Without a backward look, without a word for the French and British soldiers who had come to rescue his country at his frightened request, King Leopold III of Belgium surrendered his arms. This is unprecedented in history...

(J. Benoist-Méchin, *Soixante jours qui ébranlèrent l'Occident (10 Mai–10 juillet 1940)*, 2nd edn (Paris: Laffont/'Bouquins', 1981), p. 216.)

In a declaration made on the same day, Churchill, more just and moderate, gives the Belgian Army its due.

17

'You're Belgians, aren't you?'

Terrified, we answer as one: 'No, no, not Belgians, we are Romanians ... '

At that time, as I am passing through Montpellier, I see Frenchmen behaving aggressively towards Belgian officers and treating them like traitors. It is extremely unpleasant. As if the French Army itself had not also been crushed and captured in the north! There seems to be no solidarity, no fraternity between Hitler's defeated, between the enemies of Germany. The hope for revenge could bind them but, on the contrary, Paul Reynaud's words sowed in France an unnecessary resentment of Belgium.

On 6 June 1940, with a vague sense that our vacation is over, Gerdi and I leave Saint-Georges d'Orques to go to Lyon. I decided to apply to the university's School of Chemistry and continue my studies. I am not received well: no money, a refugee, and a Jew! It is true that the battle for France is raging, the line at the Somme has been broken, and to some extent, French public opinion is already facing possible defeat and an armistice with the Germans. That day on the radio, Paul Reynaud describes Nazi Germany as 'an oppressive regime, where men who are not of German blood will only serve as slaves. Orders, bullying ... the physical and moral destruction of the elite ... the Middle Ages without the moderating light of Christ'.[5] Fear, humiliation, uncertainty: the French don't know what to expect. And do we know?! In the general débâcle, who will worry about two Romanian-Jewish refugees?

The next day, still accompanied by Gerdi, I visit the Honorary Consul of Romania in Lyon. The Consul is a Frenchman, a veteran of the First World War, who welcomes us graciously. The radio is on as we talk. News from the French front is very bad. This is history in the making; the collapse of the French Army is imminent. The Consul bursts into tears. Moved, we remain silent.

What now? We have no job, and no money. Still, as we do have some sort of chemistry training, we start looking for work

---

5. See Benoist-Méchin, *Soixante jours*, p. 306.

18

in that field. To our surprise, we are hired by the chemical factories of the Rhône, a major enterprise that will become Rhône-Poulenc. It is Saturday. On Monday, 17 June, we set off for our first day of work only to be told that they cannot take us. The Germans are approaching, and Lyon has been declared an open city. To prevent destruction, Lyon will, like Paris, allow itself to be occupied.

We are devastated. What now? Indeed, two days later, the town is completely occupied by the Germans. We no longer know where to go so we stay put, waiting for some indication of the way to safety. The Armistice of 22 June finds us in Lyon, as undecided as ever and with no resources.

We soon learn that the Armistice provides for German refugees to be handed over to Germany. All the Jews who fled the Reich to the French zone now find themselves on German military-occupied territory and will therefore be 'returned'. We are afraid to even imagine their fate. Panic is taking over. Despite our Romanian passports, we feel that nothing is certain anymore. We must flee the Germans, as far south as possible. Fortunately, we have work permits for the Rhône factories, enabling us to get special assignment permits for non-occupied territory. They let us take the train as far as Marseilles, where we find shelter as Belgian refugees in a school serving as an accommodation centre.

The centre houses about 300 refugees, including a group of 30 Polish aviators who are waiting to leave for London and 25 Belgian rail workers. Gerdi and I are the only students and the only Jews. There are also two communist members of the International Brigade – one German, the other Romanian – neither is Jewish, although, to my knowledge, very few non-Jewish Romanian communists joined the Brigade during the Spanish Civil War. As we have little in common with either the Polish aviators or the Belgian rail workers, we mainly associate with these two communists. The organisation sheltering us treats us well. We are given lentil soup to eat, which I find inedible, but for which I will bitterly yearn later in Auschwitz! We are even given a small allowance, a few francs to spend on outings. As we have nothing to do, we go swimming in the rocky bay of Marseilles. It is wonderful!

Nevertheless, we must find something to get us out of there. Maybe we can return to Romania. On 2 July, we seek advice from the Rabbi of Marseilles, thinking that he will be able to help us leave France. We are prepared for anything, but unfortunately he has nothing to offer us. He himself is overwhelmed with the problems of the Jewish refugees in the transit camps near Marseilles[6]: 'You do understand, don't you, that I must first take care of all these families who are relying on me, families with old people and children. The two of you are young with nobody in your charge. Find your own way!'

Easier said than done! To find our own way we need money, and we don't have any. So we set off again in search of work. As most dockworkers are still mobilized, we manage to get hired in the port of Marseilles; with the labour shortage, almost anybody is hired. There is a frenzy of activity in the port; apparently, a lot of merchandise is being transported to Algiers, Oran, and the other French colonies of Africa. Four of us carry cotton balls, weighing 500 kilograms, with docker spikes. One day, I witness a fight to the death between two dockworkers, although I have no idea what sparked the fight. They go for each other with their spikes, and the fight starts looking like a tournament from the Middle Ages. The outcome is cruel. Nobody steps in until one of them is dead.

This job as a dockworker is hard work, but it would only last a few days. We are soon laid off, as demobilized dockworkers return. This is a pity, because Gerdi and I were making our fortune, earning 100 francs a day. On 11 July, I find a job in a tannery paying five francs an hour. And so, by Saturday the

---

6. The Milles camp was opened in September 1939. Between October 1940 and the summer of 1942, at the time of the major deportations, this camp was the only transit camp for emigrating foreigners. However, by the summer of 1942, 65 per cent had been unable to obtain emigration visas. Eighty per cent of the foreigners were Jewish, and the majority of the Jews (75 per cent) were from Germany and Austria. The rabbi mentioned is probably Israel Salzer, chief rabbi of Marseilles (Amicale des Déportés d'Auschwitz et des Camps de Haute–Silésie (eds), *Marseilles, Vichy et les nazis. Le temps des rafles. La déportation des juifs* (Marseilles: Amicale des Déportés d'Auschwitz et des Camps de Haute–Silésie, 1993), pp. 94–5). On the Milles camp, see A. Fontaine, *Le camp d'étrangers des Milles* (Aix-en-Provence: Edisud, 1989).

13th, I get my first pay packet: 105 francs! I work as a skinner. My job consists of taking bull skins and cow skins out of the vats – without gloves. They have been soaking in lime to let them swell, and I then have to separate the meat from the skin. It is all done by hand: I stretch the skin over easels, and scrape it with a razor-sharp tanner's knife. Of course, after a couple of days, my hands are raw, eaten up by the lime. It seems the hardest work I have ever done. However, as hard as it is, some jobs in the camp will be just as bad, and made even more difficult by hunger, beatings, fear, and general hardship. At least here I am free, and equally important, I am paid. One of the things this allows me to do is visit my girlfriend, C., in Montpellier. She remained in the Hérault until the Armistice, before deciding, like many other Belgians, to return home. For me, these are final good-byes, because I am convinced I will be able to leave France. I didn't yet know that I would see her again very soon.

In our refugee shelter, Gerdi and I are the only ones to have found work, while the others only talk, from morning to night, about how to earn a bit of money to have an occasional drink. We have the means, and from time to time we invite the men from the International Brigade to drink with us. We pay, of course.

One day, after one glass too many, the German, who has been a communist all his life, begins reflecting: 'It is obvious where the money lies, always in the hands of the Jews!'

We are the only two Jews there, but also the only ones working, and we are working hard! I am deeply hurt by his comment. The Romanian is also very embarrassed.

That is where the true anti-Semite betrays himself, I think. Here we are, sharing as friends, both facing defeat, bound by our common enemy, and still he points me out as the 'Other'. This may explain why so many of the five million German communists were able to vote for Hitler. Later, in the camps, the insults of the Germans will never touch my essence; I will know only too well who they are, and who I am. But here, in this situation, I am hurt. Why did he say that? I will have plenty of time to think about my German communist; he would have made a wonderful *Blockältester* [chief of the block], a good *kapo*, beating, denouncing, torturing the inmates in his charge, especially the Jewish inmates.

At the end of July, we learn that after the Armistice, the government in Bucharest sent a Romanian ship, the *Transylvania*, to Marseilles, to repatriate all Romanian citizens stranded in France. Aware of our rights as Romanian passport-holders, we arrive early in the morning at the foot of the ship's ladder. Bucovina's status is unclear, but I want to go back to Romania. The attendant glances at our papers, reads our names and barks: '*Jiden*? Kikes? You think my government sent me here to repatriate kikes? Forget it ... Get out of my sight!'

And that is exactly what we do.

We will not return to Romania. It is also here that Gerdi Krauthammer and I part ways. Gerdi had a Portuguese friend, studying in Verviers. As Gerdi knew his address in Portugal he wrote to him and has just received by return mail a visa for Portugal, a neutral country. Gerdi will be able to leave the zone of German influence and get out of danger. He will go first to Portugal, and will work in a factory belonging to his friend's father. Later, when that gentleman notices the romantic interest his daughter is showing in the little Romanian Jew, he will send him to Mozambique! From that remote colonial outpost of Portugal, Gerdi will find a way to Palestine before the end of the war.

I remain alone in Marseilles, with no hope of repatriation, in an exhausting job, with no money and no future. Everything is against me. I become more and more convinced that there is no point in staying. In October, I make a final unsuccessful attempt to return to my studies in Lyon. At the same time, by chance, at the local library, I come across my other exodus partner, Fred Weiss. Luckier than I, he has been accepted by the Lyon School of Silk to continue his studies. He will eventually escape from the Gestapo in a bizarre manner. He will become valet and handyman at the Hautecombe Abbey, and will spend the whole of the war hidden and happy. When he arrived at the abbey and presented himself to the Father Superior, he said: 'I must tell you that I am Jewish', and the Father answered: 'Does that mean that you won't work on the Sabbath?' Of course, France was occupied, and Jews and anyone who sheltered them were in great danger.

Since Bucovina has been occupied by the Russians all ties with the West are broken and I have no news from my parents. The last letter I receive from them mentions a transfer of 50,000 Belgian francs to Liège 'in case of war'. My father's foresight could have been due to precaution, as well as pessimism. That sum is enough to live on for four or five years: a small fortune. I decided there and then, on 24 October 1940, to go back to Liège, a decision that will again have serious consequences (the first was when I left Palestine). It is not a happy decision, and some of those around me try to talk me out of it. But I feel I have no choice. It is not an easy choice and that day I write in my notebook: *alea jacta est* [the dice are cast]. I don't need to mention how unhappy I am to go and live under German occupation. However, three factors prevail: the money my parents sent me, my ability to continue my studies, and last, but certainly not least, my girlfriend, C., who has written that she is expecting me in Liège, in our little flat. She wants to see me again.

On 26 October, I am in Paris.[7] With a knot in my stomach, I look around at German soldiers strolling along the Champs-Elysées and at anti-Semitic posters on the walls of the city. To cross the Belgian border again I need a pass that I don't have. I must go to the Belgian Consulate in Paris to try to sort out my papers.

It is here that I must confess to an act that I consider the most shameful of my life. I don't exaggerate when I say that this memory still haunts me and lies heavy on my conscience even today. In my rush to get to Liège, in the office of the Consul in Paris, I sign a declaration of honour that I am not a Jew.

It is the first time in my life that I deny my Jewishness. It

---

7. This means that W.B. crossed the demarcation line without difficulty, despite checkpoints that had been in force since 16 July, and also despite the fact that Jews had been forbidden to return to the Occupied Zone since the German decree of 27 September. This decree also defined who, in France, was to be considered a Jew; a definition that the Vichy Government restated on 3 October in its Statute on Jews. On 24 October, Hitler met with Pétain in Montoire.

will be the only time. Thanks to my denial, I return to Belgium on 30 October without any problems. Like all western Jews, from then on I will live in a mousetrap. Of course, at the time I am unaware how much the life of Jews will resemble a large, cruel game of hide-and-seek with the occupiers. Who will be caught? Who will escape? Nevertheless, I have often thought that whatever happened to me after that was punishment for my denial, and for my mistake in leaving the land of Israel.

As soon as I arrive in Liège, I go to the bank to get the money my father sent me. The clerk, who saw me every month collecting my allowance, recognises me and greets me: 'Mr Berler, what a pity! You had an important cheque waiting for you here, but you were away for so long, that we sent the money back to Romania ...'

I am now in a rather tenuous situation; I am starting a new life in occupied Belgium without a cent to my name. To survive in those first weeks I sell, one by one, all the items from my previous life that I can easily do without, like my tuxedo, my camera, and my stamp collection. It is imperative I complete my studies. I work frantically, and receive my diploma on 18 December 1940.

In that everyday life in Liège I feel a certain reassuring tranquillity on the surface, which I will soon discover is just an illusion. A few thousand Jews still remain in Liège, with whom, however, I have no contact. I feel Jewish, but I don't feel sufficiently threatened to try to escape. And, anyway: to where, and how? Didn't I exhaust all possibilities while I was in Marseilles?

During my reading at this time, I come across a passage from Arthur Schnitzler that so accurately reflects my state of mind, my anxiety and my confusion, that I copy it into my notebook, dated 22 October 1941.[8] The main character, a Jew, asks himself, not about the Jewish condition – which would have been a question of definition, a historical and sociological problem – but what it is like to live as a Jew. Schnitzler wrote that article many years before the rise of Nazism, but he would probably not have been surprised by the subsequent course of

---

8. See A. Schnitzler, *Der Weg ins Freie* (Frankfurt-am-Main: Fischer Taschenbuch Verlag, 1978), pp. 203–5.

events, the sudden appearance of total hatred, the decision to implement a Final Solution. He says that there is no solution to the problem of being Jewish, or rather, that everyone must find his own solution. Can this problem at least be named, or described? The problem is invisible, colourless and odourless. It is not a noisy, howling anti-Semitism. It reveals itself suddenly, at the turn of a letter, of a statement, of a reproach. If a person has a grudge against his friend, or a lover against his mistress, and the object of his anger happens to be Jewish, I am certain that the friend or the lover will reproach him or her for it, even if tacitly. More generally, undeniably, if the resentment or the criticism is aimed at a non-Jew – which is the case 99 per cent of the time! – there would be no mention of any religious affiliation. However, on the one occasion that the person in question happens to be a Jew, that particular fact, which has nothing to do with the object of the anger, will nonetheless most certainly form part of the criticism.

This is the way things are, says Schnitzler, since Jews are Jews and the world is as it is. Assimilation will prove only one thing, if and when it occurs – in 1,000 or 2,000 years, after immeasurable injustice and persecution – and that is, that the Jews have been the ferment of humanity. Schnitzler ironically suggests that the sacrifice needed to reach that goal is great: too great. There is no general solution to the Jewish problem. Mass emigration is no solution. What Jew would want to live surrounded only by Jews? Many would feel completely lost in Jerusalem. The way to salvation, he concludes, is personal, but where on earth could we find it?

These reflections relate to my state of mind, but during these months, my main preoccupation is to earn some kind of living. My family is still uncontactable; all communication with Bucovina, under Soviet rule, having been cut. In the ambiguous climate of the occupation, anyone living like me – I have no choice – in the 'grey' zone must make himself as unobtrusive as possible, respect the curfew, and make sure he is not caught in roundups for compulsory work; in addition to which, there are the daily worries of finding food. I concentrate on my modest survival, which becomes my daily duty from the end of

December 1940. I would have gone on like that until liberation, had I not been arrested in April 1943.

I can earn money from my perfect knowledge of German. As I already have enough knowledge of French to be able to translate, I start making a living from that, translating whatever I can find: technical texts, sometimes whole books, usually from German to French, but sometimes from French to German. I often receive work from the University of Liège, and spend nights thinking how to translate a particular expression. I also start giving German lessons. In these troubled times I have no difficulty finding students. Many Belgians need to communicate with the oppressor. Over two years, I teach at least 20 students. During that whole period, I manage to survive without ever having to resort to the Black Market.

One of my students is a lawyer, Mr Gourdet, a secretive introvert. He knows I am Jewish. In truth, and that is certainly careless on my part, I don't conceal from any of my students that I am Jewish. When I ask him why he wants to learn German, he smiles and says: 'You know, it is always a good thing to know the enemy's language.'

It is only on my return from camp that I would find out that Gourdet was a senior commander in the Resistance.

The most remarkable of my students is a man named Ernens, who, when I meet him, works in Liège as a representative of Lanson champagnes from Reims. He is badly maimed, having lost a leg in the First World War. He claims to have been in British Intelligence, and that he received the Victoria Cross. He lives in a beautiful villa in the nicest part of Liège, and has been earning a lot of money since the Occupation. The Germans, especially the Gestapo, but also other agencies, send him to Reims every fortnight with a convoy of German trucks to receive a supply of champagne. Needless to say, he has excellent relations with the Gestapo. I guess that my German lessons are meant to improve his public relations. Ernens is practically illiterate, but he is bright. Whatever he knows he has taught himself. With me, he learns German very well and very fast.

I don't conceal from him, either, that I am Jewish. We talk frequently about our respective situations. I often tell him, with some innocence, that he is taking quite a risk by appearing so openly with the Germans. He is known all over town as a collaborator. Nonetheless, I benefit nicely from our connection. Sometimes he gives me food, and he provides me with false papers. For that purpose he has connections with a network, through which he also provides papers for Resistance fighters. He sometimes uses me as a courier. It seems that Ernens has decided to hedge his bets on both fronts, the Germans and the Resistance.

Ernens must resemble most collaborators. His sense of honour is not strong, but neither is he taken by Nazi ideology, or 'ideals'. He simply chooses to take advantage of the situation and is quite successful, as will later become evident.

Conditions at the front look desperate. It seems that nothing will stop Germany's victorious advance. How and when will all this end? My fear grows, but my daily life is filled with waiting and mediocrity. My translations and private lessons usually provide us with enough to eat. C. and I live in a small student flat that a friend left me in 1940 before he left for Switzerland. Time seems to slow; life has this terrible sense of slow motion, a sense that is familiar only to those who find themselves in a paralysing situation where action has become impossible. I would like to go on with my life, I don't want to languish in my past; I want to grow. I immerse myself in the only pastime available: reading. For two years, I read one book a day on average. I read useful things, like a treatise on mechanics. But mainly I finish with delight *Les Thibault*, and read *Men of Good Will*, which I love. I read with passion, and without order: Montherlant, Irene Nemirovsky, Troyat, Mac Orlan – I don't like him too much – Chardonne, Kessel, Jean de la Varende, Dorgelès, Henri de Montfreid, Roger Vercel and Giraudoux. I also read *The Large Flock* by Giono, and Clochemerle, Sainte-Colline, *My Friend Pomme* by Gabriel Chevalier. Only literature is able to move me or make me laugh, and I read, in German as well as in French: Pearl Buck, Vicky Baum, Shalom Ash, Lewis Bromfield, H.G. Wells, Edouard Zellweger, Jack London, Axel Munthe, Hans Fallada, Theodor Dreyser, Jakob Wassermann, Sinclair Lewis, Franz

Blei, Daphne du Maurier and Karen Blixen. I even risk Rilke, but don't understand him. I am looking for answers to my life when I tackle Victor Serge's *Leningrad: Conquered City*, Antoine Redie's *Germans in our Homes*, and *Betrayal of the Clerks* by Julien Benda. Nothing can stop my frenzied reading; I even absorb Drieu la Rochelle, considered an absolute must, and to top it all off, I read *The Beautiful Sheets* by Céline. (Both will be convicted after the war as collaborators.)

And so, my undercover existence continues. I register at the Pigier School to study accounting. In July 1942, my girlfriend and I leave my student flat for 70 Vertbois Street. We live modestly: pseudo-normal mediocrity in a mousetrap.

Wearing the Yellow Star becomes compulsory in June 1942.[9] The Yellow Star is distributed by the Jewish Association, our own Belgian *Judenräte*. I receive one, but I never wear it. I still have it, shiny and new, 55 years on. Rebelliousness? Yes. I found that proclamation of my Judaism degrading. I know that some people were proud to wear it, but I was not one of them. I felt it was an attack on my dignity as an individual. What's more, as I go about without my star, I don't think of being afraid. I convince myself that they would never arrest me because I have false identity papers. In reality, the tension is building (so much so that I felt some relief when I was arrested: finally, I no longer had to hide. And so it was with Tristan Bernard, who is believed to have said to his wife, on the truck taking them to Drancy, that if, until then, they had lived in fear, from then on they would live in hope).

On 1 April 1943, I go to Ernens' villa for his regular German lesson. I move around by bike, very carefully – I have learned to merge with the grey of the walls – I take alleys where I don't risk being followed by car. I give my lesson as usual. At noon on the dot, as I leave Ernens' villa, the Gestapo car is waiting for me at the door.

---

9. On 4 March 1942, Berlin decreed that French Jews (living in the Occupied Zone) and Belgian and Dutch Jews should wear a distinctive mark. After an initial period of indecision, the Yellow Star was decreed compulsory in Belgium on 27 March 1942; this was enforced from 7 June.

They don't beat me, don't hassle me, they just ask for my papers. I show them my ID, which is false of course, although it carries my name, Wilhelm Berler. It indicates, however, that I am Swiss, originally from Lenzburg. They laugh. I don't realise that they know perfectly well who I am.

I am taken into custody, without harassment, and led to the citadel of Liège, an old Belgian military installation that the Germans transformed into a prison. I am forced to realise that somebody has denounced me.[10] They were waiting for me. But who turned me in?

During my two years wandering through the camps, I would have ample time to ponder that question, but I would only discover the truth on my return. I led a discreet life with a non-Jew, and didn't wear the Star. Only my students knew that I was Jewish. So which one was it? At no time did it occur to me that it could have been Ernens. However, the day I return, two years later, my landlord – with whom I'd had excellent relations, and with whom my girlfriend, C., had continued to live during my absence – would welcome me warmly. They congratulate me for having come back just in time to give evidence in Ernens' trial, due to take place a few days later. He was the one who had denounced me. I was astonished. I found it hard to believe that I had been betrayed by this man whom I had actually liked (and I had had the impression that it was mutual).

Here, I'll jump ahead a bit. A few days before the trial, in May or June 1945, Ernens' daughter visited me. Remembering it now, I have to laugh. She came to tell me that she was prepared to sacrifice her virtue in exchange for positive character evidence in court about her father. Do I need to describe the effect of her offer on me? Two years in hell, and I would just

---

10. In 1942, 17,000 people were deported within a period of 100 days. The Jews who observed the Statute presented themselves when summoned or allowed themselves to be taken from their homes. However, after the major roundups during the summer of 1942, and especially from 1943, people refused to co-operate, and the Nazi authorities had to track down Jews to arrest them. Over the next two years, the Nazis only managed to arrest a little over 8,000 people. Belgian Jews found accomplices within the population who helped them to hide; at the same time, the occupiers found accomplices to denounce Jews and to seek them out.

forget about it? The trial took place. I was still so weak that the president invited me to be seated to give my evidence. I was going to meet my denouncer. I was asked whether I knew the circumstances of my arrest. But I knew nothing; I had only just been told that Ernens had turned me in, and I couldn't digest it. We had been on good terms, and I didn't have the impression that he hated Jews. This deserved an explanation.

I heard the witnesses' stories. A former police commissioner who lived opposite Ernens' villa had watched all his comings and goings, as Ernens was a known collaborator living the good life. As it happened, on the day of my arrest, this commissioner had seen the Gestapo car waiting in front of the villa. He had seen Ernens come out a few minutes before me, in his shirt, and signal to them. Another witness, a member of the Resistance who had worked at the Gestapo telephone centre, carefully recorded, day after day, all conversations of known collaborators. On the day of my arrest, he had noted a call from Ernens at 11 a.m., which said: 'He's leaving about noon. Be careful, he's armed.' That wasn't true. What did he want them to believe?

I still couldn't make sense of his motives. Why did he sell me out? I was soon to find out, little by little. Ernens arrived in court with a 'B-file'. He was presenting himself as a double agent, who had been working for the Resistance. As a witness, he brought a major manufacturer from Liège, at whose factory – which had, of course, been working for the Germans – acts of sabotage had been committed. This manager covered for his workers and hid those who were to be deported. The Germans had discovered his activities and had sentenced him to death. However, thanks to his good relations with them, Ernens had convinced the Gestapo to spare this man's life. The same man came to give evidence. All this had taken place a few days before my own arrest. By then, Ernens was afraid he had gone too far, and had confided his fears to an old friend, a retired general, who also came to give evidence. Ernens had asked the general to keep an eye on his family if anything happened to him. Things slowly started to make sense. He had denounced me to save himself. Ernens had taken the initiative to give the

Gestapo something in exchange for what they did. What could be better than an insignificant Jew? Me?

To sum it all up, except for his collaboration in business, only one thing could be charged against Ernens: my denunciation. Because of that, the court sentenced him to 20 years' forced labour. At that time, the mood was in favour of purges. A few years later, he might have been decorated as a Resistance worker! In addition, he had to compensate the victim – me! – with the colossal sum of 250,000 francs. But, as the State automatically confiscated all collaborators' property, I ended up receiving nothing, despite Ernens' fortune. I saw the man five or six years later, sitting quietly on the terrace of a café in Brussels, pardoned and free.

The day of my arrest marks the real beginning of my tribulations in the concentration camp universe. On 2 April 1943, I find myself incarcerated in the citadel of Liège. I can no longer doubt that I have been denounced. They know exactly who I am, where I was born, what I do. The fact that I was neither beaten nor harassed makes me think that whoever denounced me may have requested that I not be molested. I am alone in a spacious cell. My girlfriend, C., has been notified. Through the window of my cell, I see her come into the citadel courtyard, a suitcase in her hand. But they don't let her in. They give me the things she brought. I remain in the citadel for two and a half weeks and they never let her visit me, not even once.

The citadel is a transit prison where the Germans gather the Jews and Resistance workers whom they capture. I don't stay alone in my cell for very long, but long enough to experience the loneliness of prison. It is, of course, my first experience as a prisoner. Until one has lived through this, one cannot imagine what it is like. Still, life in the citadel is the life of an ordinary prisoner, relatively strict, yet lenient compared to what I would later experience in the concentration camp universe. I am allowed to receive letters, and they give me the ones my girlfriend writes me. I walk in the yard every day. At regular intervals, an attendant brings me my daily soup. I listen for his

31

steps in the shadows, hear him approach the door and open it … but I cannot go out. I must remain there, fearful and humiliated, with a senseless and unacceptable loss of freedom.

After four days, my first cellmate arrives, followed the next day by a small man in his forties, who introduces himself and with whom I immediately establish a good rapport. His name is Michel Zechel and he is a dentist in Liège, a well-known dentist with a thriving practice. A long-term resident of Belgium and a naturalised Belgian, he is originally from Kishinev in Bessarabia. In addition to French, he speaks Russian (his mother tongue), English, because he lived in the United States for a while, and some German. It is the second time he has been imprisoned. The first time, the Germans locked him up in the fort of Breendonck,[11] where he spent several months in very tough conditions. However, he was released, but was arrested again shortly after.[12] Now we share the same cell in the citadel.

On 11 April 1943, I am 25 years old and in prison. Outside it is spring and the trees are in full bloom. How cruel and false is this spring. I am imprisoned for no reason; I have committed no crime. My only crime is to be a Jew.

We are watched very carefully. The Gestapo search us. Michel Zechel, who became my friend from the moment he arrived, confides to me in sworn secrecy that he has a $100 bill

---

11. The deserted fort of Breendonck is part of the military belt of Antwerp and, under occupation, became an SS camp, a terror camp, commonly called 'Breendonck Hell'. It was intended for dangerous prisoners, also for Jews before the Dossin barracks opened in Mechelen. The prisoners were locked up secretly, tortured and starved. Even the *Militärbefehlshaber*, von Falkenhausen himself, was upset by the conditions prevalent. At the outset, its policy of terrifying repression led to more deaths than the SS terror. Out of a total of 3,584 prisoners, 86 died in the fort or in the Antwerp hospital; 285 were shot or hanged, sentenced to death by military tribunals or declared terrorist prisoners by military authorities. See M. Steinberg and A. Verhamme, 'Assemblé de la Commission communautaire française', in M. Steinberg and A. Verhamme (eds), *Le fort de Breendonk: Le camp de la terreur nazie en Belgique pendant la deuxième guerre mondiale* (Brussels: DOB, 1997); also, the memoirs of J. Améry, *Par-delà le crime et le châtimen: Essai pour surmonter l'insurmontable* (Paris: Actes Sud, 1995), p. 51 ff.
12. The arrest of Belgian Jews led, in 1943, to violent public protests, and thereafter the authorities became slightly more restrained. At some stage, there was talk about withdrawing the deportees' citizenship, but this did not happen (see M. Marrus, *L'Holocauste dans l'Histoire*, 2nd edn (Paris: Flammarion/Champs, 1994), p. 108).

hidden on his body. He doesn't know what the future holds for him. Michel is very able and as flexible as an acrobat. He doesn't know it then, but his $100 bill will pass all the searches, in Auschwitz and in Buchenwald. I also don't know it then, but that providential bill will one day save both our lives, much later, millions of hours of suffering later.

Every day, my cell becomes more crowded. The Germans are using the citadel to gather together the Jews arrested in Liège and its surroundings before sending them elsewhere. One day, a group of Jews from Arlon arrives, accompanied by their 78-year-old rabbi. On 13 April, a member of the Jewish Council of Liège, a man named N., is imprisoned. He was a high-ranking official taking orders from the Gestapo,[13] one of those I learned not to trust. His special status does not seem to have done him any good as he is imprisoned and will be deported with me.

On 17 April, there are apparently enough Jews in the citadel. We are told that we will be leaving by transport. We are taken to Mechelen, a town north of Brussels, which has an internment camp for all Belgian Jews. When we arrive at this camp in the Dossin barracks,[14] the shock of my arrest suddenly hits me and I realise that there is something peculiar in the way that events are unfolding. I was well treated in the citadel and never beaten. But the camp at Mechelen is a completely different world. The guards are SS, armed with whips, and prisoners are kept in line by a camp commander who moves around and keeps order by waving a club. Where am I? What is this

---

13. At that time, Noe Nozyce, president of the Liège committee of the JAB, was no longer acting under German orders. Living in a quasi-legal situation, he was arrested with his wife and two children on 13 April (Steinberg, *La Traque*, Vol. 1, pp. 154–5). As long as they remained submissive to the occupiers, the officials in the JAB were relatively safe. The Germans planned to round them up in August 1944, but ran out of time (R. Hilberg, *La Destruction des Juifs d'Europe* (Paris: Fayard), p. 523).

14. The 'General Baron Dossin of Saint-Georges' barracks in Mechelen, a military building from the Hapsburg era, was conveniently situated halfway between Brussels and Antwerp (90 per cent of the Jewish population lived in these two cities); and it was on a railway line. In the second half of 1942, immediately after the first quota of Jews to be deported had been fixed, it was transformed into a camp into which deportees were gathered (see Hilberg, *La Destruction*, p. 521). Today, it is the Jewish Museum of the Deportation and Resistance.

barbarism? The camp commander is himself a Jew,[15] a German Jew! The Dossin barrack at Mechelen is my first window onto the concentration camp universe. In retrospect, it would be my first apprenticeship. However, I don't have much time to formulate questions, as my stay there ends after 48 hours. I am allowed a last civilized gesture, to send my watch and my suitcase back to Liège. From then on, things move very fast. Michel and I are added to the *Transportliste* of the 20th Belgian convoy on its way to 'the east'.[16] I was given the number 1,058.

I would discover much later that, had I not left in that convoy, I would probably have been released and sent home as a Romanian citizen. Czernowitz had again become part of Romania, in 1941, after the German victory in the east, and in 1943, the Germans signed an agreement with their ally in Bucharest stipulating, among other things, that all Romanian Jews would be sent home in a 'brotherly fashion'. For the Germans, this was an easy way to get rid of them.[17] I later met some Romanian Jews from Belgium who had escaped deportation in 1943 in this way.

---

15. Dagobert Meyer had been an Austrian folksinger, and was feared in the camp. One of the female inmates in the Dossin barracks wrote a poem about him:

    Mayer, Mayer auf der Bühne
    War stets freundlich deine Miene
    Hier ist Ernst
    Dein Gesicht glaube mir
    Es steht dir nicht.

    ['Mayer, Mayer, you always had a smiling face on stage; here you are serious; and, believe me, it does not suit you']
    (Supplied by M. Ward Adriaens, curator of the Museum of Jewish Deportation and Resistance.)
16. This list was distributed illicitly before departure by a female Jewish clerk at the Dossin barracks in order to facilitate the regrouping of the Resistance fighters.
17. On 23 April 1943, it was declared that Romanian Jews would not be deported. As a result, 2,500–3,000 people were repatriated to Romania by the end of June, among them all the Romanians from the French camps (see Georges Wellers, *Un Juif sous Vichy*, 2nd edn (Paris: Tirélas, 1991), p. 63). On the complex problem of deportation of Romanian Jews in the Reich and Occupied Territories, see Hilberg, *La Destruction*, pp. 675–94. Marshall Antonescu seems to have wanted to encourage 'his' Jews to emigrate to Palestine, in return for the State receiving some compensation. The defeat of the Germans at Stalingrad led to a gradual reversal of opinion in Romania, where anti-German feeling was growing. However, the Jews in Bucovina and Bessarabia – who were not really considered Romanian – had already been deported to Transnistry in 1941–2.

3 Buna-Monowitz: The Beginning of Death

> With the distance of time, we can today definitely affirm that the
> history of the Lagers has been written almost exclusively by those
> who, like myself, never fathomed them to the bottom. Those who
> did so, did not return, or their capacity for observation was
> paralysed by suffering and incomprehension.
> Primo Levi, *I sommersi e i salvati* [*The Drowned and the Saved*]

On 19 April 1943, we are loaded into cattle wagons. The train
leaves Mechelen for the east, heading for Auschwitz.[1] The
Germans gather the Jews of Belgium in Mechelen. As soon as a
convoy can be formed, they send a thousand prisoners. I will
learn later that we were 1,600 Jews on that train: 150 will return
from Auschwitz.

There are two young Jews in my carriage, one called
Friedel. They have already escaped once from a train leaving
Mechelen, but were recaptured. These two are the only ones
who know where we are heading, and they tell me. They are
also the only ones who have any notion of Auschwitz, and
what we can expect there. Even before our departure, they
decide to escape again. They soon succeed in loosening one of
the bars, and are waiting for an opportunity to jump out of the
wagon, when the train unexpectedly stops in the middle of the
Flemish countryside. Suddenly we hear shots.

---

1. Belgium was part of the Western Territories conquered by Germany; these
    consisted of a semi-circular arc, stretching from Norway to Romania, and before
    the war had a Jewish population estimated at two million. Most of these were
    deported to Auschwitz, the centre of annihilation for Jews of western culture and
    education (see Marrus, *L'Holocauste*, pp. 99–100; Hilberg, *La Destruction*; M. Gilbert,
    Endlösung: Die Vertreiburg und Vernichtung der Juden. Ein Atlas, 2nd edn (Hamburg:
    Rowohlt, 1995).

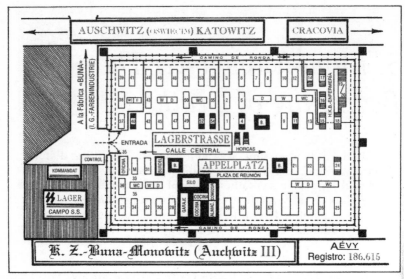

2. Plan of Buna-Monowitz (Auschwitz III).

Key:

A la Fabrica 'Buna' = To the Buna factory
Entrada = entrance
Campo S.S. = S.S. camp
Calle central = central alley
Plaza de Reunion = *Appell* ground
H.K.B. Enfermeria = H.K.B. Infirmary
Garaje = garage
Cocina = kitchen
Comedor = dining room
Almac = storeroom
Registro = register

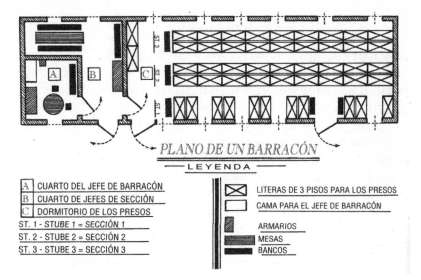

PLANO DE UN BARRACÓN

LEYENDA

A CUARTO DEL JEFE DE BARRACÓN
B CUARTO DE JEFES DE SECCIÓN
C DORMITORIO DE LOS PRESOS
ST. 1 - STUBE 1 = SECCIÓN 1
ST. 2 - STUBE 2 = SECCIÓN 2
ST. 3 - STUBE 3 = SECCIÓN 3

⊠ LITERAS DE 3 PISOS PARA LOS PRESOS
□ CAMA PARA EL JEFE DE BARRACÓN
▨ ARMARIOS
▬ MESAS
▬ BANCOS

3. Plan of a Block in Buna-Monowitz.

Key:

Plano de un Barracón = Plan of a Block

Leyenda = legend
A – Cuarto del Jefe de Barracón = *kapo*'s room
B – Cuarto de Jefes de Sección = room for the *Stubendienste*
C – Dormitorio de los Presos = prisoners' dormitories
St.1 (Stube 1) = room/section 1
St.2 (Stube 2) = room/section 2
St.3 (Stube 3) = room/section 3
Literas de 3 pisos para los presos = three-tier beds for the prisoners
Cama para el jefe de barracón = single bed for the Kapo
Armarios = cupboards
Mesas = tables
Bancos = benches

I didn't know it then, but the Dossin barracks of Mechelen had been heavily infiltrated by Belgium's Jewish Resistance, who had learnt when transports were taking place, and whose names were on the lists. Apparently, the SS felt secure enough not to try to keep this information secret. The 20th convoy was carrying a large number of Resistance members to Auschwitz.

Three communist militants had decided to rescue the people of this 20th convoy, against the advice of the Resistance Centre, although the idea of attacking a train of deportees had come from Ghert Jospa, leader of the Jewish Resistance. Such a raid seemed too risky to the armed force leaders. It was a young Jewish medic, Youra (Georges) Livschitz, and two of his high school friends, Jean Franklemon and Robert Maistriau – all three daring and wilful – who, on the night of 19/20 April 1943, attacked our train, armed with only one handgun. At that same moment, far away but in similar historical conditions in Warsaw, the ghetto rebels were engaged in their first night of battle. So let us hear no more about Jews allowing themselves to be led like sheep to the slaughter! These are exemplary acts of resistance, and they were not the only ones.

The trio waited for the convoy just before the Belgian–German border, in the region of Boortmeerbeek. With their one gun, a pair of pliers and a torch, they meant to stop the train. They carried with them bundles of 50-franc bills, 50,000 francs given by the Resistance, to give to those who managed to escape to help them survive underground. One of the attackers posted on the lower side had brandished a red lantern, causing the train to stop. Maistriau successfully opened one of the wagons with his pliers. The German guards, *Schupo*, not SS, started shooting (in later convoys, only SS guarded the deportees). It seems that 17 people managed to escape from the open wagon, 15 at that moment alone. The rescuers quickly pointed out the road to Brussels and Antwerp and distributed part of the money.

In the shooting that followed, nothing more could be done. However, after the war, it would become known that over 200 deportees from several wagons had escaped from this convoy: an exceptional event in the deportation saga.

Of course, at the time, I had no idea what had just happened. Our rescuers didn't reach our carriage, the shooting stopped, and the train moved on. We returned to our escape projects more determined than ever. We must jump out of the train while still on Belgian territory. Quickly, five or six of us decide in what order we will jump. We agree that I will jump last. In a state of frenzied tension, I watch the boy before me disappear through the opening, and then it is my turn to step through the window. As I am about to leap into the void, a most horrible sight paralyses me; the unlucky guy before me had lost his footing, got caught by the wagon, and his head, squeezed between two shock absorbers, burst open like a melon. It is the first time I see a dead man ... I feel dizzy, and I am convinced that this plunge will take me to my death ... so I don't jump. I move backwards, curl up in the wagon and decide to continue with the trip, the long trip. After all, I tell myself, we are only going to a work camp and I am young and strong. Had I known even a hundredth, a thousandth, of the reality of Auschwitz, it would have been enough to convince me to jump despite the terror of death, despite the risks. How often will I wish for that final moment where life could have taken another turn.[2]

We travel for another four days and three nights, from 19 April to 22 April. Finally, the train stops for good. We are in a train station, just at daybreak; this must be Auschwitz.[3] When the doors open, I can't wait to get out of the dark carriage. I am so relieved to be alone, just me, with no small children or elderly parents to worry about, unlike so many families on the train. But, stepping onto the platform, a strange sensation overwhelms me; who can they be, these men in striped

---

2. Many escape attempts were successful, as evidenced by the 20th convoy. Although it was relatively easy to make an opening in the wagons, the main obstacle was psychological: to dare to jump from the train and not to fear reprisals against family members left behind in Belgium (L. Steinberg, *La Révolte des Justes: Les Juifs contre Hitler 1933–1945* (Paris: Fayard, 1970), p. 281).

3. In the spring of 1943, the convoys stopped at Auschwitz station. It was a large station, about 3.2 kilometres long with 44 lines, to the west of the town and about 1.5 kilometres from the entrance to the Auschwitz camp, and at a similar distance from Birkenau. The infamous diverting track that passes under Birkenau's portal was only finished in April 1944 for the transport of Jews from Hungary.

pyjamas coming to meet us? They keep themselves busy, but why don't they say anything? Why don't they explain anything to us? This place must be some sort of prison, filled with silent prisoners, forbidden to speak![4]

On the platform, our whole convoy is directed towards a group of SS officers, waiting to examine us one by one as we go by. As the column advances and we pass in front of them, we find ourselves being sent either to the right or to the left. I am sent to the right, and after a while, I realise that the 300 or so males on the same side as me are all fairly young and in reasonable physical condition. The selection seems to be over. We are told to walk to our camp. However, the other group – those who were sent to the left, old people, women, children – go by trucks!

Do I envy them? Maybe. I certainly think that it will be less tiring for them. In my group, nobody has any idea what exactly is happening, where we are being taken, or where the other group is going. At that moment, none of us can imagine the unimaginable, that those who left in the trucks would never be seen again.

After the selection, we wait a while longer. Suddenly, a guy from my group calls out in Yiddish to the SS officer nearest to him: *'Herr Offizier, ich hob a kille'* [he cannot walk, he has a hernia].

The SS officer looks at him and tells him that doesn't matter, he should walk like the others, they will send him for surgery in the camp. As the man insists, so the SS officer makes him leave our group and sends him to the trucks. The man leaves, relieved.

He leaves straight for the gas chambers.

The group starts moving. We are led not to the actual Auschwitz camp, but to one of its *Aussenlager* [subsidiary camps], as Auschwitz is actually like the capital of a 'principal-

---

4. Thanks to a document from the underground Resistance, dated 25 April 1943, the exact number of inmates in the concentration camp is known for that date: there were 17,037 inmates in the main camp of Auschwitz, 11,671 in Birkenau (plus 12,000 gypsies), 1,194 in the Jawischowitz mine and 3,301 in Buna-Monowitz. Some smaller annexed camps had a total of 850 or so inmates (Danuba Czech, *Kalendarium der Ereignisse im Konzentrationslager Auschwitz-Birkenau 1939–1945* (Hamburg: Rowohlt, 1989), p. 477).

ity' of annexed camps and *kommando*s under its rule. I will realise later that I am interned in one of the largest of these outer camps, Buna-Monowitz.[5] We have about seven kilometres to walk.

'Buna' simply means 'synthetic rubber'. I would discover later that next to Auschwitz and its inexhaustible human reserves, the German industrial giant, I.G. Farbenindustrie, is in the process of building an immense complex of factories for producing raw materials essential to the war effort. Before the war, I.G. Farben had already begun research into, and development of, synthetic rubber, and several factories were operating in Germany.

When we arrive in the camp – behind the barbed wire fence and observation post – we are met by somebody who is clearly in charge. He is the *Lagerältester*, the fearsome camp elder – a criminal,[6] as evidenced by a green triangle, sewn pointing downwards on his uniform. He gives a speech, and I, dumbfounded, understand nothing of it. I only catch one sentence, repeated over and over as if it contained the meaning

---

5. Many testimonies describing Monowitz exist: see P. Levi, *Si questo è un homo* (Torino: Einaudi, 1958); P. Steinberg, *Chroniques d'ailleurs: Récit* (Paris: Ramsay, 1996); R. Waitz and M. Klein (eds), *De l'Université aux camps de concentration: Témoignages strabourgeois*, 2nd edn (Strasbourg: Presses Universitaires, 1989); G. Wellers, *Un Juif sous Vichy*; also G. Vallet's MA thesis, 'Étude de témoignages oraux d'anciens déportés du camp de Buna-Monowitz', unedited ms, Paris: Centre de Documentation Juive Contemporaine.

6. In April 1943, the *Lagerältester* of Monowitz – who was at the top of the hierarchy of inmate officials – was the Upper Silesian, Paul Kozwara, a criminal sentenced for a variety of crimes. According to Langbein (*Menschen in Auschwitz*, p. 177), Kozwara was a kinder chief than his predecessor, Jupp Windeck, an anti-social German who wore the Black Triangle. Windeck was a murderous despot, insatiably vicious with the weaker inmates. Kozwara, known as 'P.K.' (Waitz and Klein, *Témoignages strabourgeois*, p. 480) was also a despot, but a kinder sort:

> He lives comfortably, permits himself a daily massage, organises lavish banquets for his own birthday and presents himself as a patron of the arts and sport...He periodically reproaches the HKB inmates who suffer from dysentery of actually having caused their illness by eating excrement...His influence is enormous, and to find favour in his eyes can mean survival; to be out of favour can mean death.

Paul Steinberg, then 17 years old (*Chronicles*, pp. 104–5), tells of his mercenary idea of giving Kozwara a present; which pays 'excellent dividends' and leads to Kozwara saving him from death in the freezing cold during evacuation. It seems that Kozwara was murdered 15 days after evacuation by anonymous individuals seeking revenge (ibid., p. 160).

of all that was to follow, the definition of my new status: 'Do you know where you are? You are in a KZ! A KZ! A *Kazet*! No one leaves a *Kazet*.'

And, after a few more senseless sentences, I hear the following:

'There is only one way out of here, through the chimney.' What can he possibly mean? I have no idea where I am, and I cannot make sense of that strange word, *Kazet*. It turns out to be the abbreviation of *Konzentrationslager* [concentration camp], my first introduction to camp jargon.

What this word implies, what awaits us, we, the young and healthy, who are sent to the right after the selection at the ramp, I will find out soon enough: Monowitz is not an immediate extermination camp. We have temporarily escaped death to become their slaves, at least for as long as we will be able to work.[7]

To win the war, Germany, still convinced of its victory despite the defeat at Stalingrad, is developing its military industry in a monstrous fashion. Workers are needed; the regime is restless, struggling between two contradictory goals. On the one hand, it wants to be rid of the Jews, believed to be the cause of all the ills of the world and in particular the ills of Germany, as Hitler and Goebbels have been repeating mechanically for ten years. This resulted in the creation of a whole operation with one sole purpose: the physical extermination of the Jews as if they were vermin. On the other hand, Germany is already used to the idea of the camps as a potentially infinite source of slaves, and cannot afford to lose that workforce. The result of these two approaches, extermination and exploitation, is imprisonment in a work camp which leads to elimination. The *Kazet* inmate, the *Häftling*, is in truth far less than a slave. Statistically, the life expectancy of a Jewish inmate in Monowitz is three to four months, unless he is lucky enough to work in an indoor *kommando*, which is far less exhausting than the outdoor

---

7. Only 44.1 per cent of the inmates of the Auschwitz complex in April 1943 (32,626 men and 16,000 women) were sent to *kommandos*. The rest were sick or in quarantine (see F. Piper, *Arbeitseinsatz der Häftlinge aus dem KL Auschwitz* (Oswiecim: Éditions du Musèe d'État à Oswiecim, 1995), p. 71).

kommandos. The neighbouring coal mines, Fürstengrube and Janinagrube, had been bought immediately by I.G. Farben to ensure energy and raw material supplies; the survival rate there is just four weeks.

This healthy 25-year-old man is therefore going to serve the great German war machine for a certain period, after which he would, of course, be replaced by one of the thousands of *Häftlinge*, sub-humans, who arrive daily. He will then be disposed of or, to be more precise, his body would be disposed of, because the first lesson I learn on arrival in the camp is that we are just bodies. At the end of the expected work period, these bodies are simply burnt to ashes. Here lies the primary obscenity, from which all others follow: the loss of dignity in death, which all camp inmates suffer. Your neighbour in the next bed who dies in the night, your work companion who is beaten to a pulp by a bad-tempered *kapo*, this person is no longer a man, but just a body. A body that is turned into waste in a second. These bodies, rigid as heating fuel and piled up along the lane leading to the crematorium, have become unidentifiable waste: raw material. As I am no longer a man, my body will be burnt as excrement, as planned. Everything is programmed in the Auschwitz principality; everything ends up in the crematorium chimney.[8] The wisdom for camp survival lies in grasping the situation as quickly as possible. This is the hidden meaning behind the word '*Kazet*', which I need to learn.

After the *Lagerältester's* speech, some time passes as the SS leave us waiting in the vast central space of the camp.[9] I emerge from my numb state when they suddenly order us to hand over all our valuables. They don't seem convinced that we will comply, because they announce that we will be searched afterwards, and if anybody is found with valuables, he will be shot

---

8. There were no crematoria in Monowitz. In 1943, in Birkenau, it was essentially those inmates who were selected at the hospital to be gassed, and the dead from the camps annexed to the complex, who were burned (*Contribution à l'histoire du KL Auschwitz* (Oswiecim: Éditions du Musée d'État à Oswiecim, 1978), Vol. 2, p. 165).
9. This is the *Appellplatz*, which is shown on the map of Monowitz drawn by the inmate André Lévy, registration number 186,615.

instantly. The threat means nothing to me, as I have nothing on me. But the scene around me is impressive; men are hesitating, slowly undoing the seam of a coat, or separating a heel from a shoe, and handing the SS a jewel or money that they have kept in the fragile, human hope of somehow making things better for themselves. Suddenly, I think of Michel Zechel and look around for him. There he was, he had been selected with me. I want to see what he will do with his $100. He doesn't budge. Strength of character or insane recklessness? I will long admire him for his daring.

When it is over, I am shoved towards a barrack where they brutally shave off all my body hair, starting with my head. Then I am sent to be disinfected and to the shower. Real water flows there, but there is nothing with which to dry ourselves. Then some sort of pyjamas are thrown at me; the camp uniform.[10] Apparently, when my convoy entered the camp, orders were given to allow inmates to keep their shoes. I will later discover that this was not the usual procedure. So I am still wearing my own very good leather shoes. When I arrive at the barracks, on seeing my shoes, the *Stubenältester* who is in charge of my room tells me: 'You won't need them here.'
'Why?'
'You'll be much better off with wooden clogs.'

---

10. All Monowitz inmates seem to have been dressed in the concentration camp 'uniform', specially manufactured for the camp, of blue and grey vertical stripes; these were sometimes in tatters (Waitz and Klein, *Témoignages strabourgeois*, p. 484). In Auschwitz, and particularly in Birkenau, only those *kommandos* that worked outside the first line of armed guards were dressed in this way so that they could be more easily guarded. Inside, inmates – except those in the 'Canada' *kommando* – were usually dressed in those clothes taken from the Jewish convoys, or ragged uniforms taken from Poles and Russians, with large red marks on them. On arrival, the women in Birkenau received clothes randomly; these ranged from a Russian officer's jacket to an evening dress. The assigned uniform was, therefore, almost a privilege. Robert Waitz remembers that it consisted of a 'suit' and a synthetic coat with blue and white stripes; a shirt, usually in tatters; underwear; and, sometimes, a sweater. Not everybody had a coat. The shirts and underwear came from the 'Canada' barracks and had labels from all over the world. The shirt was changed every three to four weeks. The clogs, spiked on the inside with nails, were worn with *Fusslappen*, a kind of rag wrapped around the feet. The clothes are intentionally insufficient for protecting inmates from the cold. On the sites, the rare *Meister* civilians of the Buna who want to improve the working conditions for the Jews seem to have been prevented from doing so on orders from above (see Langbein, *Menschen in Auschwitz*, p. 510).

44

Very surprised, I answer: 'No, no, I prefer to keep my shoes on. I am used to them.'
I get my first slap in the face. Naturally, I give him my shoes ... and in exchange receive a pair of wooden clogs, the *Holzpantinen*, which make walking difficult and painful. It seems that this, Block 22, is going to be my home.

I may seem to be telling these things as if they went on in a logical order, but my brain was not registering properly what was happening. My memory of events before being sent to the barracks is very vague ... I see us in some kind of field, surrounded by barbed wire. My overwhelming memory is of dreadful thirst ... there is only one tap, a pipe coming out of the earth, from which awful water trickles, rust-coloured, or even red, and we are fighting like beasts to get to that tap, because the thirst is unbearable ...

The day after disinfection, large numbers are tattooed on the outside of my left forearm, with a needle mounted on a little stick and dipped in ink. The same needle is used for everybody – no hygiene. My number is 117,476. It is painful, but it is over quickly.[11]

There I am, stripped of everything I have, and now they have even taken my identity.

I am only *Häftling Nummer hundertsiebzehntausend vierhundertsechsundsiebzig* [inmate number 117,476]. My mind does not

11. The tattooing of registration numbers on the bodies of the inmates was particular to Auschwitz; elsewhere, only registration cards and clothes were marked with the inmate's number – a number that could be reassigned on death or departure. Until the beginning of 1943, the Auschwitz practice was not strictly applied. In principle, Jews were tattooed from 1942, but not necessarily all political prisoners; some non-Jewish female prisoners were exempted. The numbers followed each other sequentially: one series for men (which reached 202,499 on 18 January 1945, the day the camp was evacuated); one series for women (the last one, 89,235, seems to have been given to a little girl born on 29 November 1944; see Czech, *Kalendarium*, p. 936). The gypsies were given registration numbers starting with the letter Z (for *Zigeuner*): one series for men and one for women. On 22 February 1943, regulations became stricter: all inmates, male and female, had to be tattooed on the left forearm. The only inmates to be exempted were Germans from the Reich or ethnic Germans (*Volksdeutsch*), and inmates interred for provisional instruction purposes (*Polizeihäftlinge*). Then, on 13 May 1944, while the uninterrupted series continued, two new ones were begun, probably to camouflage the real number of prisoners (see Czech, *Kalendarium*, p. 733). One series started with the letter 'A', then 'B', for Jewish men; and one started with 'A' for Jewish women. In total, there were 405,000 inmates registered in Auschwitz, 261,000 registered deaths in the camp, and 60,000 known survivors.

follow this succession of events; I still cannot grasp what is happening to me, this fast sequence of dispossession and intolerable brutalities. I am in shock: numb. It will take me some time to realise that this is also part of their plan, aimed at totally annihilating the individual. Dehumanisation. It is true that I survived, because I am here to tell my story, but what does that prove? Those who carry the most serious accusations against what Nazi totalitarianism perpetrated there did not come back. From dehumanization, they slipped directly into void, nothingness, *Shoah*, havoc.

My number lives with me to this day. It has been somewhat erased with age, but it never occurred to me to have it removed. It was tattooed in such a way that it could be read by the person facing me, not by me: a sign that, as a number, I no longer belonged to myself, but only to the person who could dispose of me.

I think it is three days after my arrival that I am sent to the camp's *Schreibstube* [the administration office] to proceed with my registration. The inmate's files are meticulously kept; German *Gründlichkeit* [the German obsession with order] does wonders for organising hell. I must now be assigned a job, which will be recorded in my file. The clerks in the *Schreibstube* are inmates, and their function gives them some power as they allocate people to *kommandos*.[12] The secretary dealing with me is a German Jew about my age. He asks me in German for my profession, which he must note on my file. I answer in German that I was a chemistry student in Liège. With a dubious look at me he says: 'Friend, do you want some good advice? Do you want to live a little longer? If you do, don't register as a student. Declare any manual profession, because students are not worth much around here.'

'OK, put down that I am a tanner.'

I didn't give much thought to my answer, and he marked me down as a tanner. That will have enormous implications for

---

12. The *Schreibstube* and the kitchen were two havens of power (Steinberg, *Chroniques*, p. 61). J. Semprun tells how the allusion to the *Arbeitsstatistik* – the labour service in which he worked in Buchenwald – does wonders to tame a young *Stubendienst* who tried to harm him (*L'Écriture ou la vie*, Paris: Gallimard, 1994, p. 30).

me in the hell of the *kommandos*.[13] However, for the moment, I am at a loss as to why it is better to be a *Facharbeiter* [a specialised worker] rather than a student. I should have realised that a tanner would not find work in a camp like that, and that it would have been a thousand times better to be a carpenter or an electrician.

Jorge Semprun also tells how, similarly, in Buchenwald, a charitable clerk registered him, without his knowledge, as a *Stukkateur* [stucco worker], although he had said 'Student'. To declare an intellectual profession exposed the inmate, especially a Jew, to increased hatred, but I still have no idea of that. Jean Amery, who was also an inmate in Monowitz, describes this social twist as follows:

> Anyone with an intellectual profession was part of the sub-proletariat, which meant that he became an unqualified worker and had to work outdoors. This in itself was a death sentence. Many, therefore, tried to keep their profession a secret. Anyone who was even slightly good with his hands, courageously asked for manual work, which sometimes meant that he was risking his life if found to be lying. Most tried to downplay themselves. So it was that all these men, these university professors, these lawyers and these librarians, carried rails, pipes and timber for carpentry and, except in very rare cases, they were soon removed from the circuit and sent to the neighbouring camp where the gas chambers and the crematoria were waiting.[14]

Within the camp population, I belong to what the old-timers disdainfully call 'the millionaires' – those with a six-digit number. Here, unlike in other camps, dead people's numbers are not reassigned, and therefore one can more or less tell from a person's number when the inmate arrived. I am a novice, and I am going to learn the hard way what that means in Monowitz.

---

13. See Semprun, *Écriture*, pp. 96 and 307.
14. See Améry, *Par-delà le crime et le châtimen*, pp. 24–5.

When called, one must give one's number quickly in German. I begin to realise how lucky I am to speak German fluently. There are Greek and Italian Jews here who don't understand any of the orders and cannot even pronounce their numbers when called on. They cannot sing in German either, and we must sing, on our way to and from work. Not singing is reason enough for the SS to beat someone mercilessly, sometimes to death. The rumour circulates that this is reason enough to be gassed.[15]

For the first few days in the camp, while I'm not working, I only notice domestic issues. But already, then, I begin to see how everything is conceived to humiliate me, to starve me, to lower my resistance and my chances of survival. Unless you have lived through it, you cannot imagine the horror of waking up in the morning when the *stubowy* knock against the bunks yelling, '*Aufstehen! Wstawac! Ojfstajn!*'; the horror of getting up before 4 a.m., stumbling with exhaustion, leaving our dwellings, washing, dressing, drinking the horrendous potion called breakfast and being ready for the *Appell*.

Primo Levi will describe it so well: 'The illusory barrier of the warm blankets, the thin armour of sleep, the nightly evasion with its very torments drops to pieces around us and we find ourselves mercilessly awake, exposed to insult, atrociously naked and vulnerable.'[16]

In Monowitz, there is a *Waschraum*, a block with sinks for each group of blocks, but no lavatory. That kind of luxury is found only in the main camp of Auschwitz – which had been military barracks, and which I will come to know later. For now, it is a race to the collective latrines, the *Scheisshaus*, where the facilities consist of a hole in the ground covered with boards. No paper is provided (at the Auschwitz hospital, paper bandages were used for that purpose). To be precise, the

---

15. Primo Levi relates how the vast majority of Italian Jews died in the first 15 days because of their inability to communicate and to learn the laws of survival from the old-timers (*I sommersi e i salvati*, p. 72). German-speaking inmates have the advantage of at least understanding, linguistically, what is going on around them, and of being able to respond, sometimes judiciously, to their torturers. The second most used language of the camp was Polish (Langbein, *Menschen in Auschwitz*, p. 69).

16. See Levi, *Se questo è un uomo*, p. 69.

ordinary inmate is prohibited from entering the latrines at all times; these are carefully watched by Cerberus (guardian of the gate of Hell in Greek mythology), personified in the *Scheissmeister* [the master of shit]. The *Scheissmeister* is an important official, and it is important to stay in his good books because he can allow or prohibit entry to the location. Only the camp's 'management', the *Prominente*, have free access.

Naturally, I know nothing about behaving according to the rules, which are as harsh as they are absurd. I am beaten ceaselessly, day after day, for the first few weeks. As a novice, I am a favourite target for those in charge of us to vent their anger on: the *Stubendienste* [in charge of running the Block] and the *Blockältester* [the inmate-official who bullied the Block along]. Both are inmates desperate to keep their comfortable jobs rather than join one of the much tougher outdoor *kommandos*. One morning, I must have made my bed wrongly, so the *Blockältester* hurls himself at me with a board that, in his fury, he snatched from the bunk. The bunks are in fact just boards resting on a frame and can be removed. However, *Bettenbauen* [making the bed] is an obsession of the SS and of our *Blockältester* in particular. Undoubtedly, this was a remnant of Prussian barrack discipline, but in this case his perversion explodes. We are not soldiers, only inmates, and we already have so little strength to work that this additional morning chore exhausts us even further; what is this obsession with making our beds properly? Beds indeed – bags filled with rotten, decomposing hay! We, however, can still consider ourselves lucky. In Monowitz, everyone has his own bunk, which is better than a collective *koja* where many are cramped together in one bunk.

I soon realise that I am better off sleeping on the top bunk, because the other inmates sometimes urinate during the night, or worse, defecate, taken by dysentery caused by the all-too liquid soup. Particularly irritating is the straw dust that falls on the lower bunk and irritates the eyes and causes coughing. To top it all off, we must sleep with all our possessions rolled up in a bundle under our heads, and above all, beware of committing the disastrous mistake of leaving our shoes on the floor, lest they be gone by morning. We must constantly be on guard. The inmate who is not fully dressed at *Appell* time is mercilessly beaten, and his miserable clogs must be properly shined, another obsession of the *Blockältester*, as senseless as the one about making beds, because the ground is muddy and cleanliness as ephemeral as absurd.

We are also beaten if caught searching in the trash for leftover food; the *Blockältester* cannot stand it, and accuses us of bringing in the plague and other diseases, but how can we resist? We will do it again and again. The old-timers, better fed, call us the *Speckjäger* [lard hunters]! Hunger gnaws at me day and night, like at all of my companions, as does thirst, because the water here is revolting. (In Auschwitz, the water is actually drinkable. In Monowitz, we are not supposed to live more than six weeks, so it is considered unnecessary to improve the situation.)

In addition to other humiliations and dangers, we, the Jews, sub-humans among sub-humans, are also exposed to violent anti-Semitism from the Poles, who lord it over us. They hate us and abuse us, able to show fraternal feeling only to their fellow Poles. As I see it, I am lucky in one thing: to have arrived after the worst of winter was over. There are heaters in the Blocks. But could I have survived the outdoor *kommandos*, my feet bruised and almost bare, in the snow and the frozen mud? Getting up before dawn, followed by the long, motionless and deathly *Appell* in sub-zero temperatures? Later, I will be told that punishment *Appells* – those called, for example, when there had been an escape – were less frequent and shorter in Monowitz than in Auschwitz. But, no matter what, the *Appell* is always a crucial ordeal. Every morning and evening the number of inmates, dead or alive, must correspond to the lists. So we bring our wounded and dead comrades to the *Appell*. Anyway, dead or alive, we are only *Stücke*: pawns, puppets, just bodies, not men. '*Appell muss stimmen!*' [The number of inmates must be correct!] Every *Stück* must attend *Appell*!

On one of my first days, at the distribution of the morning coffee, which is more like a piping hot substitute hiding behind the name coffee, in the rush to drink, I spill my mug and seriously burn my hand. This is the first of a long series of wounds that prove impossible to heal.

On about the fifth day after my arrival, I start to work.[17] I am unaware that, despite my registration as a tanner, I have not been classified as a specialised worker. According to their classification, I am a *Hilfsarbeiter*, an unskilled worker; the worst possible situation to be in. I am assigned to the *Holzhof kommando*, the wood yard. I discover very soon that the *kommandos* are intended to make us work and achieve our physical destruction and, ultimately, our elimination. It is a disciplinarian grind, except that while in hard labour prisons limits are set, here they don't exist, and there is no pity. An inmate is no longer human, his humanity having been resolved administratively. The issue here is death. The chimney of the crematorium is waiting. Besides, nobody is affected by our death; dying is the norm. I don't think our work was of much economic value. Obviously, the SS consider the work more as punishment. They have perfected an elimination system that also allows them to temporarily benefit from the inmates' energy. If it were really useful work, they would try to optimise our contribution and preserve our strength! They would feed us! They would look after us! They would provide us with equipment to carry out the heavy labour without mortally wounding ourselves in the process or, at least, decent shoes and protection against the cold! However, in the eyes of the Nazis, neither Jews nor gypsies have the right to exist other than as slaves. Still, in principle, these slaves have been recruited to help Germany win the war, and it would have been logical not to waste that workforce. I jump ahead of

---

17. It seems that either W.B. was not quarantined, like Paul Steinberg and Primo Levi (who arrived some time later), or that his quarantine was very short, indicating that, in April 1943, the Buna site was short of workers. Steinberg lived through quarantine: Days of *farniente* [idleness] broken by abuse and initiation tests' (*Chroniques*, p. 62). This oppressive quarantine contributed to further weakening the inmates even before they started work, and was the scene of savage internal selections. For a small number of lucky inmates, work would also mean access to additional food. Elsewhere, the initial elimination was achieved by other means: in Buchenwald, all new arrivals were assigned to disciplinarian *kommandos* for six to twelve weeks; in which, without well-placed comrades, hardly anybody could survive (see E. Kogon, *L'État SS: Le Système des camps de concentration allemands*, 2nd edn (Paris: Seuil/Points Histoire, 1993), p. 212).

myself, but later, in 1944, they would have a completely different perspective.

The *Holzhof*[18]*kommando* is one of the many outdoor *kommandos* slaving in the Buna area. There is nothing else to do for the moment, as the factory is not yet producing. And, as a novice, I have no chance of being assigned to less strenuous work. Our job is to transport tree trunks, without any mechanical help. The trunks are so heavy that ten men are needed to lift one of them. Ten of us go to pick up the next trunk, lift it onto our shoulders, and pass in front of the *kapo*,[19] whom we call *Pieronia* [Thunder], because it seems to be his favourite curse. He is a Silesian Pole who hates Jews, and in his hatred, tends to be much more violent than the Germans. He beats us for the pure pleasure. His most subtle form of torture is to stop us when we pass in front of him bent under the near intolerable weight of the trunk, and to dismiss half the men. The trunk is then supported only on five shoulders, which is almost impossible to bear, and Pieronia, is of course, well aware of that. I can still see his eyes shining ferociously. For my misfortune, I am tall, and when only five of us are left, I end up carrying most of the tree's load. I begin to hate these short men and the advantage they enjoy![20] After three days of this exercise, my shoulder is a mess; I am carrying the trunks on an open wound. I cannot take care of it, and it reopens every day. Soon it spreads, and the bone is almost bare.

Like all ordinary *Häftlinge*, my feet are also bleeding. The wooden clogs, those horrible *Holzpantinen*, are a carefully

---

18. Marc Klein also remembers having worked in a *Holzhof* [wood yard] *kommando* at the main camp (Auschwitz II), where he unloaded tree trunks (see Waitz and Klein, *Témoignages strasbourgeois*, pp. 423–55). In the Auschwitz complex, the non-specialised workers' *kommandos* mainly did digging and the transporting of heavy materials: trunks, bricks, cement, pipes, charcoal, etc. The specialised *kommandos* recruited plumbers, bricklayers, carpenters, roofers, domestics, tailors, cobblers, etc.

19. *Kapo* or *capo*: the name is the same in all the concentration camps and refers to a *kommando* chief. The term is believed to have been brought to Germany by Italian workers. According to Marc Klein, in Auschwitz, the spelling *capo* would have been used in the registers (see M. Ruby, *Livre de la déportation* (Paris: Laffont, 1995), p. 285). We have adopted the German spelling.

20. Primo Levi found himself in exactly the same situation: when he had to carry a girder with a tall comrade he considered himself lucky to be shorter (*Se questo è un uomo*, p. 73).

planned torture. They are never the right size, never hold the foot, and keep getting stuck in the mud, where they remain. In this season in Monowitz, mud is everywhere and permanent, on all the sites, in all the alleys in the camp. Hence, we have many wounds on our feet, which more or less close during the night, only to reopen the next day. The friction from walking, the pressure of the feet against canvas and wood, causes us to limp continuously; and beware if our step is not brisk enough! In the best case, the wounds simply fester without the feet swelling. When things get worse, we naturally dream of going to hospital, but, although I don't yet know it, swollen feet are a very bad condition to have, and there is never any guarantee that we will come out of hospital alive.[21]

In the course of a workday, as if carrying trunks wasn't enough, I am constantly beaten. Sometimes it is the *Vorarbeiter*, the foreman at the bottom of the pyramid in charge of a handful of workers, who goes for me, and sometimes the *kapo*, because work is never done to their satisfaction. In this kind of *kommando*, it is impossible for work to be done satisfactorily, as the work itself is only secondary, and the main purpose is to make us suffer, to reduce and eliminate us. There is, of course, never any break or remuneration, and the end of work towards 5:00 or 6:00 p.m.,[22] certainly does not signify the end of torment. The Buna site is enormous, and my *kommando* at the *Holzhof* is some distance from the camp. The way back is interminable; bleeding feet hammering torture, head throbbing, we advance like spineless puppets, like zombies. How do I make it, how do I get back to the Block, walking every evening? To carry on, I would at least like to be able to grit my teeth, but no, we have

---

21. As Primo Levi says, death begins with the shoes (*ibid.*, p. 40). Very often, inmates had no socks or rags to protect their feet, and it was only a short step from there to frostbite, wounds and inflammation. The SS doctor, Entress, admitted in court that wearing these clogs was the equivalent of a death sentence for the inmates (see Langbein, *Der Auschwitz-Prozess Eine Dokumentation*, 2 Vols, 2 edn (Frankfurt: Neue Kritik, 1995), p. 572).
22. According to various sources, a workday in Monowitz stretched from 6:30 a.m. to 6:00 p.m. in the summer, and from 8:00 a.m. to 4:00 p.m. in the winter, with a break of half an hour to an hour in the middle of the day (however, reveille was before 4:00 a.m. in the summer and before 5:00 in the winter). A directive of 15 March 1943, from *Kommandant* Höss, specified work hours as being from 6:00 a.m. to 5:30 p.m., with a break from 12 noon to 1:00 p.m.

to sing. Next to me, Greek and Italian Jews are beaten because they cannot sing the songs in German:

Im Lager Auschwitz bin ich zwar
So manchen Tag, so manches Jahr,
Doch denk ich oft, gemut und gern,
An meine Lieben in der Fern
Ganz gleich obs schneit ob rote Rosen blühn... [23]

Behind the camp gate, it is time for the endless evening *Appell*. At each *Appell* there are the dead – some brought back from the sites – others who just drop dead where they stand. After the *Appell*, we are supposed to be left in peace to eat the evening soup, after which we will drop, exhausted, onto the bunks. But invariably, the *Blockältester* is waiting for us with a list of new grievances for which he makes us pay with further beatings.

That first week of work is endless, limitless suffering. Thirst tortures me day and night. We have to resist the temptation to drink water from the sink, as it causes dysentery. That is something we cannot afford to catch, because the *Scheissmeister* does not allow us to go to the latrines whenever we want. But the beverage we get in the mornings is not enough to quench our thirst, nor is the midday soup, although it is too liquid to alleviate our hunger.[24]

My first Sunday, at the beginning of May, should be a 'non-working' Sunday, because we are supposed to rest every other Sunday except for Block duties. But, to my horror, my group is taken from our Block and sent to the station, where wagons

---

23. 'Indeed, here I am in the camp of Auschwitz, for many days now, many years. Still, I often think with good humour and contentment about my loved ones so far away, whether it snows or whether red roses bloom ...' (see T. Geve, *Es gibt hier keine Kinder: Auschwitz, Gross-Rosen, Buchenwald* (Göttingen: Wallstein, 1997)). This 'Auschwitz Song' was one of the songs most frequently sung, and alludes only to the disciplinarian aspect of the imprisonment.

24. The SS and the board of directors of I.G. Farben co-operated fully in the construction of the barracks and the military surveillance of the factory and the camp. The inmates were lodged and (badly) fed by the camp services: 'The SS put the inmates on Auschwitz rations, I.G. Farben added some "Buna soup" to ensure production' (Hilberg, *La Destruction*, pp. 804–5). Primo Levi remembers receiving two litres of soup a day, the one at midday being given by I.G. Farben (*I sommersi e i salvati*, p. 89).

filled with construction materials are waiting to be unloaded: large blocks of stones and huge sacks of cement. I am sent to unload the cement. The only way I can carry those very heavy sacks is to let them weigh down on my already open shoulder, but on contact with the wound, the cement causes almost unbearable burning. This time I know I won't last. I must slow down. But, unfortunately, an SS sees me and hurls himself at me. I am beaten black and blue on my behind, which is apparently the 'disciplinarian' punishment.

When I return to my block, on the eve of my first Sunday after only one week at the camp of Buna-Monowitz, I am a wreck. My feet are torn and hurt terribly, my shoulder is a huge open wound, horribly burnt. To top it all off, my behind is black and blue, covered in bloody stripes. And the burn on my hand from the morning coffee is starting to look quite serious.

The next day is Monday and work at the *Holzhof* starts again. I feel I cannot go on, and I think that only one thing remains to me: let myself drop. If I just let myself fall to the ground, I won't see anything anymore, I won't feel, and one way or another, all this will come to an end. What does it matter if I die?

And still, I go on. They yell, we are driven; we keep going, one more day.

In the middle of that week, a small miracle occurs. Because of my burnt hand, I am sent to hospital.

The *Häftlingskrankenbau* (HKB) consists of several barracks. The *Blockältester* of my sleeping quarters is called Glaser. Thanks to him, I learn much that is vital for life in the camp. This first stay in hospital is a turning point. Until now, I have been in a state of shock and physical misery, which has prevented me from thinking. I just took everything. Here, while resting, I find time to inquire, and others willingly cooperate.

I will read in the memoirs of doctor Waitz, who worked as a medic[25] in this camp, that the most common diseases here are: abscesses (a pus-filled infection, common on the legs and feet, which must be lanced); pneumonia and other diseases caused

---

25. See Waitz and Klein, *Témoignages strasbourgeois*, p. 482 ff.

by the cold; broken limbs resulting from beatings and accidents; and hunger oedema, which weakens the sick. Almost no medication is available; the rare sulphas are reserved for the *Prominente* and the Aryans. Tannin is given against diarrhoea, solvent for coughs, and a wheat mash for those on special diets; but there is nothing against scabies and other skin diseases, which are common. The hospital treats all wounds, even serious ones, with oxygenated water, disinfectant and paper bandages, some of which are stolen for use in the latrines.

I am discovering what grave danger awaits those in hospital. The SS medics periodically select the most seriously ill inmates, without waiting for them to become *musulmen*.[26] These selections take place at the hospital, and the sick whose numbers are called are sent to Auschwitz, and from there, directly to the gas chamber. Even if nobody talks about it openly, everybody knows.[27] The rule to follow becomes clear to

---

26. There are various unconvincing explanations for this term. In camp jargon, it designates cachectic inmates who had reached the last stage of exhaustion. The term may have been invented by the SS – out of contempt for Arab fatalism. Inmate doctor, W. Fejkiel, reflected that, for him, the cachectic figure conjured up the image of the posture of Arabs at prayer (Langbein, *Menschen in Auschwitz*, p. 114). According to Robert Waitz, a person reaches the state of *musulman* after losing at least a third of his normal body weight. (At the time of liberation, some *musulmen* weighed 25 kilos; few weighed over 35 kilos.) The muscle structure is evenly distributed over the body, so one can be diagnosed by checking the buttocks. Oedemas develop, mainly on the face in the morning and in the lower limbs in the evening, spreading sometimes over the abdomen. Dysentery can be an aggravating factor. The most striking symptoms were psychometric and behavioural: the *musulman* went through a physiological slowdown of his movements and thought processes. He stopped understanding orders, and wounded or burnt himself without noticing. He had to be carried to the *Appell*. He stopped taking care of himself, picked up sordid leftovers to eat and relieved himself where he lay. He seemed to have lost all sense of his own humanity. Tragically, this exposed him not only to persecution from his oversees, but also from his companions. In them, instead of pity, he inspired disgust and contempt. Paul Steinberg, when promoted to honorary *Stubendienst*, surprised himself when he was tempted to slap a Polish *musulman* before withdrawing in horror at his gesture (*Chroniques*, p. 147). Many abused the *musulman*, waiting for his food ration or his gold teeth. Finally, if he was not selected for the gas chamber, he died 'like a clock that stops' (M.-Cl. Caillant-Couturier, quoted in Langbein, *Menschen in Auschwitz*, p. 125).
27. No survivor ever fails to mention the horrendous selections in the Blocks and at the hospital. The selected were sometimes penned in a Block for many days, without food, waiting for the last transport to arrive. They knew what to expect, even though the SS policy was to create a sense of doubt about the outcome of the selection (Langbein, *Menschen in Auschwitz*, pp. 129–34, ff.; Levi, *Se questo è un uomo*, pp. 130–5; Wellers, *Un Juif sous Vichy*, pp. 250–1).

me. Under no circumstances am I to become seriously ill. But how? These few days in the HKB are, for me, a stay in limbo, as Primo Levi[28] so accurately said. It is not that I am being treated, but I am no longer beaten and I don't have to slave on the site. On the other hand, I am constantly hungry. My friend, Michel Zechel, manages to visit me once and brings me a potato! It is my luck that Michel manages to get around better than I do. He learned quickly how to 'organise' the things needed for his survival.

I will never forget the striking moral distinction that prevailed in the camp between stealing and 'organising'. Stealing from inmates is *Kameradschaftsdiebstahl* [stealing between comrades]. To be caught stealing a fellow inmate's bread ration is punishable by death. On the other hand, 'organising' is the most common occupation in Auschwitz, and the SS are the first to participate in it. This distinction is characteristic of the perversion in the concentration camp universe, because in reality, there is little difference between the two activities. 'Organising' means helping oneself to supplies in the kitchen and the clothes store at the expense of the whole camp. However, the camp is, by its very nature, a perverse place, where a diversity of morals coexists with the total absence of morals. Everybody knows that the barrack chiefs and the *Stubendienste* keep, for their own consumption, part of the food meant for the whole Block. The 'organisation' in Auschwitz, with the inflow of goods from Jews exterminated upon arrival, has become a thriving business. The wretched newcomers, carefully deluded to believe that they are on their way to a work camp in the east, bring with them a large portion of their household: linen, pots and pans, clothes, money, jewellery, books. And, while their gassed bodies are being reduced to ashes in the crematorium, a special *kommando* is sorting their belongings and piling them up in the famous 'Canada' *kommando*, named in memory of the blessed country, the country of abundance. Throughout 1943, and even more in 1944, goods arrive constantly, and Canada is bursting with an

---

28. Levi, *Se questo è un uomo*, p. 56.

abundance of everything. Although, in principle, Jews' belongings are the property of the Reich and it is absolutely forbidden to appropriate them, it is widely known that the SS steal valuable goods.[29] What is maybe less known and quite characteristic of the camp's ambiguities, the 'grey zone' that Primo Levi evokes in *The Drowned and the Saved*, is that certain inmates, acting as intermediaries for the SS, sell many of these precious objects. In return, the SS close their eyes to the commissions that these agents pocket, as this is the only way for the SS to remove their stolen goods. The system functions smoothly. The 'Canada' *kommando* goes about its business undisturbed, and, a few days later, the SS comes to collect his share. The despicable Jews are still good enough to help the pride of the German race fill their own pockets.[30]

On the sixth day of my stay in hospital, I am sent to push carts, as I am slowly getting better. I still have the right to remain a few days in the *Blockschonung*, a halfway station between the hospital and work, where one is supposed to remain in the Block and not go out to work with one's *kommando*. In theory, this is to regain one's strength. In reality, it is dangerous, because of the many *kapos* whose duty in the camp is to hunt down inmates believed to have hidden in the barracks instead of going out to work. They beat up anybody they find, or send them to the *Scheisskommando*, the latrine *kommando*. I am caught once, and I am sent to empty the cesspool. To do that, one must climb down into excrement, and while submerged in filth up to one's waist, fill buckets that others pull up hell knows where.[31] Fortunately, I only have to do it once, and by a lucky stroke I am allowed to shower afterwards.

After a week of rest, I am assigned to a new *kommando*, number 32. The prospect is gloomy; no doubt the work will be as painful as in the *Holzhof*, because it is another outdoor *kommando*, transporting sacks, stones, wood. The ordeal starts

---

29. Even the incorruptible commander Höss, on leaving Auschwitz with his family at the beginning of November 1943, took several wagons with him filled with personal effects (Langbein, *Menschen in Auschwitz*, p. 352).
30. Ibid., p. 161.
31. Human excrement was commonly used for fertilizer.

all over again, the main purpose being to kill us fairly quickly with work. Hunger becomes intolerable, as rations are desperately limited. As a common *Häftling*, I am meant to die of exhaustion. I just don't know what will get me first, hunger or abuse.

Yet I slowly begin to realise that I have the tiniest power of resistance. I can, to some extent, use cunning to spare my strength. One day, I witness an example of what I should not do. A German Jew in my *kommando*, really big and in great physical shape, wanted to show how good he was. Maybe it was bravado, or maybe he wanted to impress his torturers as only a German could. Whatever it was, he decided to carry a heavy piece of machinery all on his own. It turned over, crushing him. I didn't see what happened next, whether he died right there or was transported to hospital, which I doubt. But this is common here. Every day, horrible accidents occur on the sites: hands, arms, legs are mutilated. The business is run on the understanding that the workforce is unlimited, and in truth, it is. The SS know that new convoys arrive continually.

This week of work is incredibly hard. It feels as if the blows in this *kommando* are distributed with a special enthusiasm. When Friday finally comes, we are entitled, as a supplement, to an endless *Appell*, after which we receive the surprise of the day; back in the Block, we are told to go and participate in a 'sports' session. It is one of the favourite pastimes of the SS; they come to the Blocks and amuse themselves watching men broken by the inhuman work of the day perform forced gymnastics, with hundreds of exercises, crawling under beds, jumping to attention and sprinting – a real 'gymboree'. However, against all common practice, no medal is awarded to the winner; on the contrary, those who do not perform at the required rhythm are beaten black and blue. At other times, for good measure, everybody is beaten.

Almost every day I am beaten and struck until I bleed. I am under the impression, maybe wrongly, that I am their favourite target. Do they notice me because I am still resisting physically, despite hunger and exhaustion? I have no idea, but in some obscure way I start feeling that I don't want to admit defeat.

Can they still see in me some trace of natural pride, even though I believe I will not even recognise myself in a mirror? They may have a more positive view of me than I do. I can only ponder one thing: this life, this living death, cannot go on. It is impossible for it to go on, yet it does. The limits of my strength are stretched a little further each day. And yet with each new chore I discover new unsuspected limits. Every morning witnesses my incredible survival of the past day. But how long can this reprieve go on? When I have the courage to be honest, I tell myself out loud: 'You will never go home.'

Towards the middle of my second week in *kommando* 32, on 20 May, my friend, Michel, is recruited as a dentist to the main camp of Auschwitz. For Michel, it is without doubt a happy event; his new job promises to be less demanding and better protected. At the same time, although I don't know it yet, both our paths in this concentration camp hell are curving slightly, and Michel's move is to be the first of a series of changes which will have serious consequences for both of us.

For me, change is not yet on the agenda. I remain a *Hilfsarbeiter*. Between the Block and the worksite, my physical condition continues to deteriorate; my strength is ebbing. Every day, work becomes more painful; my feet are a mess and can no longer carry me. Hunger gnaws at me every minute of my life. Yet, it is during these days that a German criminal teaches me one of the most precious lessons of camp life. He teaches me how to pretend to work, how to ape exertion to preserve what little strength I have left. This wisdom, from his long past as a convict, enabled him to withstand the most murderous *kommandos*.

'My friend,' he says, 'you have to learn not to work with your hands, but with your eyes. Otherwise, you're finished, man.'

What it means is that it is essential to unobtrusively watch the *Vorarbeiter* and the *kapo*, and to scrupulously mimic the gestures of a working man, but without exerting yourself. And, of course, you must work hard the moment you feel the guard's eyes on you. I got the message. My technique, essential for survival, improved quickly.

After a month in Monowitz, the SS gives each inmate postcards, ordering us to write to our families and close ones. We are free to choose whom to write to. I obey: I send one card to my parents in Czernowitz and another to my girlfriend in Liège. This way they will know where I am, because I am allowed to indicate the place of sending, *Arbeitslager* Monowitz. I later discover, to my dismay, the calculated thinking of the SS behind these postcards.[32] I will bitterly regret having sent the first ones and will write no more. It is a propaganda move with one sole aim: to convince the families not yet deported, and the public in general in the rest of Europe, that not only are the inmates still alive, but that they are healthy, comfortable, and busy working. Everyone writes more or less the same text on these cards, almost under dictation.

At the end of May, when I have been in the camp about 40 days, I finally have my first day of rest, not counting my week in hospital. I decide to see how I look, and I go and look at myself in a mirror that I find at one of the sinks.

How strange. I stand in front of the mirror and I don't see myself. What faces me is not me – but there is nobody else around …

I didn't recognise myself.

The next day, I approach a French civilian worker I am in contact with every day in the Buna, and ask him if he would mind sending a card for me to my girlfriend, because what I have to tell her will definitely not pass the censor. He agrees, and I write this simple sentence to C.: 'I will never come back.'

It is true that in the meantime, spring arrived; it is the beginning of June and I have been in this death factory for six weeks.

---

32. The Reich Security forwarded these cards, handwritten in German, with their standardised text. In Belgium, they arrived at the JAB, which distributed them to the Jewish families not yet deported. This poisonous indoctrination by the SS had a dual purpose: to strengthen the 'working myth' (Steinberg, *La Traque*, Vol. 1, p. 255), and to find the Jews who were hiding (they even went so far as to offer them an amnesty if they returned to their own homes). This was a routine police operation (Czech, *Kalendarium*, p. 543). Georges Wellers (*Un Juif sous Vichy*, p. 130) described the effect these cards produced in Drancy in January 1943:

> [They] came from the *Arbeitslager* of Birkenau in Upper Silesia … The text was more or less the same: the senders wrote that they were well, they were working, and they asked for an answer, a parcel of clothes and 40 marks. In Drancy, all these cards made a very good impression.

But I feel my end approaching. Their elimination programme is conceived with diabolical effectiveness. I have no strength left and, one morning at work, I hide behind a pile of wood to escape the chores. Besides not being stable on my feet, I am burning with fever and am incapable of lifting anything.

This time, it is not an SS guard who finds me, nor the *kapo kommando*, but a German civilian employee, a *Meister* of the I.G. Farben. (Until the evacuation of the camps in Upper Silesia, the Buna will remain a large site, producing almost nothing. On the site, the I.G. Farben employees and their foremen use the same language as the SS when talking to Jews, and treat them the same way. In their eyes, we are not men, not even a workforce worth preserving.) The *Meister* hurries to report me to the *kapo* and the SS guard. What happens next is standard. First, the *kapo* beats me black and blue; then he formally reprimands me by writing my number in his notebook. As the organisation has no loopholes and orders are executed without fail, I am called to face the others at the evening *Appell*, and there I get the regulation discipline punishment: *Fünfundzwanzig auf den Hintern!* [twenty-five lashes on my behind]. And these are no laughing matter.

Some people like to think that only the SS knew what was happening in the camps, and that the German population was completely unaware of our working conditions, or of what we had to put up with. However, the I.G. Farben employees working at the Buna all saw us. They saw that the inmate-workers were starved, exhausted, beaten, harmed, and they themselves contributed to it on a large scale. They saw that the teams were constantly replaced, and that the men from the previous team were never seen again.

This time it really is the end for me. A few days after my 25 lashes, my dysentery starts. My body hurts all over, I cannot stand it anymore, I am falling apart. Only willpower remains, and I try to hold on.

It is generally said that those who kept going in the camps were those who had faith or believed in some ideal. I observed that this was true for political prisoners, in particular the communists, who I must say were generally better organised.

However, this was not true for most Jews, whose fate was beyond understanding. Among them, only some believers found support in their faith, and considered what was happening to them the expression of God's anger. For me, I was not a believer, nor a political militant. I thought only that what the Germans were doing to the Jews – and thus, to me – was an injustice and an obscenity. I didn't have the slightest sense of guilt; I couldn't find the remotest justification for what they were doing. And I must admit that what stopped me, in those atrocious days of suffering and exhaustion, from drowning in a black hole of desperation and allowing myself to fall to my death, was not longing for home, nor regret for a life foolishly interrupted, nor any grand ideal. No, at the risk of sounding frivolous, I must confess that what kept me going was a desperate wish to return one day to the mountains, and hurl myself down the ski slopes onto the bright soft snow.

The beginning of June drags by. One evening, a week after the outbreak of my dysentery, my feet start swelling, caused by oedema, which is brought on by hunger. In the morning, however, my face is all swollen. The swelling moves around my body as though through communicating vessels.[33] By then, I know enough about the *Häftlingskrankenbau* to avoid being sent there at all cost. I am no longer a novice, and unlike the first time, I don't consider it luck to be taken to hospital. On the contrary, this time I will be very happy to avoid it completely.[34] I am slowly turning into a *musulman*, and I have no illusions about my chances of passing an internal selection. I don't think

---

33. If they survived their incarceration in the camps and did not die within days or weeks of their liberation, some survivors, like Robert Antelme, took months to recover from the camp's dysentery (see M. Duras, *La Douleur*, Paris: POL, 1985). Oedema is caused by a lack of protein, fat and vitamins, as well as by food that is too liquid.

34.
> The problem of admission to hospital, discussed covertly [by inmate doctors who decide who should be accepted or refused], was cruel and delicate. Under no circumstances was selection or danger to be mentioned. A number of comrades, refusing to understand our hints...insisted on being admitted and ultimately ended up disappearing in a selection.
> (M. Klein, in Waitz and Klein, *Témoignages strasbourgeois*, p. 445.)

'Not knowing is one of the most horrible things of the camps' (Kogon, *L'État SS*, p. 164).

63

I have enough flesh on my buttocks to be sent to the right side. I just have to go on struggling in that nightmarish *kommando*. I try pitifully and without hope to sneak out of work. It is obvious that the *kommando* will soon go on without me.

Still, miraculously, I manage to remain standing until the last week of June, in the antechamber of final exhaustion.

On the last evening of the month, the *Blockältester*, a German political prisoner, is serving the soup at our Block; when my turn comes, I am so weak that I cannot even hold my mug. It turns over and my soup is irredeemably lost. Yet it is unthinkable for inmates who have reached the state I am in to survive even one day without food: those few calories are more or less crucial, and going without them could send the *Häftling* irreversibly downhill. The *Blockältester* blows up in intense anger: he must have taken my weakness as a personal insult. He strikes me a terrible blow, knocking me to the other end of the room. But, immediately after that, while I am still lying on the floor, a strange thing occurs; maybe out of remorse, the *Blockältester* picks me up and carefully looks me up and down. In a reprimanding tone, he asks me what I did when I was a civilian: 'You look so stupid that I really wonder what you could have been before you came here!'

I must have answered him that I was a chemistry student, because I hear him announce peremptorily that there is absolutely nothing for me to do in his Block. 'This is not the place for a future chemist; the factory is not yet functioning. You should have been sent to the main camp of Auschwitz to work at the hospital or something like that!'

And right there, the most incredible thing happens, he seems to take pity on me. He drags me through the whole camp to the *Schreibstube* of Monowitz. Pushing me in front of him in the administration office, he forces the clerk to take out my file and to change my profession to 'chemistry student'.

Forty-eight hours later, I am called to the office and told that I will be transferred to the main camp of Auschwitz together with ten other inmates. A 'logic' in total opposition to elimination, a semblance of 'normal' logic, is acting in my favour. Once again, it is better for me to be a student than a worker.

I am convinced that another few days, at the most one or two weeks, and my life would have ended at the Buna site. Others continued to die right there.

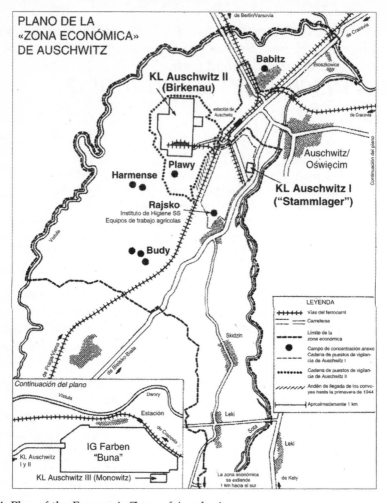

4. Plan of the Economic Zone of Auschwitz.

Key:
SS Instituto de Higiene SS Equipos de trabajo agricolas = SS Institute of Hygiene
    Horticultural Kommandos
Vias del ferrocarril = railways
Carreteras = roads
Limite de la zona económica = limit of the economic zone
Campo de concentracion anexo = camp annex
Cadena de puestos de vigilancia de Auschwitz I = line of sentinels guarding Auschwitz I
Cadena de puestos de vigilancia de Auschwitz II = line of sentinels guarding Auschwitz II
Andén de llegada de los convoyes hasta la primavera de 1944 = arrival ramp for the
    convoys until spring 1944.
Aproximadamente 1 km = distance 1 km
Continuación del plano = continuation of map
Estación = station
La zona económica se extiende 1 km hacia el sur = the economic zone extends 1 km to the
    south

4 Auschwitz: Capital of a Principality

> In Auschwitz everything was unpredictable; everything was
> possible. And yet – even from the perspective of the
> exterminators – many things remained inexplicable.
> No one was safe from surprises. Exceptionally these surprises
> could have positive outcomes.
>
> Hermann Langbein, *Menschen in Auschwitz*

On 10 or 11 July, I am transported to the main camp of Auschwitz, in German the *Stammlager* [the original camp]. That capital of the concentration camp principality was in old Polish artillery barracks, which were first taken over by the *Wehrmacht*, and then by the SS. It is next to Oswiecim, a small town of 12,000 residents, situated, as I would find out later, on the railway crossroads of Vienna, Berlin, Prague and Warsaw.

Although my changed status is thanks to the intervention of a *Blockältester* with good intentions, I am worried, because any change also means a high risk. I will have to go through a visit, a selection; my whole fate depends on the assessment of my physical condition. And I do not cut such a fine figure. If they find me too shabby to be part of a *kommando*, the walk through the gate with the infamous inscription *Arbeit macht frei* will be my last stop before the crematorium.[1] Although even this is not certain, because everything in the camp is unpredictable. Happiness and misery are distributed without any logic. Who knows, this move may well be my lucky stroke! I hang on to what I am led to believe: there are positions available for chemists.

---

1. The slogan *Arbeit macht frei* [work provides freedom], imported from Dachau, was not ironic in the eyes of the SS: according to Höss, all the world – except Jews, anti-socials and homosexuals – could be re-educated.

I tell myself I am lucky that I can leave Buna and my life as an unskilled worker in the site *kommandos;* those death *kommandos*, with their carefully planned elimination programme. But the minute I allow myself to be remotely realistic, I must admit that I am indeed in a perilous position. I am in a state of advanced exhaustion, and show almost all the characteristics of the fearsome *allgemeine Körperschwäche* [general exhaustion]. My face and lower limbs are swollen by oedema. My insides are sapped by hunger, as there is never enough bread. I feel as if all my bones are broken and I am wounded in several places. It is insane to claim that I can lift anything, or walk long distances. One thing is certain: either they find me an easy job, or I will die. But it is hard to imagine that pity exists anywhere here, so I don't think I have much of a chance.

I jump ahead a bit. The fact that I am officially a chemist again will not necessarily open the door to a specialised *kommando*, at least not at the beginning. It is a unique set of circumstances that will forge my destiny, but – and this can never be said too often – all survivors experienced special circumstances. To survive was an exception, not the rule.

I arrive at the admissions office in the large hospital sector of Auschwitz as part of a group of disabled and very ill inmates. If I remember correctly, we had to report to Block 28. Before anything else, we have to shower; the SS doctor wants to see what is left of the showered men before deciding their fate. In the abominable administrative language of the camp, the wretched individual who goes to consult a doctor is an *Arztvormelder* [a candidate for medical viewing]. It must be understood that an SS doctor does not treat; he only decides whether a prisoner is to be admitted to the hospital, gassed, or immediately assigned to work. He can therefore decide instantly whether a sick man should be liquidated. If he decides against me, I face two possibilities: either a specialised nurse will inject me with some deadly substance[2] in one of the

---

2. The liquidation campaign by intracardiac injections of phenol (or evipan sodium) was essentially the work of Entress. This work carried on through the autumn of 1941, until Himmler's injunction of 27 April 1943, which limited the number of

nearby rooms – in camp jargon, this is called *abspritzen* [to prick[3]] – but this is no longer done much. Alternatively, I will be put aside indefinitely in a Block for the dying, without treatment or food, naked, waiting without hope, for the truck to take me to the gas chamber.

After the shower, I know that I will have to wait, naked, in the hall for the doctor who does not wish to get too close to the inmates' germs and the foul smells from their putrid bodies. The hospital is not meant to treat and cure people; it is not a safe place to be. The SS doctor does not behave like a doctor, either. Actually, this world is not the world, either, even though we are living in it, or at least, are trying not to die in it.

But this is my lucky day. Although I don't know it, I arrive at the Auschwitz HKB when a new policy is in force. Germany has not succeeded in its lightning conquest of Europe, as it boasted it would. The prisoners' work will need to be exploited further, human lives in the camp, at least of registered inmates like me, will need to be better preserved. There is some relaxation of internal selections. They will, however, pick up again towards the end of the summer. The hospital is still not really

---

patients who could be euthanised. The act took place in room number 1 in Block 20 (before that, it took place either in front of the morgue, or in Block 28, or else in Block 21). As with the selections, the *Blocksperre* was announced; patients were brought into the room individually and seated on a stool. An SDG or a nursing aide then injected him directly into the heart with a solution of 10–15 cc. of phenol. Death occurred about 15 seconds later. The principal perpetrator of these murders was the SDG, Josef Klehr, who – in Frankfurt, in 1965 – was sentenced to 475 terms of life imprisonment. In court, he declared that the patients knew what to expect but never tried to resist. One witness said that Klehr killed 'like a shoemaker tearing a rotten sole from a shoe'. According to several Polish inmates, 25–30,000 inmates (90–95 per cent of them Jews) were killed in this manner between 1941 and 1943. In the spring of 1943, Klehr was moved, receiving a questionable promotion: he became the 'disinfection' *kommando* in Birkenau, in charge of keeping the gas chambers supplied with Zyklon B (see Langbein, *Der Auschwitz-Prozess*, for the court proceedings of Klehr, p. 709 ff.; Langbein, *Menschen in Auschwitz*, pp. 46–7 and 440–1; Hamburger Institut für Sozialforschung (eds), *Die Auschwitz-Hefte: Texte der polnischen Zeitschrift* Przeglad Lekarski *über historische, psychische und medizinische Aspekte des Lebens und Sterbens in Auschwitz*, Vol. 1 (Hamburg: Rogner u. Bernard, 1995), pp. 277–80).

3. The term *spritzen* or *abspritzen* [to kill by injection] was part of the camp jargon (Langbein, *Menschen in Auschwitz*, p. 47) and was probably coined by inmates before it was taken up by the SS, as was often the case (for example, the term 'Canada'). On the rich and fascinating Auschwitz jargon, see *Die Auschwitz-Hefte*, Vol. 2, p. 241 ff.

safe, certainly not for Jews, but when I appear there, in the summer of 1943, it has definitely become a less dangerous place to be.

When I enter the shower room of Block 28, the *Badestube*, an unbelievable surprise awaits me. My friend, Michel Zechel, is the *Unterbademeister* [assistant shower master]. This is still not a *Prominenter* job, but the work is undisturbed, and in warm surroundings. From the beginning, Michel showed himself to be more resourceful than I in surviving and improving his own and his friends' living conditions. In particular, he found a way to increase his income. As he had free access to hot water and soap, he offered to wash the personal dirty linen of the Polish doctors and nurses for a small fee. This gave him additional food, and I see that he is in relatively good shape.[4]

Before long, I am washed, tended and fed by Michel Zechel. And there is more to come. In the shower quarters, he is going to prove himself infinitely more powerful than I could have expected. Indeed, Michel has a plan. It is too risky for me to be seen by the SS doctor. He intends to shield me from that visit by sending me directly to the hospital unofficially, which he can do thanks to his good relations with the Polish doctors and nurses.

His plan works and I quickly find myself in a sick bed. I owe my life to Michel and his contacts. Is it possible to imagine what it means to a man at the end of the road, to have a warm shower followed by a good rest in a bed, without beatings and without being whipped like an animal to carry tree trunks or sacks of cement? After 48 hours of sleep, care and food, I start to re-emerge as a man. On the third day, as I become a think-

---

4. This situation is similar to that of the nurses (see Langbein, *Menschen in Auschwitz*, p. 237). Georges Wellers, who worked as a nurse at the Monowitz HKB, also recounts (*Un Juif sous Vichy*, p. 244):

> We were working inside closed buildings, heated in the winter...Our pyjamas were clean and often new, we had two or three good shirts each, two or three sets of underwear, proper leather shoes, socks, handkerchiefs, a sweater and gloves for the winter...We had proper sinks to wash ourselves in, and often also hot showers [while ordinary inmates] had a cold water tap to share between 50 to 60 people. Each of us had a piece of soap, a towel, and we could shave every other day with razors reserved for staff ... [and] we ate sitting at a table.

ing creature again, lying on my sick bed, I remember everything: my luck in being there, but also my suffering in
Monowitz for the last two and a half months since my descent
into concentration camp hell. In the horrors of the Buna
kommandos, I was not capable of thinking for even one minute;
the present swallowed everything, the past was suspended
and the future reduced to a struggle to allow the next minute
to still belong to the present and not become the end. Rest
returns the concept of time to me.

I will think about that later when reading Primo Levi's
sentence: 'Do you know how one says "never" in camp slang?
One says *"morgen früh"*, tomorrow morning.'[5]

The *Häftlingskrankenbau* or *Revier* should not be seen as a
real hospital. Like everywhere else in the camp, the building is
swarming with vermin: fleas; lice; bugs. At night, when coming
back from the latrines, black socks cover our feet – flea socks!
Looking down, we can see the whole floor moving, covered
with a thick rippling carpet of slowly undulating vermin …

Some time after I enter the hospital, typhus[6] – spread by lice
– starts to wreak havoc in the camp, and the SS decide to disin-
fect. Although we are required to leave the barracks during

---

5. Levi, *Se questo è un uomo*, p. 139.
6. Typhus was never eradicated, and raged in Auschwitz, on and off, from April 1941
    (Langbein, *Menschen in Auschwitz*, p. 236). The first large epidemic occurred in the
    spring of 1942 and spread to Birkenau in the summer. SS doctors fell victim to it.
    In this period, to fight the disease, whole blocks were liquidated, including conva-
    lescents (Czech, *Kalendarium*, p. 289; see also deposition from the doctor, J.P.
    Kremer, in *Auschwitz in den Augen der SS: Rudolf Höss, Pery Broad, Johann Paul Kremer*
    (Auschwitz: Staatliches Museum Auschwitz/Interpress, 1992), p. 154). The staff in
    Auschwitz were vaccinated, and in Birkenau, even the inmates were vaccinated
    (D. Haffner, *Aspects pathologiques du camp de concentration d'Auschwitz-Birkenau*
    (Tours: Imprimerie Union coopérative, 1946), p. 38). In the winter of 1943–4,
    another terrible epidemic finished off the women in Birkenau, where hygiene was
    more limited (see F. Fénelon, *Sursis pour l'orchestre* (Paris: Stock, 1976); and K.
    Zywulska, *Tanz, Mädchen … Vom Warschauer Getto nach Auschwitz: Eine Überlebens-
    bericht* (Munich: dtv, 1988). In the main camp, after another outbreak in March
    1943, the situation improved towards the summer. However, at least 10–15,000
    inmates were affected by it. The fight against the disease became more effective
    after Wirths arrived. Inmates were checked once a week and, by 1944, it was
    considered shameful to be infested with lice (Waitz and Klein, *Testimonies stras-
    bourgeois*, p. 438). By the end of 1943, steamrooms had been installed in all the
    camps for the inmates, and in Auschwitz, a shortwave delousing station had
    repalced the old disinfecting steamrooms for clothes. This was an improvement,
    as wet clothes caused many lung infections (ibid.).

71

disinfection, three or four men decide to stay in the Block. They consequently die, poisoned together with the bugs. Zyklon B – a cyanic acid-based product readily available within the camp premises and normally used for disinfecting – was probably used. Three kilometres from there, in Birkenau, the same product is being used, at the same time, for the mass extermination of Jews. However, as I am in Auschwitz, in the main camp, I am unaware of these things.

After ten days' rest, I feel better and start to work unofficially; or, rather, I start to help out. Officially, I am still on the sick list on which Michel had registered me. I help my friend in his various jobs. In addition to his other functions, he is in charge of cleaning the Hospital Block's soup pots. As the soup for the sick is thicker than the usual camp soup, some deposit of food usually remains in the bottom and on the sides. Michel improvises a scraping tool, which is nothing more than a rubber sole. With it, we manage to scrape the vats every day before rinsing them, and salvage between three and six large mugs of soup; and what soup, so thick and nourishing! Michel could easily sell these rations, as bartering is king in the camp society: a society based on absolute necessity and survival. But no! I am witness to his sense of honour; he distributes the mugs among the sick of our Block most in need, and eventually helps some of them avoid dying of hunger.

Not everyone behaves like this. In general, inmates trade what they can 'organize' against the standard Auschwitz currency: cigarettes. The value of cigarettes varies according to the supply and demand of consumable goods. There are periods of abundance, where a quarter of a loaf of bread is worth one cigarette; in periods of shortage, it can be worth four cigarettes. The principal source of cigarettes is the canteen, where certain things, such as toothpaste and soap, are for sale against job coupons. Jews, however, cannot get job coupons. This is the starting point of the economic channels for ongoing trafficking with Poles who receive parcels (any parcels that arrive for Jews are confiscated immediately by the SS). Better fed than us, thanks to the food they regularly receive, the Poles trade their soup or their bread for cigarettes.

I live in Block 28, which is part of the *Häftlingskrankenbau* barracks, and which contains, in addition to dormitories for the sick, several medical rooms.[7] In the basement is the camp morgue. All inmates who die in the Blocks or at work are brought to the morgue before being transferred to the crematorium and burned. It is essentially a bureaucratic measure, to verify who is dead, and keep the *Sterbebuch* [register] in order. *'Ordnung muss sein!'* [There must be order at all cost!] A very special *kommando* works here, the *Totenträger kommando* [undertakers], consisting of about ten individuals, especially well fed. I can watch them; their work includes unloading the trucks that arrive at the morgue with their cargo of corpses.[8]

Resting at the hospital, I recover some courage and strength reasonably quickly. As I hang about the Block more or less idle, the undertakers sometimes enlist me by force when they need help.[9] As I am there illegally, I cannot refuse. Anyway, who can say 'no' in Auschwitz? They take me with them to unload bodies. They seem used to their horrible job, but I am not. I am repelled by the sight of the bodies and they are very heavy. When the truck arrives with its cargo, two men get up on the platform, grab a corpse by its extremities, drag it to the edge, and send it flying to two men waiting below to catch it in a

---

7. Block 28 comprised the *Ambulanz* [outpatient clinic], the administration office of the hospital, a sterile operating room (Block 21 also contained another OR that was not sterile), an ear, nose and throat and ophthalmology section, a radiology and physiotherapy room, a laboratory, the inmates' pharmacy, a storeroom, the special diet kitchen (where boiled food is prepared for gastric patients), and a medical experiment room (see *Die Auschwitz-Hefte*, Vol. 1, p. 162 ff.; and Waitz and Klein, *Témoignages strasbourgeois*, p. 446).

8. For information on the number of undertakers, see Langbein, *Der Auschwitz-Prozess*, p. 722. Only inmates who died, or who were killed in the Blocks, ended up in the morgue – a room in the basement of Block 28. The undertakers' *kommando* resided in the first room. However, the victims of collective executions, and those who were exterminated, were taken straight to the crematorium. The morgue was equipped with trolleys and stretchers covered with metal to facilitate cleaning off traces of blood and excrement. Later, the undertakers were provided with hearses, as the crematorium was at the other end of the camp; when the number of the dead grew, the bodies were transported by truck. The morgue register for the period 7 October 1941–31 August 1943 was saved (*Die Auschwitz-Hefte*, Vol. 1, pp. 164–5; Czech, *Kalendarium*, p. 127; W. Kielar, *Anus Mundi: Fünf Jahr in Auschwitz*, 2nd edn (Frankfurt-am-Main: Fischer, 1994), p. 58.

9. Ex-inmate Fabian also testified that the nursing aides from Block 28 had to be enlisted to help when there were not enough undertakers (*Die Auschwitz-Prozess*, p. 722).

similar fashion, one catching the arms, the other the feet. Then they carry it off to the basement, which serves as a morgue. The procedure is well rehearsed.

Today, I am posted below the truck, and must catch the feet of the body they are throwing at me. A male corpse appears. I am expecting something repugnant and heavy, but firm. To my horror, when I catch the leg, I feel my hand pass through a pulp of putrefied flesh and close on bone. The body is decomposing, the leg completely rotten, and I didn't notice. Disgust chokes me, I think I am going to faint. And then reason returns to me. I realise that I am lucky to have no open wounds on my hands, so the putrid flesh could not infect me.

The undertakers decide to harden me. Under some pretext, they send me inside the morgue, where the bodies are piled up. They conceive the devilish plan of locking me in it, and have great fun at my expense.

I am trapped, and find myself locked up for a whole night in the company of the piles of corpses of Auschwitz, smelling of rot and chlorine, each one with its number written on its chest with a thick blue pencil.[10] In the dim light, they stare for all eternity at the moment of their atrocious death, swollen, deformed, eyes enlarged, an enormous tongue pushed with difficulty through a barrier of menacing teeth. Distorted by death, grimacing faces surround me on every side. I try to look elsewhere, and to think about something else, or I will lose my mind. I am not an executioner, nor a torturer, nor an undertaker; I am just a simple, frightened man. Yes, soon enough I will finish in here too, with my number painted on my chest. This is done to keep records straight, for the sake of bookkeeping; inmates must be identified and registered before they can be burned in the ovens. We are camp property, forever, and even in death, while our bodies are being reduced to ashes, we are being duly recorded like all the rest.

---

10. The marking of the number in blue ink on the bodies dates from the time when inmates were not yet routinely tattooed: the identity of the corpse had to correspond to the file registers. The practice was continued, and often the number was written on the chest of the sick person selected for the injection while he waited for death (Langbein, *Menschen in Auschwitz*, p. 47).

I spend an indescribable night, with death's frozen hand at my neck, in a state bordering on panic. In the morning, they come to let me out, laughing. I don't know how I avoided madness.

A few days after this incident, I am brutally beaten by a *kapo* for a reason unknown to me. Then I am suddenly catapulted into the position of nursing aide and sent to check inmates for lice. *Läusekontrolle!* Epidemics are increasing in the camp, and the SS are mainly worried about their own health. This leads to a ferocious war against lice in the sanitary blocks, where a poster proclaims: '*Eine Laus – dein Tod*' ['One louse – your death']. The hypocrisy of putting inmates on guard against disease and death when the SS themselves are masters of life and death![11] The typhus rages as much among the SS as among inmates, and they are terrified. So they introduce regular check-ups, during which all inmates are examined, especially under the arms and around the penis. It is not a very painful job. When I find lice on a *Häftling*, I mention it to him to allow him to try to get rid of them, in so far as that was possible. However, some of my 'colleagues' immediately inform the *Blockältester*, who then gives hell to the wretched victim. Of course, all these measures are mere tinkering. We could go on forever looking for lice in underwear and squashing them; we will never be able to eradicate nits, and for all our efforts at disinfecting, vermin proliferate.

Meanwhile, I discover another facet to my job as nursing aide. On Monday, 28 July, the SS summons me for the first time to the yard facing Block 28, which is between Block 10, the experimentation Block,[12] and Block 11, the prison Block – the

---

11. According to Langbein, this poster testifies less to SS cynicism than to their real effort to eradicate typhus by gaining the inmates' co-operation (*ibid.*, p. 157).
12. Block 10, luxuriously equipped, housed 250–300 women who were used as medical guinea pigs and subjected to various experiments from April 1943. The women of the 20th Belgian convoy seem to have been the first to be selected for this purpose. The gynaecological experiments performed by Wirths and Weber, for uterine cancers, were criminal because of the conditions in which they were performed; and those of SS doctors Carl Clauberg and Horst Schumann (see below) are perfect examples of the murderous licence of the regime. Clauberg, a renowned gynaecologist, suggested to Himmler that they perform sterilisation experiments by injecting substances that caused inflammations in the womb,

fearsome *Bunker* [dungeon]. There, for the first time, I witness a most horrible and unforgettable event: a collective execution.[13]

Of course, only after my liberation would I discover what this collective execution was really about. However, at the time, what I witness inside the yard is the ultimate act; a *Standgericht* [mobile court] comes once a month from Katowice to sit in Auschwitz and decide cases. In the space of two hours, sometimes over a hundred death sentences are pronounced, for acts of resistance (transmission of news, association with a Resistance movement) or for criminal acts (theft, black marketeering). 'Interrogation' sessions – under torture – precede the 'court' session, which in itself lasts less than a minute, and in which the accused has no right to speak, or to be defended.[14] The death sentences are all prepared in advance, blank documents pre-signed by the *Gauleiter* of Silesia. The accused are mainly Poles, and the executions are in fact a liquidation of the Polish intelligentsia and Resistance. The president of the mobile court is *SS-Standartenführer* Rudolf Mildner, a judge in charge of the Katowice Gestapo, who sits in the Nazi government of Upper Silesia. But, in the camps, the person really responsible for executions is the Chief of the *Politische Abteilung*

---

which would cause adhesions. The results would be observed under X-ray. Himmler was excited by the idea that the Reich would have a quick and cheap means of sterilising the 'inferior' races while at the same time exploiting their work force. He therefore provided Clauberg with the 'human material' he requested: women between 20 and 40, preferably mothers. After treatment, they were to be expected to submit to forced sexual intercourse to prove their infertility; however, this part of the experiment never took place. The experiments, often performed by the chemist Goebels, caused tremendous pain and often led to death from infection. Some women, however, did submit to it to escape from the hell of Birkenau. Those who refused to participate were sent back and usually gassed; as were those who did not recover. The number of women sterilised by this method is difficult to estimate: according to Jan Sehn, there were between 700 and a few thousand (*Konzentrationslager Oswiecim-Brzezinka* (Varsovie: Wydawnictwo Prawnicze, 1957)). Clauberg was sentenced to 25 years in prison by a Soviet court, freed in 1955, charged again, and died in 1957 before his trial (Langbein, *Menschen in Auschwitz*, p. 385 ff.; R.J. Lifton, *Les Médecins nazis: Le meutre médical et la pscyhologie du génocide* (Paris: Laffont, 1989), p. 306 ff.).

13. On 28 July 1943, prisoners from Silesian prisoners were executed, together with four inmates registered in Auschwitz, whose names are recorded (Czech, *Kalendarium*, p. 556).

14. Langbein, *Menschen in Auschwitz*, p. 210; *Auschwitz in den Augen der SS*, p. 104 ff.

[Political Section][15] of Auschwitz, the *SS-Untersturmführer* Maximilian Grabner, an uneducated Austrian police officer with sadistic tendencies. The well-informed know that, as a civilian, he kept cows in high mountain pastures, but he is without doubt one of the most powerful men in Auschwitz.[16] The executions, preceded by summary sentencing, reflect an illegal policy, even in the context of the SS State. Grabner is well aware of the illegality, and he conceals those deaths in the death registers under the names of various diseases.

I am standing in the relatively large yard between Blocks 10 and 11. I stand on the side, against a Block. At the end of the yard, on the opposite side to the entrance gate, is a breezeblock wall painted black: the execution wall. Witnessing the execution is a *Blockschreiber*, whose insignia is the oddest Star of David I have ever seen: a yellow triangle crossed with a green triangle, meaning that he is a Jew and a criminal. Many years later, at the 1958 World Fair in Brussels, I will recognise this man as the consul of a Latin American Republic, an important official in his new country. On that day, he will look me straight in the eye and assure me that he was never in Auschwitz. Who knows what he felt guilty about![17]

At the time of execution, which had to remain secret, the wooden blinds covering the windows of Blocks 10 and 11 are closed on the side overlooking the yard; however, some inmates can still see what is happening, either through the cracks, or because, like me, their job requires them to be present. While I stand there, I am so frightened that I barely

---

15. According to the administrative subdivision of the Auschwitz complex, the commandant is responsible for seven divisions: (1) Kommandatur; (2) Political Section; (3) Camp Management; (3a) *Arbeitseinsatz* [Labour Section]; (4) Camp Administration; (5) *Standortarzt* [Garrison Physician]; and (6) *Truppenbetreuung* [Troop Management] (*Contribution à l'histoire du KL Auschwitz*, 2 Vols (Oswiecim: Éditions du Musée d'État à Oswiecim, 1978), Vol. 2, p. 7).
16. On Grabner, see Broad, in *Auschwitz in den Augen der SS*, p. 100.
17. We will come across this dubious character again in Gross-Rosen. He may have been arrested in 1938, when Heydrich, Chief of Criminal Police, made a point of increasing the grounds for imprisonment in order to fill the recently created camps – more particularly, interning all Jews with a police record in Buchenwald. The length of his imprisonment may explain why he qualified as a 'high-ranking official'.

notice the SS. In Auschwitz in general, it is unthinkable for a *Häftling* to stare an SS in the face: even more so here. The convicted who are ignominiously executed in this yard – there is no firing squad, they are murdered by a single bullet in the back of the neck – are mainly Polish officers and civilians, but also Yugoslav partisans. All are political prisoners. They come from different prisons, not from the camp, and this is quite obvious; despite the torture they have endured in prison and in the *Bunker*, their bodies show no trace of the atrocious deprivations and physical misery of the common *Häftling*. Their sham trial takes place on the same day the death sentence is pronounced. When the moment comes, they are brought up from the basement of the *Bunker*, and ordered to undress. Then they are forced to go out naked, two by two. One especially sturdy *Häftling*, Fat Jakob,[18] *kapo* of the *Bunker*, grabs the men under the arms, one on each side, drags them to the wall, and straightens their faces against the black surface. This is the best position for committing the murders. On either side of the two men stands a member of the SS, each pressing a small calibre gun against the back of their necks, and then they shoot. The two men fall as one. The whole thing happens very quickly. While two condemned men are being shot, the next two witness the execution. From the entrance to the *Bunker* where they stand, they are facing the spectacle of their own inescapable destiny.

After the bodies fall to the ground, our *kommando* takes over. We must quickly remove the bodies from the foot of the execution wall. We drag them to the other end of the yard towards the exit, where the gate is obviously locked. There they

---

18. Jakob Kozelczuk, a semi-literate Polish Jew of athletic build, had been a boxer, and arrived in Auschwitz in January 1943. He is remembered by all those who survived incarceration in the *Bunker*. Because of his physical attributes, the SS gave him the important job of *Kolfactor* of the *Bunker* [Block 11], which meant he was the caretaker, furnace assistant and assistant executioner. Despite his job, 'Fat Jacob' was a basically good man, helping where he could, hitting lightly when he had to inflict punishment, taking care of the wounded, passing messages and food, lying to the Political Section, and showing compassion to those who were to be executed. In an inquiry after liberation, almost all testimonials were favourable to him. After the war, he emigrated to Israel (Langbein, *Menschen in Auschwitz*, pp. 215–18; F. Müller, *Trois ans dans une chambre à gaz d'Auschwitz* (Paris: Pygmalion, 1980), p. 90).

remain, piled up and bleeding. One *Häftling* with a small shovel covers the traces of blood with earth and gravel. In the meantime, the next two condemned men are already being slaughtered. After the execution, a truck will come to collect the bodies and transport them to the crematorium.

Whatever I do there is in the strictest secrecy. I am forbidden, on pain of death, to talk about it to anybody. I am terrified; I have unwittingly become an accomplice in the abominations of the camp, the bearer of a heavy secret, and am seriously threatened. The SS would not like witnesses to such abominations to remain alive.

At the second execution in which I am forced to participate as assistant to the undertaker, some 40 prisoners are slaughtered. This isn't the last execution for me; I will still have to go several times, between the end of July and the end of October 1943.[19]

Gradually, I come to be surprised at the attitude of those partisans, who are hardened underground fighters and often also officers. I would have expected them to proclaim with their last breath their *raison d'être* in the face of their torturers. However, only one prisoner, a German, once yelled '*Es lebe Deutschland!*' [Long live Germany!] Langbein recounts that while he was inside the *Bunker*, he thought a lot about what words he would call out in the very likely event that he were executed. It would have been: 'Long live free Austria! Down with fascism!' But fortunately, Langbein was released. I never saw a condemned man display a final sign of protest or resistance. Knowing that all is lost, that their fate is sealed at that moment, they could have done anything: yelled, spat in the face of the SS. Almost no one I saw fall ever did.

There I witness enormous differences in the attitudes of Jews, although it has often been said, especially during the first years of the war, that they all went to their deaths like sheep to

---

19. On 20 August, 38 political prisoners kept in the *Bunker* were executed (Grabner called the procedure 'dusting the *Bunker*'). On 4 September, a further 53 prisoners from the *Bunker* were executed: two of them German criminals (a rare event). W.B. is probably referring to this execution. More executions took place on 21 September (29 men); on 28 September (18 men); on 11 October (54 men, notably a group of high-ranking Polish officers from the Resistance); 9 November and 29 November (see Czech, *Kalendarium*).

the slaughter. I witnessed the last moments of a group of men sick with tuberculosis, selected at the hospital by the SS medic, and sent to their death before my eyes. Among them was the brother of Maurice Goldstein, who will soon join the players in my story. Those Jews knew exactly where they were going when they were put in the trucks: they were all *musulmen*, at the extreme stage of physical deterioration, in that state of total apathy where they no longer expressed anything, and perhaps no longer felt anything, even as they approached death. Still, at that moment, I saw magnificent evidence of those men's persistent dignity and moral resistance; the instant the truck moved, they struck up *Sh'ma Israel*, the basic prayer of the Jew, which is first of all an assertion of his identity. I believe these people retained their humanity until the last moment of their lives.

After each execution, I come back to the hospital covered in blood. The freshly slaughtered men bleed for a long time. From the hole in their necks a fountain of blood pours out, soaking the ground in front of the wall, and other inmates are busy spreading sand on these pools of blood. In the Block, I return to my friend Michel, but I am not allowed to talk about what I have seen. The SS warned all the inmates present at the executions: 'You see nothing, you hear nothing, you say nothing.' We are *Geheimnisträge* [the secret bearers], the carriers of a dangerous secret. To talk probably means immediate death, and I was much too afraid to disobey. Just thinking about what I have seen on these execution nights, I am choked by a cold terror that will not leave me. Michel guesses something, he has probably guessed where I have been, but he doesn't talk about it. Only much later, when we meet again in Brussels, after infinite suffering, will we openly talk about it.

Nevertheless, when there are no executions, and I manage to forget for a while the threat hanging over my head, I must admit that this period of my detention is not the most painful. As long as I am still officially hospitalized, I am better fed than the common *Häftling*, and I am slowly regaining my strength. Our shower hall is like a small haven of peace inside Auschwitz, where we gather quietly. One day, a Polish prisoner in our Block, a violinist, who must have enjoyed some kind of privilege, because he still had all his hair, comes to play his violin in the showers. Although, in civilian life, I was not particularly sensitive to music, on that day, I experience the most intense musical emotion of my life. It is not that the music opens up a new world for me, it is rather that it made me feel a powerful magical presence beyond the barbed wire, reminding me of the real and unique world from which I have been removed. I understand through my emotions that the virtual space opened by art is in fact the real world, and that Auschwitz is the nightmare.[20] But the minute he stops playing, an iron hand falls on top of me and holds me down, like a million others, within the nightmare, alas, more real than anything else.

I also have a German friend called Ludwig, a *Rotspanier* [Red Spaniard], so called because he fought in Spain against Franco's supporters as a volunteer in the International Brigade. Everybody likes Ludwig. In the Block, we sometimes talk politics; when we can talk normally, we feel a bit human again. One evening, in this relative haven of the *Badestube*, a lively discussion occurs between some Brigade old-timers and a number of Jewish doctors and nursing aides, including Michel and me. Ludwig suddenly blurts out in a reproachful tone: 'Where were you, the bourgeois Jews, and what were you doing while we fought the Spanish fascists?'

As a real *Zugang* – this occurs at the beginning of my stay at the HKB – I foolishly answer: 'There were also other ideals. Myself, after completing high school, I left for Palestine to realise my Zionist ideal and return to the land.'

If I had a little more camp experience, I would have avoided putting myself forward so carelessly. Indeed, the left-wing political prisoners considered Zionism a middle-class aberra-

---

20. The strong emotional impact of music in the camp is widely documented. Musicians would sometimes play informally in the Blocks on Sundays. There were orchestras in most camps: one in Auschwitz (to which Jews were not admitted); one in the men's camp of Birkenau (see S. Laks and R. Coudy, *Musiques d'un autre monde* (Paris: Mercure de France, 1948); and one women's orchestra in the women's camp of Birkenau, directed by the German-Jewish violinist, Alma Rosé, Gustav Mahler's niece (Fénelon, *Sursis pour l'orchestre*).

tion. I put myself in the precarious position of being badly regarded because of that.

While we talk, a man is quietly listening on the side, Miki Korn,[21] *Kapo* Korn. This man is about to play a major role in my life in Auschwitz, and I will long ask myself why he showed such an interest in me. Like me, *Kapo* Korn is, I believe, from a middle-class background, and may also have been a Zionist. Was he touched by my naïveté?

One morning, in autumn, a young man, barely 20, arrives in the *Badestube* in a miserable state. Even more wretched and broken than I was in July, he comes to be showered before selection by the SS doctor. Naked under the shower, he is surprised to hear Michel and me speaking French. We discover that he comes from Belgium, and we establish an immediate rapport. His name is Maurice Goldstein.[22] The deportation of Jews with Belgian citizenship was long deferred, then brutally fixed for 3 September 1943. Maurice Goldstein was caught in Brussels during the roundups of Jews of Belgian nationality, and deported with the 22nd Belgian convoy on 19 September. With him were deported his parents, his young, pregnant wife and his older brother. His other brother managed to escape the roundup and hide in Brussels, where he was killed in a bombardment. At the ramp, his mother and his young wife are sent directly to the gas chamber, while the three men find themselves selected for work. The father, an old man – he is 40 – holds on for three months before dying of exhaustion. The brother will contract tuberculosis in the coalmines at Fürstengrube and be brought back to Auschwitz in 1944. Very ill, he will be selected as incurable and sent to the gas chambers.

---

21. Doctor (in medicine or chemistry) Mikulas (or Mikolaj) Korn, a Slovakian Jew, was *Blockältester* and, at least in the first week of May 1943, when the Hygiene Institute was set up in Rajsko, he was *kapo* of the *Laboratorium Rajsko kommando*, which had been put together at the beginning of 1943. There are very impressive testimonies concerning Korn. During the campaign of lethal injections, the SDG asked him to take the place of prisoner Panszczyk, who later boasted of having killed 12,000 people. Korn refused, knowing very well what risk he was taking, all the more so as he was a Jew. However, he was not punished and survived Auschwitz (Langbein, *Menschen in Auschwitz*, p. 213; *Die Auschwitz-Hefte*, Vol. 1, pp. 214–15).

22. See A. Israel, *Le Passage du témoin:Portraits et témoignages de rescapés des camps de concentration et l'extermination nazis* (Brussels: La Lettre volée/Fondation Auschwitz, 1995), pp. 240–3.

It is of him – his transport and his dignity – that I was thinking earlier when I mentioned human resistance. On arrival, Maurice was sent to Fürstengrube together with his brother, where he worked for a few weeks in the mines and at the blast furnace site. He became weak very quickly, which was normal, because in those camps, a man's physical resistance lasts only three weeks. He has just been brought back to Auschwitz when we meet him. He is a *musulman*, and has no illusions about his future. He knows he doesn't have much longer to live and expects to be gassed.

We must save Maurice. He is little more than a child. He arrived with parents, with a wife and child-to-be; he has almost nothing left of what a human being can claim in life. The camp has taken everything from him, except life itself. I ask Michel to do whatever he can for him, as he did for me when I arrived, and once again, Michel takes over the organisation; we will put Maurice in a bed and hide him at the hospital.

We will personify destiny for Maurice. He will be one of the few Belgian survivors, and will become president of the International Committee of Auschwitz. He will also become one of my best friends. He likes to say that I saved his life when he arrived in Auschwitz. In reality, it is Michel and his connections that saved his life. I only drew Michel's attention to this Belgian boy, so touching, so emaciated.

Michel and I find ourselves in one of the cruellest and most guilt-ridden situations of the camps. We are very conscious of our privileged situation which allows us to do something for a friend, but that is also where our power ends. We cannot save more than one person, we cannot hide everybody at the hospital, because the strategy might eventually turn against us, betray us and bring us all to our death. It is clear to us what we can do. If we save one *musulman* because he is Belgian and likeable, we are at the same time condemning any of the others with exactly the same right to life as the one we saved. And among the *musulmen*, only Maurice is saved that day.

The balance of forces at work in the camp, the perverse logic of the concentration universe, forces us to make choices that anyone with a healthy mind would consider immoral and inhuman, and which would be so in any universe but this one. These choices are pragmatic, but do not prevent painful remorse. If a prisoner survives, he quickly reaches the position of being in charge of something he does not necessarily want, but from which he cannot escape. David Rousset calls it the bronze law, the law: of the concentration camp universe to which anybody with any power to protect others is subject. As a result, some find themselves forced to assist the SS at some point in any of their many murderous tasks. Jewish doctors working at the *Krankenbau* must accompany the SS doctor on his rounds of the Blocks for selecting the sick, and it is they who must make up the list of the most hopeless cases. They hold the balance of life. If they refuse to perform, the consequences could be even more tragic; the SS doctor may then decide to send the whole Block to be gassed, or select blindly among the sick some who might still have a reasonable chance of getting well and surviving. Maybe any gesture giving rise to some slight improvement should be modestly considered an act of resistance, one more step towards the survival of a prisoner, be it just one in tens of thousands. In a world where death is all powerful, an act can be recognised as moral only if it favours life.

In the unstable oasis of the hospital and the showers, life for Michel, Maurice and me continues quite peacefully for some time. I receive great news from home. I get seven postcards at one time from my parents, and am greatly relieved to learn that they are still alive and free. However, one beautiful morning, the calm of our existence is almost shattered. Michel is responsible for his own misfortune. He is a heavy smoker, and when he manages to procure some tobacco for himself, he cannot resist smoking at work. Inmates are strictly forbidden to smoke at work and the inevitable happens. An SS officer catches him in the act in the hospital hall. (The camp regulations forbid just about everything, and it is impossible to observe all the rules. This gives the SS, *kapos* and *Blockältester* numerous opportunities to punish and abuse the simple *Häftling*: a bed badly made, shoes not properly shined, a button missing – of course, no shoe polish or thread is available. We must find our own way to 'organise' supplies.)

84

The SS officer hits poor Michel very hard and knocks him to the ground, but this devil of a man rolls himself into a ball, and like a jack-in-the-box, he jumps back up in a split second. Stupefied by the agility of this 45-year-old man, the SS officer stops beating him. Had Michel remained on the ground, he might have been beaten to death. His mischief, however, is not totally forgotten; the SS officer writes a report, and the next day he is sent to the *Bunker*.

Anyone sent to the *Bunker* takes leave of his friends and makes his will. Michel has only one thing to entrust me with, but it is very precious – his famous $100 bill. Nobody believes he will return from the *Bunker*, but it must be the beginning of a new, more liberal era, because, after a few days, Michel comes back to his previous job. He is not even sent to a punishment *kommando*, which would definitely have been the case a few months earlier. With his job, he also takes back his war treasure, the $100 bill.

Yet we are not going to stay together. A short while after he leaves the *Bunker* in November, Michel is sent as a dentist to the nearby camp of Jaworzno,[23] where he remains for the whole of 1944. We will only meet again during evacuation, when we are forced to retreat to Gross-Rosen. It will be a fairly danger-free year for him, as he will genuinely work as a dentist. An outstanding and much-appreciated practitioner, at Jaworzno he will take care of the SS and the *Prominenter* as well as the inmates.

Shortly before his departure, Michel – much better at learning the secrets of the camp than I am – gives me some important advice. Without ever having talked about it, he knows that I was enlisted several times to carry corpses during executions. He fears for me, and for good reason. It isn't my fault, but I have become a secret-bearer initiated, a *Geheimnisträger* – one

---

23. The annexed camp of Neu-Dachs in Jaworzno, 40 kilometres from Auschwitz, was built in the summer of 1943 to house the inmates who were working in the *Dachsgrube* coal mine and constructing a large electricity factory for the *Energieversorgung Oberschlesien*. After Monowitz, this was the largest camp of the Auschwitz III complex, with barracks for 5,000 inmates, but holding on average 3,000. For information on Jaworzno, see H. Bulawko, *Les Jeux de la Mort et de l'espoir: Auschwitz-Jaworzno. Auschwitz 50 ans aprés* (Paris: Montgoueil, 1993) and J. Heinemann, *Auschwitz, Mein Bericht* (Berlin: Das Neue Berlin, 1995).

who knows too much for his own good about the dubious secret practices, one who has seen too many things that must remain secret. He knows that liquidation awaits all witnesses to the butcheries in the camp. He urges me to leave the hospital as soon as possible, where my status as officially sick has become too dangerous. But to get out of this privileged cocoon means certain return to an ordinary *kommando*. In other words, elimination: a return to harassing work that may kill within six weeks. It is not an easy decision to take.

Somebody else gives me similar advice at the time: the mysterious *Kapo* Korn, an influential Slovakian Jew who has been interned in Auschwitz for many years and is respected by everybody. Miki Korn's number is very old and he has been a *kapo* for a long time. To my knowledge, in my experience of Auschwitz, no Jew has ever been a *kapo*. *Kapo* Korn takes to me and advises me most insistently to leave the hospital, where I am at serious risk of being coldly liquidated.

Before taking this difficult decision, I must still face death twice. The Nazi concentration camp is, by definition, filled with dangers for a *Häftling*, particularly a Jew. It cannot be compared with a Soviet Gulag or any forced labour camp of any other totalitarian regime.

In Auschwitz, there is an SS soldier called Oswald Kaduk,[24]

---

24. The *SS-Unterscharführer*, Oswald Kaduk – butcher, fireman, soldier and German nationalist militant from his youth – joined the SS in 1940, began his service in Auschwitz in 1942 and was very quickly promoted to *Rapportführer*. As an ethnic German, this man seems to have overcompensated for his 'inferiority' by being even more brutal than Germans born in the Reich. He was decorated with the second class War Cross with swords on 20 April 1943 (at the same time as SDG Klela and Scharpe, inventors of the lethal injections, and Lachmann, Grabner's vicious assistant in the Political Section). He would continue his cruelty even during the death marches. Brutal and unpredictable, dangerous when drunk, he was the incarnation of SS terror for many inmates. Tried in 1947 by a Soviet military court, he argued that he was just following orders. He was sentenced to 25 years and pardoned in 1956. After three years of quiet life working as a nursing aide in Germany, where he seemed to have been appreciated by his patients, he was arrested in Berlin and tried in Frankfurt in 1964. At the trial, he showed himself to be cynical, unrepentant and arrogant, and was sentenced to life in prison for having participated in the selections in Auschwitz and Birkenau (he took part in gassings in the 'small houses'), and for an undefined number of murders. The revelations of the court proceedings of 1964 make the name of Kaduk synonymous with beastly extortions (Langbein, *Menschen in Auschwitz*, pp. 337, 438, 552, 563 and 571; Langbein, *Der Auschwitz-Prozess*, p. 249 ff.).

who is more hated and feared than the others. He is a *Volksdeutscher* [an ethnic German], and I know from experience that these Nazis are the worst of the German Reich.[25] Poles and Ukrainians are more abusive and cruel towards Jews than are Germans, but when a German lashes out, it is usually a *Volksdeutscher*, those notoriously ferocious anti-Semites. Kaduk is a *Rapportführer*, a secretary-general in charge of some sort of labour. He keeps a close count on the number of prisoners present at the morning and evening *Appell*. However, in the autumn of 1943 in Auschwitz,[26] policy definitely seems more lenient towards the *Häftlinge* and few selections take place, to the displeasure of this sadist; and is he a sadist! When he is drunk, he sometimes organises spontaneous, savage selections. One day, at the beginning of October, Kaduk arrives in the hospital sector and announces a roundup. He ensures all exits from the Block are locked, gives the order for a *Blocksperre* [curfew], and starts a random selection of the gathered prisoners. It is pure gangsterism, and he doesn't even bother to camouflage it by enlisting a doctor for the selection. I am

---

25. National Socialism could be quite attractive to the average German – mostly rural, anti-modern, anti-communists with strong anti-Slavic and anti-Semitic racist tendencies. The glorification of his German nationalism was an answer to the repressions that these groups had suffered under the nationalist regimes that governed following the collapse of the Austro-Hungarian Empire (V.O. Lumans, *Himmler's Auxiliaries: The Volksdeutsche Mittelstelle and the German National Minorities in Europe, 1933–1945* (Chapel Hill, NC: University of North Carolina Press, 1993)). In all, 360,000 ethnic Germans were 'repatriated' to the Reich by the *Volkdeutsche Mittelstelle* (VOMI) created by Himmler.

26. Arthur Liebehenschel was commander of Auschwitz from 11 November 1943 (when he replaced Höss) until May 1944 (when he was moved to Majdanek and was replaced by Richard Baer). During those seven months, there was a relatively liberal atmosphere in the Auschwitz-Birkenau complex, at least as far as the registered inmates were concerned (the extermination of the RSHA convoys of Jews continued as before). Liebehenschel ordered the destruction of *Stehzellen* ['standing' cells] in the *Bunker*; abolished the torture instrument called the 'Boger swing'; systematically reduced by half the Political Sections' punishments; curbed violence against inmates, in particular Jews; dismissed cruel *kapos*; and made SS men sign a service note, specifying that murder of inmates was forbidden (Czech, *Kalendarium*, p. 662). Attempts to escape were no longer necessarily punished by death. Generosity alone cannot explain these changes; the Nazis were starting to worry about the effect that certain revelations were having on public opinion in Germany and abroad, particularly regarding executions. Under Liebehenschel, internal selections in Auschwitz also decreased (Czech, *Kalendarium*, p. 695); under his successor, Baer, conditions worsened again (Langbein, *Menschen in Auschwitz*, p. 67).

87

trapped like a rat and will have to endure his visit. I am not very sick or especially exhausted; rationally, I know that I don't run a high risk, but Kaduk is unpredictable.

A miracle occurs. That day, Miki Korn is watching Kaduk's moves and sees him begin the roundup. He also notices that I am caught, and manages to get me out of the Block through a window. I escape a brutal selection.[27]

Around the same period, I survive an ordeal probably even more dangerous than this last one. In the first two weeks of October, I am ordered to report to the Political Section, the fearsome *Politische Abteilung*, which is the internal Gestapo of the camp.[28] Such a summons is a terrifying event in the life of a *Häftling*, who is unlikely to be seen again after that. The Political Section initiates collective executions and also many sudden and mysterious 'treatments' on *Häftlings*. In nine out of ten cases, the *Häftling* is taken to the *Bunker* then liquidated, one way or another. In very rare circumstances, a prisoner is released, and it is the Political Section who decides on his release. However, that happens only to Germans, and never, ever to Jews.

The next day, I am escorted to the office of the Political Section, and you can guess my state of mind. An SS police officer, apparently highly placed, receives me: can it be the fearsome Grabner himself?[29] After studying me for a while, this high-ranking SS officer announces: 'Listen Jewboy, you have been given a Romanian passport from the Romanian embassy in Berlin. You will sign a release declaring that you have received it.'

Of course, I am given nothing. What can I do? Terrified, I signed.

---

27. This selection is not mentioned in the *Kalendarium*. Many events, particularly those that led to deaths, are recorded only in the individual memories of survivors. There are more testimonies of selections performed by the SS Kaduk and Clausen in 1943 and 1944 (Langbein, *Der Auschwitz-Prozess*, p. 268 ff.). Kaduk often seems to have acted on his own initiative, selecting only Jews.
28. The Political Section, present in most of the labour camps, was especially watchful in Auschwitz because of the high risk of contact between Polish prisoners and the Polish Resistance.
29. Probably not, because that same SS officer received him a second time in February 1944 (see Chapter 5). By then, Grabner was far from Auschwitz, having been sent away in October or November 1943.

Once I have signed my execution order, the police officer adds mockingly: 'Now that you have a passport, we will keep it here for a while. To get out of the camp you still need a visa.'

After this sinister joke, I return to the Block, furious.

Only after my liberation, when reunited with my family, will I find out what was behind what had happened. In Czernowitz, my father did not rest until he had lobbied all his connections in the hope of helping me. Once he discovered where I was, thanks to the postcard I sent him from Monowitz, he made several attempts, the first being to solicit a close business acquaintance, a *Volksdeutscher* who could travel freely to Poland. My father, who didn't even know the name of Auschwitz, asked him to find out about this camp, Monowitz, where I was, and if possible – pure madness – get in touch with me. This man came to the area, discovered that the camp he was looking for was near Oswiecim, and also understood that, once inside the camp, a Jew must be considered lost. Returning to my parents, he advised them to forget me.

However, my father made a second attempt through a childhood friend, the Romanian ambassador in Berlin. They had grown up in the same village. He asked this important person to intervene in procuring me a passport. Not only did he feel it was his duty towards his imprisoned son, but from a civilised perspective, the idea made perfect sense, as Romania was allied with the Axis powers. Under any regime except the barbaric Nazi one, this would have got me straight out of the camp. Besides, the Jews of Romania itself (which did not include Bucovina and Bessarabia) had not been deported and owed their life to their Romanian nationality. However, if a Jew had already entered the gates of Auschwitz, his fate was sealed; he had fallen into the large secret extermination project. And, of course, the regime refrained from informing the public, and had no intention of letting any witness survive. No passport, or any other intervention, could ever enable a Jew to leave the camp. Obviously, my father could neither know nor understand this. In Europe at that time, who could know or understand? With his solicitude, my father actually put me in grave danger by making the formidable Political Section aware of me.

After this episode, and while I am still pondering my decision to leave the hospital, somebody named Hacker, a political prisoner from Austria, comes to see me and suggests I take up training. He himself is in charge of organising the training of nursing aides inside the camp.[30] Hacker is an interesting character. He comes from an anti-Nazi Austrian family, but after the *Anschluss*, had enlisted in the German Army at the age of 17-and-a-half. Stationed in Belgium under the German banner, he did a crazy thing. He actually organised an anti-Nazi campaign inside his unit and distributed anti-military leaflets. Caught and sentenced to death, his punishment was commuted to *Festungshaft* [life in prison], due to his youth. He started serving his sentence in a German prison, and was later transferred to a concentration camp – as a *Sicherheitsverfahren*, I believe, a class of prisoner with a chance of release – because they were short of staff. Finally, he ended up in Auschwitz as a nurse.

If I accept his offer, I could officially become a *Pfleger*. I am tempted, because life as a nurse offers an infinite number of precious advantages. But *Kapo* Korn warned me: it is essential that I disappear into anonymity as soon as possible, because the initiated who have attended executions run a risk from one day to the next of being eliminated. He insists I leave the hospital immediately. It is a difficult decision to take, and time is running out. I will have to give up the relative comfort of the Hospital Block, a fairly easy job where I am not beaten, and especially the shower room, where conditions are almost human. What's more, I will have to report to the *Appell* again, something I have been exempt from while I was sick. Although the *Appell* was shortened in 1943, it is still harassing and murderous when added to the day's hardships.

I opt for caution; they must lose track of me. To provoke my dismissal from hospital is child's play. It's enough to answer back impertinently to a Polish doctor – I think it is to Dr

---

30. Professional training courses for inmates were sometimes organised in the camps when there was a shortage of qualified workers. It is known, for instance, that a school for builders was set up in June 1942 in Birkenau for men between the ages of 15 and 25 (this did not prevent more than half the students being gassed almost immediately).

Dering[31] – and the next day, 18 October 1943, I am thrown out of the hospital and sent to Block 4.

I am back in a Block and a horrible *kommando*, so similar to everything I left behind in Monowitz: inhuman work conditions, calculated sadism turning each painful day of work into one more stop on the road to death: *Vernichtung durch Arbeit* [programmed elimination by work]. I named the *kommando* that worked at the methane gas station *'Faulgasanlage'*. Six months before, it had actually been a disciplinarian *kommando* (*Strafkommando*),[32] in which survival rates were barely more than a week or two.

But, after all this time in the camp, learning its ins and outs as well as the dangers to beware of, I have evolved. I am no longer a total novice, and I have learned to recognise the small things that can still work to my advantage. My *kommando* has become less aggressive, death is held at bay a little longer, and if one is just a little bit tough, one can even adapt to the work. Besides, it offers the additional advantage of putting us in

---

31. Wladyslaw Dering, a Polish inmate-physician and virulent anti-Semite, was interned in Auschwitz in the summer of 1940. He became a nurse, then a doctor, and then *Lagerältester* of the HKB in August 1943. In this capacity, Dering did nothing to improve conditions for Jewish patients: quite the contrary. His 'career' as a doctor at Auschwitz led him to be servile to, and adopt the ways of, the executioners. He did refuse to administer the lethal injections, but worked together with the SS doctor, Horst Schumann, in sterilizing young men and women – mainly 17-year-old Greeks – by heavily irradiating testicles and ovaries with X-rays. Surgeon Dering's task was to perform ablation of these glands within ten minutes of irradiation, without any sterile precautions, using rudimentary anaesthesia. He boasted of how fast he could work and proudly paraded his tobacco pouch made from an inmate's scrotum (Langbein, *Menschen in Auschwitz*, pp. 255–6; Lifton, *Les Médecins nazis*, pp. 281–4 and 318). Dering was freed in January 1944 and was recruited by Dr Clauberg. He retired after the war to the British colonies. In 1959, the writer Leon Uris accused him in *QB VII* of having performed 17,000 sterilization procedures in Auschwitz. In his subsequent libel action, the sterilization experiments performed in Auschwitz and the names of the perpetrators were revealed to the world. Ordered to be paid a symbolic halfpenny – the number of victims could not be proven – Dering died shortly after. Schumann took refuge in Africa and stood trial in a German court in 1966, but he was released on grounds of ill health.

32. According to T. Geve, it was another *Hilfsarbeiter kommando* of 200 inmates (*Es gibt hier keine Kinder*, p. 89). In 1942, this *kommando* enjoyed a sinister reputation. 'Hat throwing' was a popular game: after snatching an inmate's hat, the SS would throw it beyond the barbed wire and order the inmate to retrieve it. The inmate would then be shot either for having tried to escape, if he obeyed, or for disobeying, if he did not try to retrieve it. Every inmate shot while trying to escape would bring the SS a reward. The disciplinarian *kommandos* were disbanded at the beginning of 1944 on direct orders from Berlin.

touch with Polish civilians who work in the same place, located two or three kilometres from Auschwitz (a distance we cover every morning and evening, on foot, of course, dragging ourselves painfully through the autumn mud). By now, I know how to 'organise'; I find linen and sweaters in the camp, which I exchange for food with Polish civilians, and by evening, I return to the camp with some margarine, sometimes even a bit of butter or some sausage.

I have indeed absorbed the unspoken camp rules. For my own good, I have learned how important a *Häftling*'s appearance is for his survival, and I have managed to obtain a striped outfit giving me a relatively well-dressed look. I even have quite a becoming beret, and proper shoes. I could almost be mistaken for a *Prominenter*. Thanks to my continued good relations with the hospital, I receive supplies of soap and hot water and I can shave properly. It is amazing what a difference appearances can make, just how much clothes maketh the man. One learns quickly in the camp, provided one doesn't die first. The distribution of rags on arrival is in itself part of the programmed reduction of the person. Few grasp this concept immediately; unconsciously, they expect pity, but what they get instead are beatings. Shaved, tattooed, dressed in rags, the person himself becomes a rag in the eyes of the SS and the *kapos*. That person has earned the status of *Stuck*, *Scheisse*, excrement, less than nothing, a corpse with a temporary reprieve. On the other hand, with a neat appearance and shiny shoes, one can avoid the violent reactions of the *kapos* and other officials, and thus preserve life a little longer. As Langbein says, these could even gain respect from the SS. '*Kleider machen Leute*' ['Clothes maketh the man'].

The *kapo* of the Faulgas *kommando*, his insignia a green triangle, keeps beating his men. However, from the first day, I notice that he is wary of me – probably because he knows I worked at the hospital. It is well known that the hospital is a place of power, where an undesirable *kapo*, if he is unlucky enough to become sick, can be quietly liquidated by an influential *Häftling* … He therefore chooses to be cautious, and makes an effort to build good relations with me. This is not difficult, we talk in German, and things go reasonably well. After only a few days he offers me a promotion, the position of *Vorarbeiter*, which puts me in charge of a group of ten inmates. I am not very pleased with the prospect, but as I am interested in good working conditions, I accept.

The *Vorarbeiter* does not work, he watches. In exchange for his effort, he gets an extra bowl of soup. On the other hand, he is responsible for ensuring his team does a good job. This is the fundamental element of the concentration camp system; this first modicum of power over other inmates means that one must beat them when they don't work or work badly. It is my misfortune to be entrusted with gypsies, and gypsies are so hungry for freedom that they keep running away, in the most crazy and dangerous ways imaginable.[33] Rather than do the job required, they hide anywhere they can, under a haystack, in a hole ... They don't even try to avoid being caught; they take no precautions and even miss the *Appell* ... They are always found, but as their *Vorarbeiter* is responsible for them, I am the one who will be punished.

Soon enough I have had it. I cannot be responsible for their absurd escapades, nor do I want to have to beat them. I am not a torturer, and abhor this system. The only thing I can do is resign and go back to work myself, which I do without a second thought. It is not a heroic act. Fortunately, it is no longer 1942, where the ordinary prisoner dies quickly, while the foreman survives because he exerts no physical effort. I don't need the extra bowl of soup either, because I get one anyway every night from my friend Maurice Goldstein, who has become a nurse at the hospital. So, during the autumn of 1943,

---

33. See the paradoxical testimony of Höss on the gypsies, who were:

> ... his preferred inmates ... They couldn't cope with any work for very long; they loved their gypsy ways far too much. Their preferred *kommandos* were the transport *kommandos*, because this allowed them to go everywhere and to satisfy their curiosity.
>
> (*Kommandant*, p. 165)

> When the liquidation of the gypsy camp of Birkenau was ordered on 2 August 1944 (the same day the 26th, and last convoy, arrived from Mechelen), the gypsies' restlessness was their last and most extraordinary gesture of resistance against death. The 2,897 surviving gypsies did not give in and the SS had to use extreme force to get them into the trucks (Czech, *Kalendarium*, p. 838).

I no longer feel directly threatened by death. Actually, refusing the responsibility has no negative consequences. I am no longer a novice and I have friends, which is not the case for everyone.

I do wonder sometimes if I would have behaved the same way a year earlier, when an extra bowl of soup could have meant the difference between life and death.

One morning, when I am working at the methane gasworks, I receive a large parcel of food, which is incredible. No Jew in Auschwitz has ever received a parcel. Anything sent by families is simply confiscated by the SS. This rare favour is again due to my father, who again asked his friend, the ambassador of Romania in Berlin, to intervene on my behalf. He sent him a parcel for me asking him to forward it to me in Monowitz, where he thought I still was. So, in a way, I get this parcel through 'the diplomatic pouch', and for some reason, the SS preferred not to confiscate it. It is indeed a treasure: sugar and bacon. Immediately, the most crazy (although unfounded) rumours spread through the Blocks. A Jew got a parcel! This means that Jews are going to have the right to their parcels. Alas, the SS policy remains unchanged, and, as always, parcels for Jews are not distributed.

The atmosphere in this Faulgas *kommando* is a little better than in those in Monowitz, but nevertheless, I find myself back in the reality of Auschwitz, which is the reality of elimination by labour, the gradual decline towards extermination from which I was miraculously exempt for a few months. It is imperative that I spare my strength, and for that purpose, I try to use all the tricks I have learnt from the questionably selfish camp wisdom. I make friends with some Frenchmen who arrived in 1942, tattooed with older numbers, with whom I get along very well. I manage to 'organise' a lot. Thanks to my good contacts with the hospital and the disinfecting *kommando*, I sell underwear every day to Polish workers, and exchange with my suppliers from the camp what I receive in payment, essentially food. I am sure the SS are aware of what is going on, or at least suspect it. The trick is not to be caught.

On 23 December, the night before Christmas Eve, our

kommando is searched. It is a serious and frightening search. The SS move the prisoners forward in a line, and search each row, man by man. I have a treasure on me, a block of butter, which I keep hidden in my mittens. However, they don't seem to punish us very severely, maybe because it is almost Christmas and they probably just want to confiscate the goods for their own use. My comrades, certain they will be caught, throw their loot on the ground just before the search. The SS need only bend down and pick up all sorts of goods. They reach the man before me, a resourceful Ukrainian. As he lowers his pants, a rabbit escapes, running for its life under the furious eyes of the SS ... the guy had 'organized' a live rabbit! Nobody wants such loot to escape, and the scene that ensues is the funniest rabbit chase imaginable, right there in the middle of an Auschwitz camp.

They search me, my hands up ... my mittens are still on my hands, and they don't notice anything. I come back to the camp with my butter, still laughing happily from the rabbit scene.

I remain assigned to this *kommando* from October to December 1943. Towards the end of December, I feel very weak and obtain a *Blockschonung* [permission to remain in the Block and thus in bed] for the whole day. During this whole period, *Kapo* Korn is working quietly for me, and, following his intervention, on 28 December, I am moved to the disinfecting *kommando*. This is a good *kommando* to be in, not strenuous and not very dangerous. I finish the year there, while still living in Block 4. At the beginning of January, a postcard from home reassures me again that my parents are still alive. On 6 January, I am assigned to the clean laundry *kommando*, the *Neuwäscherei*, also a very good *kommando*, where we wash the inmates' laundry. I am part of the night shift, which is propitious for 'organising'. There is not too much work at night, and part of the time is spent playing chess with my night guard, a Polish professor.

Still I never let my guard down. Selections have started again in the camp, and when I hear yelling, '*Alle Juden antreten!*' ['All Jews come forward!'], I hide.

Eventually, on the last day of January, I am called to the *Arbeitsdienst* [the labour service], the body responsible for job distribution in the camp. I am called as a chemist, not yet aware that my new 'career' in Auschwitz has been decided.

5 Rajsko: The Hygiene Institute of the SS

> When one reads the concentration camp testimonies... beyond the suffering all the inmates described, and beyond a certain number of constants, we are struck by the enormous diversity of situations. These differences are fundamental because ... they either implied survival or they led to death.
>
> Annette Wieviorka, *Déportation and génocide: Entre la mémoire et l'oubli*

On the eve of 1 February 1944, I discover unexpectedly that I am assigned to a new place. My guardian angel, *Kapo* Korn, secretly worked for my safety, and recommended me as a chemist at the *Arbeitsdienst*. As a result, I am assigned to the SS Hygiene Institute, a medical and biological research centre set up – like the neighbouring centre for agricultural research – next to the village of Rajsko, about five or six kilometres from the main camp of Auschwitz inside the wide belt of armed guards. I am also moved to a new Block where I join the rest of my new *kommando*.

The Hygiene Institute of Rajsko is quite an imposing building, completely isolated in the middle of fields and fenced off with barbed wire, guarded on all sides by SS. Although he is no longer a *kapo*, Miki Korn is known to everyone as *Kapo* Korn – actually, nobody really knows whether or not he is a *kapo*. He is part of the Hygiene Institute personnel, where he takes care of various things and is very influential. He obviously enjoys the confidence of the chief of the institute, the SS doctor, Weber, who is very much feared. Everybody knows that if he even looks at a *Häftling* the wrong way, the *Häftling* risks being sent on the next transport. Our *kommando* works under three SS officer-doctors: Weber, Hans Münch, and a young Belgian man,

Delmotte.[1] They are surrounded by several NCOs and SS. In addition, there are five SDG (SS nurses), who are supposedly doing 'scientific work'. In reality, they do nothing, because they are incompetent for lab work. However, I quickly realise that their main job is to watch us and try to harm us.

The director of the institute, the *SS-Hauptsturmführer* Bruno Weber, is a doctor of Medicine and Natural Sciences with a degree from the University of Chicago. According to André Lettich,[2] a young French doctor with whom I will have dealings every day in Rajsko, and who will later write his memoirs of the camp, Weber is 32 in 1943. Even if Lettich – with hindsight – judges him to be culturally and intellectually mediocre, the director is, nonetheless, admired by his subordinates, especially by Münch. He is also utterly convinced of the importance of his institute. He makes an effort to develop it and furnish it with sophisticated equipment and prestigious researchers. This is not difficult because the RSHA (Central Administration Office) convoys deliver them in large numbers. Weber is also ambitious, seeking his superiors' appreciation of his value to promote his research and further his career in peace. He is really there, in Auschwitz, for career reasons. Langbein confirms that one

1. The *SS-Obersturmführer*, Hans Delmotte, of Belgian origin, came from a family of industrialists, with many relatives highly placed in the Nazi hierarchy. He seems to have been sent by Mrugowsky to Auschwitz at the time when Münch was categorically refusing to participate in the selection of Jews on the arrival of convoys. Delmotte accepted his assignment in return for a promise that he could write his doctoral thesis while in the camp (a Jewish inmate doctor would help him to write it). Delmotte had neither Münch's strength of character nor his skill, and as he was partially dependent on Wirths, he had to do his 'duty' at the ramp. The first selection left him distraught. However, Liebehenschel, probably helped by Weber and Wirths, sent him to work under Mengele, who within two weeks convinced him of the patriotic and racial need for the exterminations (Langbein, *Menschen in Auschwitz*, pp. 405–6). In addition, Weber arranged for Delmotte's wife to join him. Münch describes her as a heartless creature with no soul. She may have been the woman that W.B. saw sunbathing from the roof of the villa. Delmotte was in charge of selections until the end, but seemed relieved when the gassings stopped. Deeply affected, he had a brief period of training at Dachau, where the Hygiene Institute relocated. On liberation, just before being captured by American troops, he shot himself in the head (Lifton, *Les Médecins nazis*, pp. 346–7 and 362).
2. Dr André Lettich of Tours was also deported to Birkenau on 17 July 1942; his wife and child were gassed there in September. He was assigned to the Hygiene Institute in July 1943 and bore the number 51,224. He described his experiences in the camp in a doctoral thesis (see Lettich, *Trente-quatre mois*).

could sense some repugnance on his part for what was going on in the camp, but nothing in the world would have induced him to exchange his place for a mission at the front. Being a perfectionist, he makes the inmate-doctors take tests, and those who fail lose the enviable opportunity of working in the protected climate of the institute. He is also an elegant man, haughty and cold with the inmates. Some say that he behaved the same way with the SS. We are afraid of him, but he does behave correctly at all times and with everybody.

Even in the early days, I am aware of the special status of this institute, and the *kommando* working in it, compared to the rest of the camp. The atmosphere there resembles nothing I have known, either at the outdoor sites, of course, or at the hospital, or in the disinfecting hall. Is it because they are almost all doctors or scientists and there are no brutes? Weber went to a lot of trouble to set up his institute, and he equipped his labs with sophisticated equipment 'organised' from all over Europe.[3] He seems to believe in his project. The *kommando* remains housed in the main camp, and every day we walk to Rajsko. However, even in the camp, our life is different: much more human than in the other Blocks. The constant pressure of the fight for survival is felt less intensely.[4]

---

3. Like Klein, Lettich notes that the labs were state-of-the-art, and equipped almost entirely with French instruments, some of them marked 'JOUAN-PARIS'. For the origin of these materials, see Kogon, *L'État SS*. Kogon describes how three officers of the Hygiene Institute, under the leadership of the physician Ding-Schuler from Buchenwald, were sent to Paris in 1942 to buy medical materials for Berlin. Having easily spent their budget of 30,000 Reichsmark, they nonetheless dispatched the medical equipment to Germany for much greater amounts. The debt, however, was never paid. Ding-Schuler silenced the suppliers with threats of concentration camps (ibid., p. 334).

4. In October 1944, this *kommando* totalled about 100 inmates, and Marc Klein describes life there in detail (*Témoignages strasbourgeois*, p. 450): get up at 4 a.m. in the summer and at 5:45 a.m. in the winter; half an hour to make one's bed and swallow the breakfast liquid. Then gather together in front of the Block in rows of five, form columns, the orchestra arrives playing military marches, and the *kommandos* depart in a setting both tragic and grandiose, tightly guarded by the *kapos*, stiff, hands on the seam of their pants, hats low over the nose, exit, then relax the pace and atmosphere so that it is almost human for the 40 minutes it takes to walk to the lab. Return to the camp before nightfall for a less formal ceremony and sometimes a search. The evening *Appell* is exhausting and danger-ous: sometimes, prisoners are hanged; evening meal; various activities; treat-ments; curfew at 9 p.m. And the terror of the night selections.

The SS had actually founded its Hygiene Institute some time earlier to fight typhus, one of the worst curses of the war period, an extremely contagious disease with a death rate of over 50 per cent. The disease is transmitted by lice, and appears wherever people are crowded together in poor sanitary conditions. So, naturally, it thrives in the camps, and in the ghettos, and at the Russian Front among the *Wehrmacht* soldiers. When the Lemberg[5] ghetto was about to be liquidated, Weber discovered that, in its Jewish hospital, a specialist was working on perfecting a serum against typhus, which at the time affected 70 per cent of the ghetto's Jewish population, and many of the soldiers guarding them. In German, this disease is called 'Fleckfieber', and, ironically, this specialist was called Fleck. One week before the Lemberg ghetto was liquidated, Weber, well aware of the fated date, sought out Fleck and offered him the option of being exterminated with all the Jews of the ghetto, or joining him and pursuing his work in Auschwitz in very good conditions with modern equipment. Fleck thought it over for a few days then agreed, on the condition that he could bring his wife and 12-year-old son, Ryszek, as well as five of his colleagues and their wives and children. Weber accepted, and Fleck's team arrived in Auschwitz with the status of exceptional prisoners, *Sonderhäftlinge*, at least at the beginning. Later, their privileges were gradually reduced and, finally, withdrawn. For some time, they were allowed to keep their hair and to live with their families in a Block strictly separated from the others. Later, their position weakened, they were shaved, separated from their wives and sent to join the rest of the inmates. It is true that their specialization also encouraged their isolation. The SS from the camp avoided contact with them as much as possible because of their exposure to the fearsome and contagious disease of typhus. Fleck and his team could at least enjoy the relative

---

5.   Lvov (Lemberg) in Galicia had been part of the Austro-Hungarian Empire since 1772, and was a Polish town from 1918. As in all major towns in Poland (for example, Warsaw, Krakow, Vilna/Vilnius, Lodz, Bialystock, etc.), the Germans regrouped the Jews in Lvov soon after the invasion, in a ghetto that consisted of several small blocks of housing cut off from the rest of the town. The liquidation of the Lvov ghetto began in August 1942 and ended in March 1943 with the murder of all the survivors and its destruction by fire.

advantage of their situation while they worked in the very different atmosphere of their separate world.

Yet, while working there, I soon discovered that this Hygiene Institute did not produce any serious or scientific work.[6] It served, first and foremost, as cover for the SS, who were better off there than anywhere else. It was a cushy haven for the three medics and the five SDGs who lived there like pashas, exempt from all kinds of repugnant jobs. This cushy existence of the SS in the camps was well known and well documented. The SS of Rajsko enjoyed the services of two brothers, excellent Jewish tailors from Warsaw, who made them superb uniforms and sometimes also civilian clothes which they sent to their families in Germany. They had a Jewish shoemaker who made them magnificent boots, a Jewish barber who shaved them daily. For some of them, their very high standard of living must have been incomparably higher than their life as civilians, let alone life at the Russian Front.[7]

André Lettich described in detail the working conditions at the Hygiene Institute. He was a *Häftling* from 1942, with whom I had daily contact in the *kommando*. Lettich and Landau were two French doctors, an inseparable pair who were always seen together in the biology section. I believe Landau came from Berck-Plage.[8] Both arrived in 1942 and had low ID numbers, between 40,000 and 60,000. They were conducting bacteriological tests. Their work included blood tests for SS officers who had committed some offence or who had been involved in

---

6.   Lettich (*Trent-quatre mois*, p. 34) is of the same opinion:

   It was in the interest of the SS in charge of them to perform as many analyses as possible, to justify not being sent to the front line. For that reason, they also took samples of blood, urine, faeces, saliva and throat swabs from inmates who would be sent to the gas chambers a few days later. We who knew the futility of these tests, had to carry them out with a semblance of seriousness.

   Marc Klein agrees; he notes that, in 1944 alone, 110,000 were performed, all duly signed by the SS (*Témoignages strasbourgeois*, p. 450).
7.   See Kogan, *L'état SS*, Ch. 18. Even at the height of the war effort, in Auschwitz there was a *kommando* called *SS-Schneiderer*, where female inmates sewed clothes exclusively for SS wives and female SS staff. This *kommando* was expanded and obtained its materials from the 'Canada' barracks.
8.   For information on Léon Landau, who worked in the Hygiene Institute from spring 1943, see *Die Auschwitz-Hefte*, Vol. 1, pp. 214 and 280.

accidents while drunk. The blood alcohol level tests took longer and were more complicated to perform then than today. Needless to say, our doctors often found alcohol in those blood samples, as SS officers drank plenty. The biology section performed an enormous number of all kinds of tests, sometimes up to 5,000 a day – one can imagine with what precision – whose results were sent to Berlin. This frenzy of activity was meant to justify the existence of the Hygiene Institute and thus preserve the hidden life of luxury that the assigned SS officers enjoyed.

Lettich describes very well the life we lived: how the inmate doctors performed examinations with the utmost care, because the SS was lurking, watching, waiting to catch them doing wrong. Although everybody was cheating, if anyone had been caught, it would have had terrible consequences. Yet the inmates of this *kommando*, all specialists, some university professors, regularly took risks for ethical reasons. If the blood sample was from a prisoner they never gave a positive result, because this would have been a death warrant. Whatever the result, the person was not going to be treated. The logic of Auschwitz required the tests, mainly Lettich's diphtheria tests, to be conducted like in any university hospital. The consequences, however, were very different, as the sick person, convinced that he had an incurable contagious disease, was usually selected and gassed. The wisdom of Auschwitz meant postponing, as long as possible, the selection of their *Häftling* companions. The lab also performed tests on SS personnel and their families. Lettich once had to test the wife of an SS officer for diphtheria (some SS were stationed in Auschwitz with their spouses), and the result was positive. The woman threatened to hang my friend with her own hands if he ever produced a positive result again ... Needless to say, the result of the next test was negative.[9]

The further the Russian Front advanced, the more the SS felt defeat approaching, and the more frenzied their research became and the more blood tests they performed, anxious to

---

9.   See Langbein, *Menschen in Auschwitz*, p. 517.

prove how indispensable the institute was. Shortly before evacuation, they started a programme for analysing faeces, designed to discover what caused diphtheria. Of course, the real origin was the disgusting food, malnutrition, and the inmates' weakened state. They performed several thousand tests every day, and SS NCOs seemed to get particular pleasure out of conducting rectal tests on women. In order not to declare anybody sick, Lettich and his colleagues injected all the cultures with the same swab sample so that all the results would be negative.[10]

The Institute also performed *in-vivo* and post-mortem tests on Doctor Mengele's twins. Lettich testified in 1946 that Mengele had no qualms about killing these children for studying a particular problem more closely.[11] At the same time, the bacteriology lab was in charge of jobs that left one stupefied: for example, they were trying to determine what caused the death of rabbits and chickens in farms and private SS yards. For each death, a written report was required explaining its pathological cause. These cases were submitted to Lettich using the word 'deceased'. Where men were considered less than animals, these animals were treated humanely. In the course of July 1944, the four large crematoria of Birkenau were working day and night to reduce to ashes 400,000 Hungarian Jews, more than half Hungary's Jewish population. As the installation couldn't cope with the massive load, bodies were also being burned in open pits. In the midst of this horror, chief doctor Wirths sent the Hygiene Institute a small dead rabbit, about five days old, so the lab could determine the cause of the poor animal's death. Luckily, once veterinarian autopsies were done, the inmate-doctors were allowed to eat what remained of these animals, which represented a very appreciable food supplement.

---

10. Lettich, *Trent-quatre mois*, p. 33 ff. Another French doctor, Désiré Haffner, also deported in 1942, and who would also write his memoirs in the form of a thesis, seems to have studied the dysentery tests in more depth. He says that no specific agents were found, that the dysentery (40 to 50 motions a day) was accompanied by fever and was due to impurities and to the drastic change in diet, and not to the unfiltered water (*Aspects pathologiques*, p. 30).
11. On Mengele's research and methods, with his 'guinea pigs', see Nyiszli, *Auschwitz: A Doctor's Eyewitness Account* (New York: Arcade, 1993), Chapter 29 ff.; and Lifton, *Les Médecins nazis*, p. 384 ff.

But, I return to my arrival: to the moment where I will discover my new place of work.

In addition to the biology section where the two French doctors work, the Hygiene Institute also has a histology section, in which the SS personnel have use of a tomograph, a rare piece of equipment at the time. There is also a significant chemistry section, managed by a first-class Dutch chemist, Dorus Wolf, who, before long, will become my friend. As I soon find out, the chemistry lab is no more serious than the others. It is true that tests are performed, but these only serve to cover up the lab's principal function: the distillation of strong alcohol. The processed alcohol is retrieved in test phials and then distilled to produce pure alcohol. I conclude that the only purpose of the chemistry section of Rajsko is to provide the SS with strong alcohol.

Any chemist knows that it is not easy to distil a good yield of pure alcohol. Nonetheless, the Dorus Wolf lab has an excellent specialist, a Slovakian chemist from Brünn, who built a cleverly designed refinery, three to four metres long. This huge device links an impressive number of stills, one to the other. At the output, the alcohol dripped down slowly, drop by drop, a fascinating sight that strikes me when I come to visit Dorus. In its Hygiene Institute, Auschwitz actually houses a real distillery for producing alcohol, except it is not clandestine; on the contrary, as its bosses are the SS themselves, who exploit it for making the final product.

At this point, it is my first day in Rajsko. I join the institute as a chemist, and as a matter of course am taken to the chemistry section to meet its chief. Dorus Wolf immediately tests my knowledge.

Tragically, those first few months of camp life have emptied my mind. I cannot recognise any chemical formulae, I cannot remember anything I studied; the only thing I recognise is the formula for water. I stutter; I am a hopeless case. It becomes horribly clear that they will not be able to give me a job as a chemist. My situation is desperate. I might as well return to the outdoor sites and die.

Dorus then does something I will never forget. He doesn't

send me back, but goes to talk to *Kapo* Korn. Naturally, the head of the chemistry section is very embarrassed. He cannot keep me, because there is no way he can continue to hide my ignorance from *Obersturmführer* Weber, and even if he does, it could cause him a lot of trouble. Nevertheless, I am incredibly lucky not to have been interrogated by an SS chemist, as was Primo Levi.[12] An ingenious solution is eventually found to the problem I pose. They will assign me to the serology section, an incredible opportunity for the ignorant man I have become.

The serology section employs only four inmates: a university professor of mathematics, a Polish pharmacist named Fabicki, Doctor Träger, who is part of the Lemberg medical team, and me. Our job consists of counting red cells in blood samples that are brought to us. I work all day, glued to a microscope. The blood tests that are sent to our lab are taken from inmates on whom Auschwitz SS doctors perform experiments *in-vivo* to test substances and medicines. Indeed, the pharmaceutical firms, Bayer, I.G.-Farben, etc., have agreements with the camp management to use inmates as guinea pigs.[13] Within the framework of a research programme, we also study alterations in the blood resulting from changes in diet. An SS man in our *kommando*, Kirmeier, makes daily trips to Block 10 in the main camp, the Experimental Block, where women serve as guinea pigs. They are either given medication to check its effectiveness (or toxicity), or they are subjected to specific diets. Every day, Kirmeier comes and takes small blood samples, and puts them in small phials, which he then brings to us for red cell counts. We must report the exact numbers as well as the daily variations.

After a while, I realise that our 'scientific' observations are useless. It is ridiculous to consider that under the conditions in which they are performed, they can advance science in any way. Even worse, the inmates from whom the blood samples are taken don't even benefit from our results. Whatever the result, no change to their sanitary and detention conditions

---

12. Primo Levi and Paul Steinberg were tested by a German chemist, Pannwitz (from I.G. Farben?) (Levi, *Se questo è un uomo*, p. 112; Steinberg, *Chroniques*, p. 117).
13. See Lifton, *Les Médecins nazis*, p. 327.

follows. I quickly come to consider my work a sinecure.[14] The results being of no importance, I stop counting the cells, although I pretend to, and put down approximate numbers. However, I still have to be careful to keep my numbers within acceptable limits. The Polish professor of mathematics to whom I give my results, and who represents them graphically, knows very well what my data are worth. I think that the SS guards know it, too, just as they probably know that everything going on at the institute is pure rubbish, except the distillation of alcohol. Everybody knows, but of course nobody talks. The truth would send the whole *kommando* to their deaths.

During the day, my *kommando* works in the building of the Hygiene Institute in Rajsko, a few kilometres away from the main camp, but at night we come back to sleep in Auschwitz in Block 11, the *Bunker* Block. Still in February, we move to Block 13. Our *kommando* is carefully isolated from the others and our living conditions are totally different from what I experienced in Monowitz. Indeed, by comparison, they are almost human. I immediately feel at home in this *kommando*, with its unusual atmosphere, comprised almost exclusively of intellectuals. In addition to *Kapo* Korn, who is as unofficial as he is essential, we have our official *kapo*, Reichel,[15] a relatively older man, exceptionally civil, who was, I believe, a high school teacher and a member of the social democrats. He must have been a *Häftling* for many years. He is a delightful man, respected by everyone. In the last two months of the institute's existence he will, unfortunately, be replaced by *Kapo* Bertram; a rough and brutal Pole. From the minute he arrives, he will contribute to the deterioration of the generally peaceful atmosphere of the *kommando*.

At work, I sit next to Fabicki, the pharmacist – a Polish nationalist who supports Pilsudski.[16] He has been an Auschwitz

---

14. Ibid., pp. 394, 399 and 408.
15. Paul Reichel, of Ceiplice, was a German from the Sudetenland, who had already been interned for seven years (*Die Auschwitz-Hefte*, Vol. 1, p. 214; B. Klieger, *Le chemin que nous avons fait (Reportages surhumains)* (Brussels: Beka, s.d.), pp. 66–7). Marc Klein doesn't like him (*Témoignages strasbourgeois*, p. 452).
16. Marshal Joszef Pilsudski ran the Polish State between 1918 and 1923, a period of resistance against the Russian Bolsheviks. Returning to power in 1926, following a *coup d'état*, he ran an authoritative and nationalist dictatorship until his death in 1935. After the German invasion of 1939, the Polish Resistance was very divided.

Häftling for a very long time. I know from experience, having been subjected, in the camp, to more abuse and oppression from the Poles than from the Germans, that most Polish nationalists are anti-Semitic, and Fabicki is no exception. Yet, with me he makes an exception. I become 'his' Jew, his 'good' Jew. He adopts me, and almost treats me as a friend. As a Pole, he has the privilege of receiving parcels, and he receives many. Some nights, after such an arrival, under my bedcover I find a stoneware pot sealed with wax with tinned lard inside! Fabicki knows very well that for me this is gold, because, although our work is uninterrupted, our rations are as meagre as ever. What I appreciate most in him is his total discretion. He never speaks about these presents. He behaves like a perfect gentleman in a world of brutality and indifference.

When I feel like cursing Poles, I refrain from doing so because of him. In my eyes, Fabicki is one of the righteous.

Besides, honesty and proper behaviour are the norm in our *kommando*; theft is unknown, as are beatings, fights and foul language. I don't know any Block where a genuine treasure like this pot of lard could remain hidden a whole day, just rolled in bedcovers, rather than disappear as soon as it is put there. Our evenings are almost human. We can borrow books to read in the Block from a library in the institute's chemical section. One night, for the first time since my arrival in Auschwitz, I find myself with a book in my hands. And what book? Disraeli's *Tancrede*, which had survived the *auto-da-fé* of forbidden books, nobody knows how! This is not my only surprise in that respect. I also find half of Marie-Antoinette's biography by Stefan Zweig; the other half had been torn off, but that didn't matter. I find books written by Jews – that is, by 'degenerates'; prohibited, banned books, and I find them right here in Auschwitz. I savour my reading page by page, and it brings me incredible peace and relaxation. What a pleasure! Some nights we play chess. Some humanity is recaptured, which helps me forget for a while where I am.

The following morning, after only a few days in my *kommando*, I am summoned again to appear before the Political Section.

107

I cannot sleep the whole night, torn between a justifiable fear for my life and, I dare hardly admit it, hope for that cherished visa with which they teased me the first time I came, the exit visa which could mean my freedom. No Jew had ever been freed from Auschwitz, as far as I knew. Yet, against all odds, for a whole night I wish for a miracle. Didn't I get a parcel when no other Jew received theirs, and didn't they also mention a passport my father had sent me, so maybe ... insane wanderings of the mind.

Of course, this has nothing to do with what awaits me at the Political Section. When I return the next morning, safe and sound, my companions cannot believe my story, especially since they know it is the second time. That day, the members of my *kommando* develop a certain mistrust of me. They find that my relations with 'them' are too good to be innocent. They suspect me of being an informer. I don't know it at the time, but they never fully trust me again. Their uneasy feeling about me will last until our liberation, but I will only learn about it from Dorus Wolf in Brussels in 1945.

When I come into the office of the Political Section, the same SS officer as before[17] is waiting for me. He recognises me and hands me a register: 'You got a parcel from Liège. Sign here that you received it.'

Dumbfounded, I breathe in sharply, registering at once the intensity of my crazy disappointment: I had so hoped for an 'exit permit' from this hell. All in vain; how ridiculous!

My reaction is insane. I answer in a cold rage: 'I didn't receive anything, so I can't sign anything.'

The SS officer's reaction equals my madness, and paradoxically, I owe my life to it. Flabbergasted, he yells: 'Out!'

I turn around and run for my life.

This was more than enough to send me to the *Bunker* and to my death. After my liberation, I meet the Slovakian prisoner who served as secretary and translator at the time in the Political Section. She was still trembling at the thought that, without the excuse of being a novice, I could have dared such

---

17. It follows that it was not Maximilian Grabner who was sent away from Auschwitz in October 1943 (see previous chapter).

an awesome thing. It was only after I came back to Liège that I got to the bottom of this story. My girlfriend, C., who knew my address from the one and only postcard I had sent her, regularly sent me packages and was never thanked for them, for good reason. Her patience exhausted, she had gone to Malmedy, a Belgian border town annexed to the Reich, and had given her parcel to a German courier. He had conscien-tiously delivered it to the concentration camp of Auschwitz and demanded a properly signed delivery receipt from the camp administration. Unfortunately, all that attention put me in great danger. One of the fundamental laws of survival in the camp was to keep a low profile. It was a principal of prime importance. In fact, the perversion of Auschwitz was such that, in wishing to help me, my parents and my girlfriend – by insist-ing that their parcels be delivered to me – could have been the actual agents of my death.

On 6 March, after a month in serology, a surprise: a new member joins our team, a woman. My new colleague's name is Trude Müller. She comes from Prague and speaks German. (Not surprising, as Prague was a bilingual city until the war. Two events combined to cleanse Prague linguistically: the Nazis' extermination of German-speaking Jews, and the Czechs' retaliation by expelling the German-speaking non-Jews.) Trude is a political prisoner, a long-time communist. She is also a courageous woman, who was in prison for a long time before being deported to Auschwitz.

Seeing her, it strikes me that I have not seen a woman for a whole year since my deportation, except for the wives of the doctors of the Fleck team. They come to us daily with their children to find refuge from the terror in the Blocks. And on that morning, a woman is brought to my side, and an attractive one, too. We sit side by side at our work posts. Attraction is immediate and mutual. But this doesn't happen by chance. I soon suspect SS Schumacher of having contrived this fate to 'scientifically' observe what happens between a male and a female when brought together, and, if anything does happen between them, to punish them instantly.

But nothing can stop life flowing through us. The imposed

109

proximity is as delicious as it is embarrassing. We are tense and constantly watchful. Auschwitz is a physical universe. I have recovered quite well from the beatings and abuse I was subjected to, I am relatively well-fed, and I spend the day in warm surroundings as part of a useless, but relatively safe, *kommando*, at least for the time being. In Auschwitz, there is no such thing as 'long term'. And fate comes and places an attractive woman next to me.

Physically, Trude seems in relatively good shape, which in Auschwitz means that she has enough to eat. Every day after her arrival, as we sit working side by side, electricity flows between us. Our senses are heightened, and when we move test tubes and our fingers touch, this light contact gives me the physical sensation of sparks flying. A mood of love is taking hold of us, yet we never touch. It is impossible even to think that we can kiss. In this world, to get close to anybody is out of the question. Any gesture would be a death sentence if we were caught. The trapdoor is wide open under our feet, and we must avoid falling into it. The funny thing is that the God of chastity has taken the shape of *SS-Unterscharführer* Schumacher, who appears in our lab at any time, certain he'll catch us at fault, anxious to exercise his power of life and death over us. We must resist, and we do.

Trude, sitting next to me, must feel the same way.

At the end of March, they ask us to write to our families again. This time I refuse. I know now that these letters are used to spread lies about our well-being. I don't want to serve the Nazi propaganda machine.

Spring begins with mild weather. The atmosphere in the lab, however, is being poisoned irretrievably. SS officer Schumacher, who has hated me from the day I arrived, is no longer happy just watching Trude and me. It becomes obvious that he is trying to provoke an incident that will allow him to have a go at me. I must protect myself, as well as Trude. I must find a way to remove us from this persecution. The wisdom of Auschwitz whispers in my ear to return to the ranks and become anonymous again, retaining, if possible, the privileges I have been able to acquire. The opportunity arises the day the

SS announce that they are creating a vegetable garden in the Hygiene Institute grounds, and that they are looking for volunteers to work there. I am immediately aware of the advantages of this new position. Here is a legitimate way out of the institute building while still remaining in its vicinity. The SS will get used to seeing me around, and that could be an added advantage for 'organising'. Some time later, I will naturally enjoy the fruits of my first crop: radishes, tomatoes and other vegetables. I will eat of this godsend as soon as the SS turn their backs.

The work in the garden is not very hard, and even brings with it some diversion. One day, as I am digging quite a deep pit to fill with compost, my dearest enemy suddenly appears, *SS-Unterscharführer* Schumacher. Even here he comes to watch me. He stands at the edge of the pit, his shiny boots at the height of my nose. I feel that I am confronted with the living incarnation of the triumphant SS power.

I must not react, I must continue digging. He also remains quiet and watches me work for a long time. He savours his superiority. Then, after a long silence, he suddenly asks: 'Tell me, Jewboy, where did you learn to dig like that?'

And I answer without thinking: 'In Palestine.'

Schumacher stays on for a while at the edge of the pit without uttering a word; then turns round and leaves.

Did I make him doubt his racial perceptions? I know that the propaganda with which he has been indoctrinated depicts Jews only as moneylenders or merchants, and I don't fit the image with which he was brainwashed and which he has tried hard to believe. Or maybe he really thinks that Germany should be cleansed of its Jews by sending them to Palestine, and that I am here only because of a historical mistake.[18] I will never know what my answer inspired in him, but he never bothered me again after that day.

In the camp, the Germans never succeeded in destroying me, or touching my essence, my identity. The fact that I have

---

18. A somewhat anachronistic notion in 1943, after plans for forced resettlement of the Jews in Madagascar or elsewhere had been abandoned. The SS members were so indoctrinated that he must have internalised instructions on the Final Solution: extermination, or elimination by labour.

always felt a Jew means that I have always been strongly aware of my Jewish national identity (my mother tongue was German, my papers were Romanian, my residence was Belgian, but my people was Jewish). This certainly helped to protect me from breaking down. In this way, I avoided feeling threatened in the deepest part of my identity when they spat in my face and beat me. This was very different from the German Jews, who felt that they were German before they were Jewish, which had become impossible. These people suffered terribly at the thought that their homeland, Germany, wished them all dead. I always knew exactly what to expect from Nazis.

One day in April, at noon, they ask for a volunteer to get the soup. The churns for our *kommando* come from the kitchen of the main camp and are brought to the Agricultural Research station, the Gärtnerei Rajsko, at the same time as those intended for the women working there. The man from our *kommando* who usually brings our share back is sick that day. Again, I apply my principle of grabbing any legitimate opportunity to get out of where I am. This time, thanks to my mission of *Suppenträger* [soup carrier], I am able to make contact with the women's *kommando* of Rajsko, in particular with the biologists of the *Pflanzenzucht*, where they are experimenting with dandelion cultures to obtain indigenous rubber. The Germans are hoping for a large-scale development of the culture of this plant to obtain the raw material the Buna so desperately needs. As I fulfil the function of soup carrier for some time, I successfully establish contact between the women's and the men's camps. In Auschwitz, the opportunities for contact between the women's and the men's camps were quite rare. Meanwhile, a biologist from Belgium, Robert Mandelbaum,[19] joins our *kommando*. His wife was lucky to have survived the entrance selection and she works at the *Pflanzenzucht*. I act as messenger between them. I also carry letters for other comrades, and bring news of the women's camp back to the main camp of

---

19. On the Belgian Resistance fighter, Israel ('Robert') Mandelbaum, born in 1913, founder and influential member of the Committee for the Defence of the Jews, and his wife, Estera Waynman, see Steinberg, *La Traque*.

Auschwitz. Of course, this involves a certain risk, but the people of our *kommando* are rarely searched. In general, although the surveillance and threats to which we were subjected in the past haven't completely disappeared, they have become much lighter.

Robert was deported from Brussels, and this is reason enough for me to have a friendly chat with him during his first night in our Block. He was given the bed under mine. I have retained my habit of sleeping on the top bunk to escape the dust falling from the straw mattresses and the effects of my neighbours' dysentery. I work at raising his spirits for a good part of the night. The welcome the newcomers receive is generally in keeping with the spirit of the camp, and it would be wrong to believe that in Auschwitz, we receive the *Zugang* with open arms, material aid and moral support. Quite the contrary is true. Arrival is horrible for most newcomers. They are bullied and despised, leaving them quickly disheartened, which immediately plays a part in the elimination process.[20] As soon as I can, I try to dampen this initial shock for Robert. Yet he was very lucky on his arrival in Auschwitz. He has been assigned directly to our *kommando*, without going through any of the abominable elimination *kommandos*. Despite that, for weeks he will behave like a real *Zugang*, constantly amazed at everything he sees, living in a kind of stupor day and night. I cannot help thinking that he has seen nothing of Auschwitz's reality. In Brussels, after liberation, Robert will reveal to me how the friendship I offered him on that first day in Auschwitz meant much more to him than the risks I took taking his letters to his wife. But before we can exchange those confidences, I will be destined to meet Robert again in Buchenwald in disastrous circumstances ... The situation that day will be turned around, and he will be the one to help me.

One spring day in 1944, a French political prisoner joins our *kommando*. He arrives in a convoy from Compiègne; his name

---

20. See Levi, *I sommersi e i salvati*, p. 26: the novice [in German, *Zugang*: an abstract noun and not a man's name] is exposed to cold treatment, even hostility, from other inmates, either because they are jealous, although this seems totally absurd – unless the scent of home still lingers on them – or because of a regressive phenomenon where the 'We' becomes stronger with the arrival of the 'Other'.

is Marcel Thibault, and he has been imprisoned by the Germans for acts of resistance. Usually, French convoys come from Drancy and are essentially convoys of Jews, but his, at least this is what Marcel believes, reached Auschwitz due to an administrative error.[21] As they are Aryans and non-Jews, they did not go through a selection on arrival and are quarantined for an endless period. Every day he tells me that he is there by error and that it will not be long before he goes back. There is even talk that he, and all of his group, will be freed. Hope can be very tenacious. But,as the days go by, this notion becomes more ephemeral; time passes and no liberation is decreed. To cut a long story short, Marcel joins the *kommando* of the Hygiene Institute as a telephone clerk; a most privileged position.

Although Marcel is older than me, we immediately become friends thanks to the shared language. We talk in French for hours, and among other things, I explain my Zionist ideals to him passionately and in depth. Marcel, a man of the Resistance, understands me. He has an additional advantage over me; as a French Aryan prisoner, he is entitled to receive parcels from home, and he does. At home, in Mayenne, he has an extraordinary wife, who sends him such delicacies. At the beginning, I just accept the presents he offers me, but later, we decide to pool our resources. We become *Kumpel* [friends and associates]; it is a term that originated in the mines, and became part of the camp jargon. He will contribute the contents of his parcels, I will 'organize' what I can find.

If Marcel has food to exchange, I must find something to contribute to our resources. I think of the alcohol that is

---

21. Out of the 52 convoys of Frenchmen deported from the Compiègne-Royallieu camp – essentially a political camp – only four were destined for Auschwitz. Marcel Thibault probably arrived in the convoy of 20 April 1943, which brought together again 1,655 Resistance fighters (Czech, *Kalendarium*, p. 763). Pierre Nivromont, a survivor of this convoy, known as the 'tattooeds" convoy, testified that the camp administration seemed surprised and embarrassed by their arrival. Most of them were interned for a short period and then transferred to Buchenwald (see [Pierre Nivromont] and Didier Epelbaum, *Matricule 186140: Histoire d'un combat* (Paris: Hagège, 1997), pp. 140 and 186). On the controversy over the French political convoys sent 'by mistake' to Auschwitz, see Wieviorka, *Déportation et génocide*, pp. 224–5 and note 23. The communist historiography states that pressure from the Resistance on the Germans was not enough to free them. However, it was strong enough to have them transferred: the men to Buchenwald and the women to Ravensbrück.

distilled every day in the chemistry labs. I get very excited with this recklessly bold idea. I am going to 'organize' alcohol. To understand the minds of inmates, one must understand the values by which they live. At the beginning, the *Zugang* is starving to death and dreams only of soup. Then, if he is lucky enough to survive and be assigned to a *kommando*, where he gets enough soup, he dreams of bread. Once he has enough bread, he dreams of margarine to put on his bread. Then, if he is lucky to have enough of these two ingredients, which is rare for Jews, he starts dreaming of a little *kolbassa* [sausage]. Finally, if he is German or Polish, and sufficiently fed, he starts wishing for alcohol. (Only after all that does he start asking for women.)

Alcohol is available in the camp, but at an exorbitant price on the black market. If I manage to get some, I will have a highly desirable article for our exchange business. We were going to be rich ... The obstacle to our success is Dorus Wolf, a charming man, but cautious to the point of being a coward. In reality, he has a thousand good reasons to be cautious. If we are caught, we will both be executed immediately. Still, after thinking it over for some time, he lets himself be convinced and agrees to provide me, periodically, with two phials of what they are distilling in the lab. Under our deal, I will discreetly come to the door of the chemistry lab but not enter, and Dorus will give me the alcohol, two small phials each time. We must solve the transport problems, because we cannot overlook possible searches. But I have a great idea. I attach the two phials to each other and let them hang inside my trousers, next to my natural appendices. Once safely inside my Block, I 'christen' the alcohol, which is over 90 per cent; that is, I dilute it with water. Then I sell it at a high price to the Poles, who are rich and who are prepared to pay a good price for a bit of alcohol in the form of sausages, lard, margarine, bread and cigarettes. In this way, Marcel and I get ourselves some precious additional food supplies, not to mention cigarettes, which are used as exchange currency to acquire other goods. With Dorus I share, in a brotherly fashion, all the products I get from selling the alcohol. I am never caught transporting my precious phials. Indeed, it is easy for me to walk around the *kommando*; as a volunteer gardener, I always carry my shovel on my shoulder, and the SS are used to seeing me. Our trafficking allows Marcel and me to slightly improve our living conditions.

Every morning, when I go to work, walking the few kilometres separating Auschwitz from Rajsko, and every evening on the way back, my *kommando* walks past the four large chimneys of the Birkenau camp, which was renamed Auschwitz II. Our path on the south borders the huge camp, and we can see perfectly well the flames rising up from those chimneys that never stop smoking. From the end of April until autumn 1944, these chimneys are constantly active. I know that these are the crematoria, where women and men are being burned: but who? How many? I know that they burn *musulmen*, and probably also the sick (who are not necessarily at the end of the road yet), as well as the prisoners declared undesirable; not counting all the victims of typhus, hunger and abuse. However, I live in Auschwitz, not in Birkenau, and therefore cannot see what the members of the 'Canada' *kommando* or the *Sonderkommando* see. Whole convoys of Jews – men and women, children, old people, who arrive daily in enormous numbers – are unloaded on the new ramp inside the camp, and most of them, sometimes the whole convoy, are immediately pushed to their annihilation. They don't even have a chance of becoming a numbered slave.[22] Only much later will I find out that during that spring and summer, half of the Jews of

---

22. See Marc Klein, who was in the same *kommando* (*Témoignages strasbourgeois*):

> Although located four kilometres from the *Stammlager*, the installation of the gas chambers and their operation established the tone of our life in Auschwitz I. It was absolutely forbidden to speak about it, and yet we did so incessantly, in disguised language...it was a real obsession.

SS Kaduk's evidence at his trial reveals how much the Germans, who were passing through the region, knew: the Auschwitz station was filled with civilians and soldiers on leave, who saw the five-metre high flames coming out of the chimneys, and they couldn't have missed the smell of burning flesh (according to all testimonies, the smell wafted for kilometres). A Reichsbahn clerk in Auschwitz testifies that the flames coming from the chimneys could be seen from 15 to 20 kilometres away: everybody, he said, knew perfectly well that the Germans were burning human beings there (Langbein, *Menschen in Auschwitz*, p. 502; Langbein, *Der Auschwitz-Prozess*, p. 249ff.). However, the German public took no notice.

Hungary[23] were gassed *en masse* in these crematoria with their glowing red chimneys. After them, the last large Polish ghetto, Lodz,[24] is liquidated, and several tens of thousands more follow them, exterminated with meticulous care and a rare sense of organization. I will not enter the Birkenau camp until 1970, when I return to these places to remember. At that moment, seeing what Birkenau was and having heard my wife's story, who was there from May 1944 until evacuation, I realised that, by comparison, Auschwitz was a health spa.

23. Extermination of the Jews of Hungary began with the German invasion in March 1944, and the Jews in those zones newly annexed to Hungary were the first to go (Hilberg, *La Destruction*, p. 724 ff.).The first two convoys of 45 wagons, 70 people per wagon, arrived in Auschwitz on 2 May (Czech, *Kalendarium*, p. 764). Between that date and 11 July, 437,402 Hungarian Jews were deported to Auschwitz (these were the numbers given by the German plenipotentiary in Hungary, Veesenmayer (see Hilberg, ibid., p. 738). The number of those selected for work is unknown; following negotiations with Eichmann, 18,000 of them were taken to Austria (ibid., p. 736). The liquidation of the Jews of Hungary was carefully planned by Himmler, who assigned Rudolph Höss to Auschwitz as superintendent, with Otto Moll – his second in command – as technical chief, to resolve the constant problem of incineration of the bodies. Moll optimised the crematorium's production, and ordered trenches to be dug to absorb the surplus bodies and put Bunker No. 2 back into service (Czech, *Kalendarium*, p. 776). However, a succession of events contributed to saving some of the Jews from Budapest from deportation: the advance of the Russian Front; Regent Horthy's lax attitude because of international public pressure; and, later, a greater willingness on the part of his successor, Szalasi, to compromise; as well as some rescue operations, like those of the diplomats Raul Wallenberg from Sweden and Carl Lutz from Switzerland (Hilberg, *La Destruction*, pp. 742–7; Y. Bauer, *Juifs à vendre ?* (Paris: Liana Levi, 1996), pp. 203 ff. and 321 ff.)
24. The industrial town Lodz, renamed Litzmannstadt (after the German general who conquered it in 1914), situated on the Gau Wartheland, was part of the Polish territory annexed to Germany. There, in April 1940, the Nazis established one of the first large ghettos. In addition to the Jews in the region, deportees from Germany, Vienna and Luxembourg were concentrated there in 1941 (Hilberg, *La Destruction*, p. 187). Of over 200,000 Jews crammed into the ghetto, 45,000 died there (ibid., p. 234). They worked for the Germans in several factories. After the liquidation of the Warsaw ghetto in 1943, the Lodz ghetto became, by default, the largest. Over a third of its population disappeared in 'operations' during the first five months of 1942. After September 1942, the remaining 80,000 survived until August 1944, with a longevity record of four years and four months in a Nazi ghetto (ibid., p. 195). Liquidation began in August 1944 with the posting of the notice of 'transfer' signed by the German *Amtsleiter* and the Chief of the Jewish Council, Rumkowski. There was no Resistance, and, until 15 September, the 80,000 Jews took the road to either Auschwitz or Chelmno, which was briefly reopened with its gas trucks. Eighty per cent of the last convoy consisted of children aged between 13 and 16 (ibid., p. 444; Czech, *Kalendarium*, p. 882). The proportion of inmates selected for work is not known; some were 'parked' in reserve in Birkenau without being registered. The destruction of the Jews of Lodz was one of the last large operations of the RSHA.

117

June is approaching. The war is turning more and more against the Germans, and we, the inmates, are all convinced of their defeat. Still, nothing changes in the day-to-day life in the camp, except that the SS seem more nervous. News, true or false – and it is often just rumour – circulates quickly. Certain inmates, for example, the Jehovah's Witnesses,[25] who do domestic work in SS villas, have access to the *Völkischer Beobachter*, the Nazi newspaper, or find a way to listen to the official radio. The Polish Resistance also has a clandestine wireless receiver in the camp. We have just heard of the Allies' triumphant entry into Rome, 5 June 1944. From the window of our serology lab on the second floor, we sometimes look down into the yard, even though it is strictly forbidden. When the weather is good, on the flat roof of the villa where Münch and Weber live, we see a woman lounging on a deck chair, in a bathing suit. I cannot help thinking that she knows she is being watched by the prisoners; and that she enjoys it.

That day, NCO Zabel[26] is displeased with our attitude. Is it because he is nervous? NCO Zabel, one of the SS employed at the institute, a notorious drunk, is usually in charge of taking blood from inmates and bringing back human flesh for growing cultures. On that day, a day of defeat for the Germans, Zabel is patrolling the yard of the institute and he sees one of us at the window, and must have thought that we were mocking him. In my case, he is not exactly wrong. He rushes to the staircase, races up the two floors, bursts into the

---

25. The Nazis sarcastically referred to the Jehova's Witnesses as *Bibelforscher* ['Bible scholars']. In 1933, 19,268 were registered in Germany and a few thousand in the other European countries, where, however, they were not persecuted. Hitler's propaganda, which equated them with the Jews, labelled the sect the *Jüdische Internationale Bibelforscher-Vereinigung* [The Jewish International Bible Scholars Organization] and reproached them for being impossible to assimilate – even though they were all Germans – because they refused to swear allegiance to the Aryan State and were fierce conscientious objectors. Their discipline and their courage were to be admired. They could have bought their freedom by renouncing their faith, but they refused to do so, for which they would pay a high price. Their wives were in great demand by the SS as household staff.
26. The *SS-Unterscharführer* Johann Zabel, house painter or shoemaker, was trained in sanitation in the Hygiene Institute in Berlin (*Die Auschwitz-Hefte*, Vol. 1, p. 215). He is described by Lettich as a brute. Responsible for taking blood samples from already weakened patients, he took up to a litre of blood at one time. He also accompanied Weber to the crematoria to cut off human flesh to be used for growing cultures (Lettich, *Trente-quatre mois*, p. 33).

118

lab, pounces on Trude Müller and slaps her rudely on the face. This has never happened before in our *kommando*, which is normally spared these brutalities. When the first slap sounds, I am standing in front of the sink, rinsing test tubes with concentrated sulphuric acid. Blinded by fury, my arm, as if it has a will of its own, lifts itself, holding the bottle of acid, and just a fraction of a second is needed for me to crush it on Zabel's head. But quick as lightning, Fabicki tears the bottle out of my hands. The SS notices nothing. We are safe. Our Polish pharmacist has just saved me, and maybe the whole team, from certain death.

Zabel is boiling with fury and goes on hitting; the whole group passes through his hands, and when my turn comes he breaks my glasses (the only personal object I still have from Monowitz after they took my shoes away). But he will be punished. *Obersturmführer* Weber hears about his violent outburst and reprimands him a few days later. Zabel disturbed the work of the institute. Didn't he incapacitate me from performing my important scientific mission? How am I going to count the red cells of my samples without glasses?

Summer passes slowly. Our *kommando* is definitely privileged. The third SS doctor of the institute, Delmotte, is very correct and humane with us. He saves one of us from a selection in which the poor man was caught up while in the main camp. As soon as Delmotte learns that a member of our *kommando* has been selected, he hurries to the Block where all the selected are waiting for their transfer to the crematorium. There, in a peremptory tone, he demands that his colleague be given back to him, because he is indispensable to the institute's work. He succeeds. Another memorable thing Delmotte does is to authorize Robert Mandelbaum's wife to come to our institute, under the pretext of using our tomograph for biological analyses for the *Pflanzenzucht*. Robert can therefore see his wife: an exceptional event in camp life.

Yet, in the second half of 1944, I will still live through a series of terrible disappointments. First, my friend Trude is removed and assigned to the labour services, the *Arbeitseinsatz*. For her, it is a valuable promotion, but for me, it means that she is leaving our lab, and I don't know whether I will ever see her again. Our idyll, completely platonic, lasted five months. I will be able send her notes, and I will do so, because I will always find a kind friend, willing to risk being a messenger. But, from then on, something will be missing in my life. And I must have been destined to lose all those who are closest to me here. In autumn, Marcel Thibault, my best friend, comes to tell me that he is leaving in a transport.

Trude will survive the camp and go home to Prague, but I will never see Marcel again. He, the optimist, always so sure of his liberation, will be sent to one of those deadly *kommandos*. We were so well off in Rajsko, so lucky, so well fed, thanks to our trafficking. Marcel will get weaker and weaker, then fall sick, and die in Mauthausen, just after liberation, just as he is listed for repatriation. My best companion ... courageous, loyal, idealistic but not dogmatic, and without any sectarian spirit. He sincerely believed in a better future for humanity, a future for which he was prepared to sacrifice himself.

Our *kommando* may well be enjoying exceptionally favourable working conditions, but when evening comes, we return to the ordinary life of the camp, its dangers and its horrors. Sometimes, at the night *Appell*, the SS decide to put on a show for the assembled crowd of inmates standing to attention. The show consists of hanging some of the rebels, especially runaways who were unlucky enough to be caught. One night in October, while we are watching the repulsive spectacle of the hanging of three men who tried to escape, one of the ropes breaks at the crucial moment. Was there a conspiracy? Did somebody damage the rope in the desperate hope of giving the condemned man a last chance? Under civilian law, the custom is to pardon anyone whose rope refuses to hang him.[27] But that night, the runaway does not benefit from any reprieve. He is not hanged again but is kicked to death in front of our eyes.

---

27. See a similar episode as described in *Die Auschwitz-Prozess*, p. 259. The custom of pardoning does not seem to have been respected in the camps, while it was - sometimes – in prisons (see M. Borwicz, 'Ma pendaison', in *Ecrits des condamnés à mort sous l'occupation nazie (1939–1945)*, 2nd edn (Paris: Gaillimard/Folio, 1996), p. 29).

From the end of the summer, the camp is regularly bombed by Allies,[28] causing deaths among SS as well as inmates. Yet we rejoice at each air raid alert, almost wishing, with a kind of unleashed happiness, for the bombs to fall on our heads, as long as they help destroy the whole camp, the SS and the Nazi rot. In the east, the Russian Front is inescapably approaching. And yet, despite all the portents of defeat, in its megalomania, the SS continue planning and devising the expansion of existing installations. One day, I discover that Delmotte has been named director of a new Hygiene Institute to be erected in the Fünfteichen camp.[29] I am personally recruited to be part of the personnel of this new service, which will never be created. The countdown for the Germans has begun, but they refuse to admit it. We, on the other hand, are waiting anxiously for the end to come.

In the meantime, autumn slowly gives way to winter, the horrible winter of the camp. However close, the end is slow to come, so slow. It seems I will have to spend another winter in the camp.

One winter's day, when there is a lot of snow and it is very cold, I take advantage of my relative freedom of movement and

---

28. From July to December 1944, especially between 7 and 29 August, the Silesian industrial curve (including the industrial zone of Auschwitz) was bombed intensively by the Allies. They wanted to destroy the synthetic production of petrol, as the petrol war was expected to accelerate German defeat. On 7 July, an American mission of 452 bombers of the 15th division flew over two of the five rail tracks leading to the Auschwitz-Birkenau complex. On 20 August, 127 Flying Fortresses, escorted by 100 Mustang Hunters, dropped 1,336 bombs on the Auschwitz factories, less than eight kilometres from the crematoria. The toll was 38 dead and many wounded among the prisoners; and one Allied bomber was shot down. On 13 September, 96 'liberators' bombed the factory again; concentrated DCA shooting brought down three planes. Two bombs fell accidentally near the crematorium, damaging the railway leading to the ramp. The American press commented on these last two raids. The Allied Air Force took many pictures of the Auschwitz-Birkenau site on 25 August, in which columns of Jews on their way to the crematorium II are clearly visible (Czech, *Kalendarium*, p. 862). There would be two more air raids, between 18 and 26 December. Nonetheless, although there was ample information on the mass extermination of the Jews in Birkenau, and the imminent deportation of the Hungarian Jews was transmitted through the report of two escaped inmates – Rudolph Vrba and Alfred Wetzler, in April 1944 – the American Ministry of War took no decision to bomb the death installations nor the rail tracks leading to them (D.S. Wyman, *L'Abandon des Juifs: Les Américains et la solution finale* (Paris: Flammarion, 1987), Chapter 15).
29. Fünfteichen or Meleschwitz, an external camp dependent on the main camp, Gross-Rosen.

go down to the basement of the boiler room of the institute, probably intending to hide or 'organize' something. To my surprise, I find myself face to face with an SS guard from Rajsko, who must have stepped in to escape the biting cold and warm his limbs. As I come closer, I am even more surprised, as I knew him. He is a German from Bucovina, a *Volksdeutscher* from my hometown of Czernowitz, where we went to the same school for a whole year.

He also recognises me, and starts talking. He doesn't find it out of order to speak to an inmate; at this stage, we are far beyond Stalingrad, and only a fanatic could fail to see the war's new direction. This SS officer, a simple man, tells me how, together with other *Volksdeutsche*, he was 'repatriated' to the German Fatherland, although his community had been settled in Bucovina for the last 150 years. They had been transferred to Warthegau, a region in East Silesia. Without being asked his opinion, he was incorporated in the SS from his arrival. And by now, he's had more than enough of it.

Our talk remains nonetheless cold, and doesn't last long. He doesn't offer to help me, and I don't ask him for anything. Anyway, what could he do?

I never saw him again.

In truth, if I had known what that winter had in store for me, I would have been filled with terror. As incredible as it would have seemed to me at the time, I would come to yearn for the life I had in Auschwitz in my *kommando* at the Hygiene Institute. All things considered, life there was relatively decent.

6 The Death March

For the duration of the war, of the total number of camp victims,
half died in the death marches and from the massive famine that
raged in the camps by the end of the war.
Yehuda Bauer, 'The Death-Marches, January–May 1945',
in *The Nazi Holocaust*

Auschwitz is in turmoil. Under pressure from the Russian
advance, the SS decide to evacuate the camp. The order is
given during the night of 17–18 January 1945. As I will later
hear, the secretaries were called to the *Schreibstube* to submit the
lists of those who could not walk. The sick and incapacitated
will remain, but all other prisoners will be evacuated.[1] Once the
evacuation order is given, the camp authorities start burning
documents, work files, reports from the Political Section,
medical files. Fires burn everywhere. Fortunately for memory
and history, not everything is destroyed.

The Russian troops, for whom we waited and hoped for so
long, are only a few kilometres away.[2] But the Red Army, if it
ever reaches this place, will not relieve us from our torturers,

---

1. See Klieger, *Le chemin*, pp. 51–2. Some 1,500 sick people and their carers remained
   in Auschwitz. At the 17 January *Appell*, the SS registered the Auschwitz-Birkenau
   complex inmates for the last time, and the numbers were: 16,226 inmates in
   Auschwitz (about 65 per cent men and 35 per cent women); 15,058 in Birkenau
   (about 28.5 per cent men and 71.5 per cent women);10,233 in Monowitz and 22,551
   in the annexed camps; and a few thousand in Blechhammer, Jaworzno, Gleiwitz,
   Jawischowitz, Eintrachthütte, Fürstengrube and Golleschau. In total, 64,000 men
   and women (Gilbert, *Endlösung*, Map 280). The chaos in the remaining camps
   would be increased not only by defeat, but also by the large numbers of arriving
   prisoners.
2. To break the German Front, the Russian offensive was launched on 12 January and
   was continued throughout Poland. The first Ukrainian Front, under the orders of
   Marshall Koniev, and the first Byelorussian Front under Marshall Joukov,
   reinforced in the south by the fourth Ukrainian Front under General Petrov, took

because we are retreating before their advance. Our sufferings are not going to end in the way we hoped for so long. The Germans are retreating, but it is obvious they are taking us with them in their collapse. What are they going to do with us? The announcement of the evacuation may just be a trap, and maybe they are assembling us on the *Appell* square to finish us off, thousands of powerless prisoners, with bombs, or even more simply with machine-guns. We are at their mercy; no resistance is possible. Or maybe they will just lock us up inside cattle wagons, without air, without water, without food, indefinitely, until we reach another Auschwitz ...

That day, destiny does not place my friend, Maurice Goldstein, on my path. He is still working as a nurse in the *Häftlingskrankenbau*. Had destiny intervened, I would not have been propelled into this extension of hell that the SS were preparing for us with the evacuation of the camp and the death marches that followed. Maurice would probably have convinced me to stay. He decided to remain in the camp with the sick, and I would have stayed with him. Maurice knows, as we all do, that any important choice in the camps is a tragic lottery, and that the good and bad choices bear a striking resemblance, like two infernal sisters. There is no way we can predict that the sick, who are given permission to stay, or to be more exact, are abandoned to their fate, will not be liquidated at the last minute with a bomb or a flame-thrower.[3] However, Maurice's luck – or his instinct – proves him right. The Auschwitz complex will be liberated ten days later by Soviet troops, and Maurice will be repatriated to Belgium fairly quickly, via the port of Odessa.

Kielce on 15 January, Warsaw and Czestochowa on 17 January, and Krakow and Lodz on 19 January. Auschwitz could be taken in three different ways: the Russian troops could have come from the north through Czestochowa, from the east through Krakow or from the south through the Beskides.

3. Rumours in the camps were rather pessimitic. Auschwitz Resistance workers knew that during the liquidation of Majdanek in July 1944, the Jewish inmates were killed and the Aryans taken away (Langbein, *Menschen in Auschwitz*, p. 304). And so, Élie Wiesel, faced with a similar choice in Auschwitz, allowed himself to be persuaded that the hospital would be liquidated together with the patients and doctors, and chose evacuation with his father, who did not survive for long after (See *La Nuit*, 2nd edn (Paris: Minuit, 1988), pp. 128–30). Krystina Zywulska says that the women of Birkenau expected a bombardment camouflaged as an Allied attack, and death (Zywulska, *Tanz, Mädchen*, p. 363).

On 18 January, no *kommando* goes out to work. We wait, worried, filled with apprehension. When the signal to depart is eventually given, the stores of food and clothing are assaulted in enormous confusion. As we are warned that we are going to walk, everyone, with what strength and ability he still has, rushes to equip himself for departure to the unknown in relentless snow and cold. The temperature is about 15° C below zero during the day, and it isn't difficult to imagine what the nights will be like. I am very lucky, as I manage to get a fine pair of shoes. I don't take anything else, so as not to be burdened during the walk. I wear only my prison uniform, a sweater and a coat.

We are given our food ration for the trip, one full loaf of bread per *Häftling*. As night falls, our column starts moving, and we pass through the gate of Auschwitz for the last time. It is a strange departure. This is not how I imagined leaving the camp. We take the same familiar path I have been taking for months to go to work and we stop in front of the Rajsko[4] Institute for the last time.

I am reunited with the rest of my lab *kommando*,[5] who have been regrouped and are waiting in a column. I realise what a useful asset we have for the walk ahead, the handcart on which we carried our soup churns, the 'Rajsko Express', as Klieger nicely puts it. The whole *kommando* loads the cart with their belongings and we hitch up in turns to pull it. This is a real privilege, because in addition to their bags and parcels and whatever miserable belongings they carry with them, the other prisoners are also loaded with the belongings of the SS. All that weight means additional strain.

---

4. The Auschwitz and Birkenau inmates were regrouped in Rajsko to form evacuation columns. The women in Birkenau were first regrouped in Auschwitz together with women from the main camp. The last column from Auschwitz (2,500 inmates) left on 19 January at 1 p.m., and in Rajsko merged with the last Birkenau column (1,000 prisoners). The prisoners of Monowitz who were able to walk were evacuated in columns of 1,000 towards the annexed camps of Gleiwitz, then, after a few selections, evacuated to Blechhammer and Gross-Rosen, which could not take them in. They then re-embarked, in open wagons, to Buchenwald, Sachsenhausen, or Dora-Nordhausen (Czech, *Kalendarium*, pp. 969–94).

5. See also M. Klein, 'From Auschwitz to Gross-Rosen and Buchenwald', in Waitz and Klein, *Témoignages strasbourgeois*, pp. 501–10. It seems that Klein walked in the same death march as W.B.

Our *kommando* stays together as a group: a good thing. Somehow, this team is more civilized and more human than others; the people in it have shown themselves to be more caring, despite the hell we are in.

We start walking in rows of five, tightly guarded, as always, by *kapos* and SS.[6] The commotion of departure takes all day. Thousands of men must be lined up in rows (the women left before us). It is night, the night of 18–19 January 1945. The column walks on. Our guards take whatever they can with them. If I look back, I see an endless column of men. Where are we going? Rumours may have circulated, but I have heard nothing. We are heading more or less northeast. The Russians are very near, and I assume that we are moving away from the front. But won't we meet another front head on? Nobody knows for sure what kind of strategy our torturers have devised to evacuate us. 'Evacuate' is indeed the best word to describe what is happening. They are making us disappear to prevent us from taking revenge. They do not want to risk being held responsible, after the defeat, for what they have done. Therefore, by the time the enemy arrives, they need to be rid of all evidence of men tortured, of places of torture. I believe they are powerful enough to erase all evidence of what they have done to us. Faithful to their ideology, they will take us somewhere inside the Reich, out of reach of the Russians in the east and the Anglo-Americans in the west. They will create new camps, and will eventually bring about the total annihilation of the Jews. I have no further illusions.[7]

After about 15 kilometres, it becomes more and more difficult to advance; the march becomes more and more painful. The cold is tremendous. It must be 20° C below zero. Legs and

6.   Klein (ibid., p. 502) states that there was one SS to every ten men in his column. Krystina Zywulska (*Tanz, Mädchen*, p. 380) remembers seeing an armed man (with a dog) on each side of the column at every third row of five walkers, as well as sleighs with SS armed with machine-guns in several places along the convoy. One witness at the Frankfurt trial saw two SS men to every ten to fifteen rows (*Die Auschwitz-Prozess*, p. 261). By the end of the war, the SS lacked the men to guard the camps. Some of them had been moved to the front (Langbein, *Menschen in Auschwitz*, p. 318). Nevertheless, on 15 June 1944, Oswald Pohl had authorised 10,000 soldiers of the *Wehrmacht* to enter the Waffen-SS to reinforce the troops guarding the camps.

7.   The retreat was for both economic and political reasons:

feet are slowly transformed into ice blocks and no feeling remains. The tramping of thousands of men in front of us has turned the snow into ice, and we keep slipping and falling. We cannot take much more. Suddenly, I hear a shot behind me at the back of the column, soon followed by others, more numerous. This is it; I have no more doubt. The SS are finishing off those who fall behind.[8]

I go on walking, like a robot. Those who can still walk advance, some even sleeping as they walk. But many others simply let themselves fall to the ground, wanting to be forgotten, and in some obscure way, without giving it too much consideration, I understand them. Let the herd go on without them. It is an ultimate gesture, both a refusal to obey and final obedience to death. But the SS has been ordered not to forget them, unless they are dead. So shots continue to ring out.

We have left Auschwitz, but the selections continue. I am not surprised. I am convinced that, even outside the barbed wire, the power of the SS remains absolute. We, the prisoners, especially the Jewish prisoners, will remain at their mercy anywhere on earth, as long as the Reich[9] endures.

And yet, within the ranks of the column, people are whispering. Some are still not sure what these shots mean.

The idea of freeing these creatures was absolutely absurd. They were enemies of the Reich ... their place was inside the camp, and if the camp to which they had been assigned was full, they were to be marched to another one, as long as there was a superior to order the destination.
(Bauer, 'The Death-Marches, January–May 1945', p. 497.)

The SS responsibility was solely negative; no case is known of an SS officer who would have fed those prisoners presumed to be useful for the war effort, for example, by requisitioning food.

8. Commander Baer himself chose the column chiefs from among the Auschwitz guard troops, and gave them orders to finish off all prisoners who tried to escaped or remain behind during evacuation (Czech, *Kalendarium*, p. 966).

9. Bauer notes that some SS chiefs, without specific orders on the subject, just acted according to the indoctrination they had received, and took advantage of those marches to get rid of prisoners through exertion, hunger and cold, shooting only the last ones, those who hadn't wanted to die and hadn't been able to escape. One could say that the death marches were the natural continuation of the elimination process, but through different means (Bauer, 'The Death-Marches, January–May 1945', p. 498). Langbein states that many SS behaved even more brutally than inside the camps because they no longer had anything to lose; realising that punishment was near, they took revenge by exercising the power they still had for as long as possible (*Menschen in Auschwitz*, p. 500).

127

Klieger tells that when he shares his fears with his neighbour in the column, a German Jew called Auerbach, the latter retorts: 'To kill the stragglers? Do you mind? A civilized nation does not do such a thing!'

Auerbach has gone through the same hell, through fear, hunger, murders, selections,[10] but he is a German Jew, and he goes on believing that the German nation is the incarnation of civilization.

The whole time we walk, from both sides of the column, the SS yell at and abuse prisoners who do not walk fast enough, or do not stick to their ranks. One of the SS, who is walking next to me, calls out to one of my companions: 'Dirty Jew, hurry up, or I'll knock you out.' His accent leaves me breathless. This man is from my native Bucovina, I would recognise that accent anywhere. I would even swear that he came from Czernowitz.[11]

For the second time since the incident in the basement, I forget the usual rule of caution in the camp, which forbids us, sub-humans, to look at an SS, and certainly to address him, and I ask him: 'Mr *Scharführer* [group leader], are you by any chance from Czernowitz?'

I have the presence of mind to give him a title, even though he seems a simple man. This ploy always works, as vanity is universal. I hope to avoid his anger, because I expect nothing from an SS except spite and abuse. But he looks at me curiously. He must not have met many inmates from Bucovina during his service, as there aren't many in Auschwitz.

'Yes, I am from Czernowitz. But you also, it seems?'

And as we walk at the same pace, exerting the same effort,

---

10. See Klieger, *Le chemin*, p. 63. Auerbach's incredulity exasperates Klieger, who calls him an 'unfinished Nazi'. However, the Western Jewish middle class's incredulity about Nazism was much greater. 'No matter what happens [the enlightened Jews of the west] thought, barbarism has no place in central Europe in the middle of the twentieth century' (Dobroszycki, *Jewish Elites under German Rule*, cited in Marrus, *L'Holocauste dans L'Histoire*, p. 117).

11. See the deposition of two Auschwitz SS, Bilan and Bareyzki, on the way ethnic Germans were recruited in Bucovina – and probably also in Occupied Territory (Langbein, *Menschen in Auschwitz*, p. 317; Langbein, *Der Auschwitz-Prozess*, p. 298 ff.). Whole companies of *Volksdeutsche* between the ages of 20 and 40, some of whom had even fought in different uniforms beforehand, were automatically assigned to guard the camps.

we start talking, almost as equals.

'Indeed I do come from Czernowitz.'

'Where did you live?'

'On Gregor Street, next to the university. And you, Sir, Mr *Scharführer*?'

'I come from Roscha.'

Roscha is a suburb of Czernowitz I know well. Encouraged by our almost friendly exchange, I have the incredible cheek to ask him: 'Don't you think the war will be over soon? What will you do then?'

As we continue in silence, beyond the marching of the column we can hear the sound of shots from the Polish Resistance, the Armija Krajowa.

I am staggered by his answer.

'What will I do when the war is over? Well, believe it or not, I won't have any problems. I speak Yiddish. The minute I see that it is over for us, I put on a striped *Häftling* uniform, and they can come and look for me.'

It is the last thing I expect. Of course, he could not know that the Allies would set up special brigades to look for SS men and that they would be identified by the tattoo with their blood group, under their arms (many war criminals will have the tattoo removed). As proof, he speaks to me in Yiddish, and I must admit that he speaks it much better than I do: me, the 'modern' Jew, who only knows a few scraps learned in the camp.

About 20 kilometres from Auschwitz, in the middle of a column of exhausted and frozen prisoners, walking what History will call the 'Death March', a strange, almost friendly, dialogue develops between a *Häftling* and an SS, both from Bucovina. We are not exactly equals, because I use the polite form of address of 'Sir' and '*Sie*', while he addresses me with the familiar '*Du*'. Even if he does speak Yiddish better than I do, he still belongs to the master race, while I remain a sub-human, whose right to exist has been refused by decree.

'How is it that you speak such good Yiddish?'

'Let me explain. Did you know the Jewish barber N., in the Russischengasse?'

'Of course I knew him.'

'So you must have known his daughter, Miss Rosa?'

'Yes, I knew her too.'

'Well, Miss Rosa was my fiancée,' my man tells me proudly. Everybody in Czernowitz knew this lady Rosa. She was a well-known lady of little virtue; a good address that men passed around. It was thus most probable that my SS was none other than her pimp, her *maschornik*, as we said back home.

'And as her fiancé,' continued the SS, 'I was often invited by her parents. I was there at all your Jewish festivals – Pesach, Purim – sometimes, I even accompanied her to the synagogue. So, you see, I am quite well acquainted with all your Jewish stories ...'

A little more of this and I will be tempted to believe that this SS man and I have something in common. But just then, somebody in my row falls in a ditch. Was he trying to run away, did he fall out of exhaustion? My pleasant SS from Czernowitz raises his gun and aims at the man on the ground.

I shout: 'Sir, Mr *Scharführer*, please, don't shoot! Let him live! What good will it do to kill him?'

He looks at me, and says something like, 'Orders are orders,' then presses his weapon against the poor man's neck and shoots him. I lose sight of him after that incident.

Hours have passed since my conversation with the SS and the shot that ended it. We go on, in a semi-conscious state. Walking by my side in this infernal march is a young French Jew. Although he is taller than I am, he cannot be more than 16 or 17. He cannot take much more. His shoes have fallen apart; his feet are bloody stumps. I am also exhausted, but I can feel that he is weakening with every step. He is so young and he is going to die because he has no shoes and no strength, and soon he will join the bodies strewn beside the column. Maybe I will, too. But for this young man, who is still a child, fate is unkind. I support him under his arms and drag him. I will surely get even more tired, but then I make a phenomenal discovery. By helping him, I help myself. I drag the boy for kilometres and it helps me get through the night, if it will ever end. It may be normal for me to feel better in my head while I help somebody, but why does my body cope with this added effort? It is

130

strange, but I feel less tired.[12] I have just learned a very important lesson: alone, the boy would not have made it, but I
wouldn't have, either. It is not pure self-interest that necessarily helps men survive better.

At the end of the night, as dawn is breaking, the column
stops. We shouldn't be seen from the air by the enemy, and we
are given permission to lie down on the ground for a while. I
am only half-conscious; my body hurts as much at rest as in
movement. I even have trouble remembering that there has
been any interruption when we are told to go on. And the
march starts all over again for a second night.[13] Will there be no
end to this! No peace, no rest on the surface of this earth, ever,
only suffering and death: the perfect definition of Hell. The
column's advance has slowed considerably, and shots ring out
throughout the night. Bodies fall; the column abandons them
to the left and to the right of the road, along the faltering tracks

---

12. See Klieger (*Le chemin*, p. 75), who reports an experience as strange as it was
moving. During the march, he was dragging a friend from Brussels, and suddenly
notices that his legs no longer hurt. Testimonies recount many acts of solidarity
during the march, which were as much acts of resistance against dehumanisation.
Likewise, Maurice Cling remembered having been placed back on his feet and
comforted (V. Pozner, *Descente aux Enfers: Récits de déportés et de SS d'Auschwitz*
(Paris: Juillard, 1980), p. 216).

13. The death columns followed two different routes between Auschwitz and Loslau
(Wlodislaw Slaski). After the town of Cwiklice, having covered about two-fifths of
the distance, some columns turned northwards, passing through Zory and
Sweirklany. The last column leaving Birkenau on the afternoon of 18 January took
this route; four members of the *Sonderkommando* joined it undercover. The other
route goes more southwards, passing Porembia and Jasztrembia; that was the one
followed by the women's gardening *kommandos* of Rajsko and, after 19 January, by
the last evacuated column from Auschwitz I. Along this southward route, civilian
Poles would note 262 corpses, which they found and buried in pits. In Silesia,
along the roads that the columns took, Poles buried at least 1,101 corpses, of which
they notified the authorities (Czech, *Kalendarium*, p. 971 ff.; Gilbert, *Endlösung*, p.
281). Marc Klein (*Témoignages strasbourgeois*, p. 502) and Bernard Klieger (*Le
chemin*, p. 66) – who were in the same column as W.B. – remember passing through
Pless (Pszcyna), a little town near the fork of the two roads. From there, the routes
diverged on the second day. A companion of Klieger counted 600 shot corpses
during the first night of the march (Klieger, ibid., p. 69).
        It seems that the columns from Rajsko did not all walk in the same direction,
because Allied planes were flying overhead and they kept stumbling across the
German Army and fleeing citizens. They covered about 100 kilometres during
those two nights (ibid., p. 503). Klieger guesses 55 kilometres for the first night ('an
amazing feat') and 25 kilometres for the second one, during which the inmates,
exhausted, advanced much more slowly. Many stopped for a break in Poremba, in
sheds or in the snow. In the morning, the SS searched haystacks and shot those
who tried to hide; some succeeded in escaping (Czech, *Kalendarium*, p. 979).

that our convoy of ghosts leaves in the snow. Death has surrounded us; it is everywhere, behind us, in front of us, inside us. One can go no further than death.

After an eternity, daylight appears. It is the morning of 20 January. In what is not yet dawn, I can make out chimneys on the horizon. In a flash, the truth dawns on me – of course, this is why we have walked so long. Ahead of us, there are crematoria with gas chambers. Those at Auschwitz have been destroyed, so it follows that we have been led in rows of five all this way, through indescribable suffering, straight to other gas chambers which are still functioning. Here we will at last be delivered to our final destiny. They have driven our group of cursed individuals to walk to the crematorium. With a last superhuman effort, we have been given the right to fly from chimneys.

Their logic is most powerful, invincible.

I am caught in their trap. I feel so helplessly bitter that tears come to my eyes, maybe for the first time since I was taken to the camps. I walk with the others; we have been walking like sheep to the slaughter. None of us has the intelligence to understand that his destiny was, in fact, sealed from the beginning. It has taken me a long time to finally understand that this time I am going to die. Their victory over us is total; no witness will remain. The last *Häftlinge* are being sent to the slaughterhouse.

Finally convinced that I am going to die within the hour, for a brief moment, temptation to pray overwhelms me, the atheist. I have never before felt the need for God. And even if a spark of conventional belief remained in me when I arrived in Auschwitz, I've had more than one occasion to lose it since then.

Doubt, then? Maybe I have lived in guilty ignorance of what God can do for me? Very little time remains to me for repentance; maybe God can really do something for me in this final moment, maybe He will consider me His child, if right now I believed in His salvation? Maybe I should pray, and I will be relieved, maybe the sacred words will dispel this panicky fear that is rising inside me and is going to choke me?

No. I am a free man. I am going to die, but I am free. I refuse to give up what I have believed in, or rather what I have not believed in, my entire life. I don't give in to temptation. I don't pray.

I am proud to have been free at that moment. It is one of the proudest moments of my life.

Very shortly after that the day breaks, and I realise that what I see is not smoking crematorium chimneys, but train engines. We have arrived in Loslau, a village in Silesia, west of Auschwitz. It is a train station, and trains are warming up while waiting for the rest of our miserable troop.[14] They are coal wagons, flat cars with no roofs.

Stunned, I am stuffed onto one of those wagons with the rest of my *kommando*, which has miraculously more or less regrouped. This wagon has been reserved for our *kommando*, luckily, because horrible scenes take place when other, totally exhausted, inmates are squeezed, howling, into wagons far too small to contain them all.[15] Surprisingly, in my *kommando* spirits are still holding up, because we know each other. These are exceptional conditions that favour survival and leave no room for barbarism, the kind of barbarism that creeps up on inmates indifferent or hateful to each other.[16] The wagons start moving, and it is a relief not to have to walk anymore. I am so tired that I don't even have the strength to be surprised that I am still alive. Rumours circulate that we are being transported to a camp near Breslau, in the far west of Silesia, the Gross-Rosen camp. In the open wagons, we suffer terribly from cold and hunger. We haven't been fed since we left Auschwitz. The

---

14. Marc Klein also tells of his hallucinations during the march (*Témoignages strasbourgeois*, p. 503).
15. For more information on these transports, during which the mortality rate was terrifying and barbaric behaviour broke out among the inmates, see – among others – P. Francés-Rousseau (*Intact aux yeux du monde* (Paris: Hachette, 1987), pp. 22–39.
16. Marc Klein has similar memories (*Témoignages strasbourgeois*, p. 503). In Loslau, the first columns that arrived from Auschwitz left for Gross-Rosen; the last ones reached Loslau on 22 January, and left through Brünn towards Mauthausen (Czech, *Kalendarium*, p. 987). The forced evacuation advanced in stages, the inmates were often sent back from one camp to another without ever leaving the wagons. All moves were chaotic because there was no longer a functioning central administration. This, however, didn't lessen the strong hand of the SS over the inmates.

journey seems to last forever. After passing Ratibor, we arrive in Gross-Rosen on 21 January.

Arriving in the camp of Gross-Rosen, we immediately re-enter the pure, harsh, concentration camp hell. A climate of terror prevails unlike anything I have known elsewhere, even in Monowitz. I have fallen into raw horror, for the simple reason that the camp is run by murderers. It seems that from autumn 1944, small groups of inmates with green triangles, as well as other dubious prisoners, were transferred from Auschwitz to Gross-Rosen to prepare things for other inmates in case Auschwitz would be evacuated. We constantly fear for our lives. The climate of murder is such that the old Auschwitz *kapos*, who had softened somewhat during the last months, start beating the completely weakened inmates again, without reason. Even our *kapo* from the Hygiene Institute *kommando*, the bully Bertram, starts hitting the men of his Block, something he never did in Auschwitz.[17] Obviously, they want to be well regarded by the new lords of the manor, the under-world who are the undisputed rulers here. I even meet an old 'acquaintance' of mine, the infamous Jewish criminal from Auschwitz, the one with the yellow and green star. He has found his place among the *Prominente*.

In almost all other camps, in the fight for internal power, the political prisoners triumphed over the criminals. In Gross-Rosen, this fight never occurred, or was aborted. The secre-taries, the *Blockälteste*, the *kapos*, are all criminals with the green triangle. To expect them to show even the slightest passive resistance to the system is out of the question. Quite the contrary, they compete in ferocity and sadism in their behav-iour towards the inmates. The atmosphere in this camp is of absolute murder, as I never knew elsewhere, in any Auschwitz *kommando*. No doubt, their reputation and respect derive from their cruelty and inhumanity. I have become a convict in a prison. Nobody will protect us like *Kapo* Korn had protected me; there are only coarse bullies around. In Gross-Rosen, the

---

17. See Klieger, *Le chemin*, p. 102.

green triangle is a person's main asset,[18] and the sadists reign supreme.

Over 1,000 of us (between 1,300 and 1,500) were crammed onto the floor of unfinished barracks, without windows or provision for sleeping, not even boards. According to Klieger, these barracks had been dismantled in Birkenau and brought here.[19] During the day, we don't work, as, fortunately, nothing was planned. Nevertheless, there is no relief from the terror inflicted on us. We must remain seated on the floor in the Blocks from morning to evening. We are not allowed to talk[20] or get up, except for *Appell*. The commotion is incredible. I don't know how many convoys have been dumped here, under the ever-approaching threat from the Russian Front.[21]

The nights, however, are much worse than the days. We are crammed so tightly together on top of each other that we can never lie down at all. This lack of space is torture. Each of us pushes his neighbour away, without pity, to find somewhere for his legs. The Block wails, howls, gasps and dies.

Violent fights break out every night. As soon as they hear noise, the *kapos* spring into action and hit anything that moves, and anything else for the same price. This is Gehenna, Hell; there are no guilty or innocent, there is only absolute death and

---

18. Ibid., Ch. 4. The camp was in total chaos due to the mass arrivals of evacuees. Marc Klein's *Blockältester* had five of his ribs broken for not running fast enough to get the coffee (*Témoignages strasbourgeois*, p. 505), and Klieger recorded as fact the rumour that volunteers for soup duty who went down to the kitchen in the middle of the night were electrocuted on barbed wire and died; and that those who tried to escape death by electrocution were routinely assassinated by the *kapos* (*Le chemin*, p. 108).

19. To some extent, withdrawal from the Upper Silesian camps had been technically prepared. In Gross-Rosen, the camp was enlarged with a space called 'Auschwitz 2' (Roger Monty, an NN French deportee, quoted in J. Manson, *FNDIR/UNADIF: Leçon de ténèbres. Résistants et déportées* (Paris: Plon, 1995), p. 178), separated by barbed wire and managed by an old *kapo* from Auschwitz promoted to be 'chief of camp' (Klieger, *Le Chemin*, p. 91).

20. 'The only work we were forced to do was drag corpses to the crematorium' (Klein, in Waitz and Klein, *Témoignages strasbourgeois*, p. 507).

21. Marcel Guillet, a French deportee, witnessed the arrival of the convoys evacuated from Auschwitz:

    The living dead had to line up in the *Appellplatz*, and many fell on the way, despite the short distance to the *Appellplatz*. The *Sonderkommandos* picked up the dead and piled them in a corner of the quarry ... The pile was 1.5 metres high, 20 metres long, and 4 metres wide at the base.

    ('Gross-Rosen')

it beats us down. With my own eyes I see an older *kapo* from Birkenau, a giant who was evacuated with us, blindly knock down with an iron bar[22] anybody who moves around him. Every morning, the Block spews up the dead.

Some of the inmates, who retained some humanity during the last days, are now losing it. The *Blockälteste* trade the soup against whatever is available; rations are miserable. A simple *Häftling* is here to die, the sooner the better. That's all there is to it. Every day, men die by the dozen, from exhaustion, from abuse, and from dysentery, which is spreading rampantly. Klieger describes Gross-Rosen as something that became more like a madhouse every day, and this is undeniably true. The last remnants of human dignity, which some worthy creatures carried with them despite the conditions in the camps, and which prevented them from sinking into madness, finally give way here, and they sink into oblivion. Four days and four nights go by in this manner, in terror, with no hope ... On the fifth day, as a new group of evacuees is being stuffed inside our Block, I recognise my friend, Michel Zechel.

What joy! Michel is still alive. He comes from Jaworzno,[23] where he worked as a dentist for many months. My happiness very quickly turns to serious worry, because Michel is in a terrible state. He has just walked for 16 days in the snow and the cold. He was first evacuated from Jaworzno to Blechhammer, a very tough disciplinarian camp, and only then to Gross-Rosen. He walked the death march the whole way. He didn't benefit from a transport by train like we did. When I see the state he is in, I have to admit that I don't think he can survive. He has

---

22. See Klieger (*Le chemin*, pp. 115–16). He is referring to someone called Alfred, who in Gross-Rosen was nicknamed 'tiger', and who paradoxically would save Klieger's life a few days later. W.B.'s testimony allows us to think that this 'tiger' is a *kapo* of the quarantine camp of Birkenau, with the same nickname, who enjoyed publicly hitting the inmates with leather gloves, for the pleasure of the sound it made (Langbein, *Menschen in Auschwitz*, p. 172).

23. Of the 3,600 inmates of the annexed camp of Jaworzno/Neu-Dachs, 3,200 were evacuated on 17 January to Gross-Rosen, where they arrived on 21 January (Czech, *Kalendarium*, p. 968), then transported to Buchenwald. M. Zechel seems, however, to have arrived with an earlier transport. Marc Klein mentions the arrival at Gross-Rosen of totally exhausted evacuees from Jawischowitz and Blechhammer in the last week of January and the first week of February. They had wandered on the road for 18 days (*Témoignages strasbourgeois*, p. 507).

reached the end of the road. He never looked his 45 years, but now he has become a very old man. And what frightens me most is how low his spirits have sunk.

We replay the scenario of our reunion in Auschwitz, but in much worse conditions, and with our roles reversed. This time, Michel is the exhausted one in despair, and I am the one doing my best to take care of him. But I am at a total loss. I have no power here, I cannot 'organise' anything to improve our lot. The only thing left to me is to talk to him. I am a little better off than he is; to some extent, I have already recovered from the fatigue of the march. I tell him then that food is scarce but that if we don't have to use our strength to work, we might have enough not to die. I also tell him that as we are two, we have a better chance of survival, and that is true. Michel should not die. I must do for him what he did for me when I arrived at the showers in Auschwitz on the verge of becoming a *musulman*. And more importantly, I must give him back some hope.

As soon as I can, I ask him a question that is puzzling me. I want to know if he still has his $100 bill. Michel nods, he still has it. His work as a dentist protected him from searches in Jaworzno. Thanks to his status, he reached a relatively high position in the hierarchy.

Gross-Rosen is becoming unbearable. The whole concentration camp machine is stuck, and it is obvious that the SS has no idea how to administer the growing influx of evacuees. Day and night it is getting worse. In retrospect, Auschwitz seems almost viable. Nothing that was possible there is possible here. We no longer receive food every day. Supplies arrive irregularly and are insufficient. These are probably being traded between the *Blockälteste*. To top it all off, it has become totally impossible to 'organise' anything, because we are penned in and cannot move around the camp. It is also impossible to sleep, because of the relentless crowd. Besides, there are *Appells* at night. We haven't washed for days, and to go to the latrine is an almost impossible ordeal. We have reached the point of wishing for anything that will end this nightmare, even an Allied bombardment.

Ten days have gone by. We hear rumours that Gross-Rosen

will soon be evacuated. Evidently the front is closing in. On 31 January, in the middle of the night, we are ordered to get ready; Jews are going to be evacuated, Aryans are to remain. The sick are ordered not to leave their Blocks.

Hearing this, Michel decides to stay in Gross-Rosen. He considers himself sick, and rightly so. He has no strength and is convinced that he will not survive another death march. I, on the other hand, decide differently. If there is the slightest possibility to get out of this hell, I must grab it. To remain here, even as a sick person, is unthinkable. I have recovered enough strength to be able to consider a new evacuation. The problem is Michel. To leave him behind is out of the question. So I must force him to come with me, and this is no simple matter, as he refuses to listen. He's had it. And yet, I finally convince him to try.

Without knowing it then, I saved my friend's life. Jews who reported sick when Gross-Rosen was evacuated were liquidated the next day.[24]

In the middle of the night, the *Appell* for Jews takes place. All those who are leaving receive half a loaf of bread and a slice of sausage. We haven't eaten anything for 48 hours, and as I am ravenous, I swallow my whole ration in one go. Michel keeps his bread in reserve, which is a terrible mistake. In the camp's state of moral disintegration, he should have known that the only thing that doesn't risk being stolen is what you have in your stomach. We are crammed, 100 per wagon, and our third 'big trip' begins.

It is the most unbearable trip of all. There is no space for 100 inmates. It is impossible for all of us to be on the floor of the wagon, either lying or crouching. We therefore have to crouch in turn, group by group. Scenes of incredible violence break out for the right to crouch, and fights for a piece of bread are

---

24. See Klieger (*Le chemin*, p. 118). The Jews who arrived from the camps of Silesia seem to have all been evacuated to Gross-Rosen before 8 February. According to his chronology, W.B. must have been among the first to arrive. Klieger says he left on 6 February, and Marc Klein on the 7. The rest of the inmates (over 31,000) were evacuated between 8 February and 26 March 1945 to Buchenwald, Flossenbürg, Ebensee, Dachau or Dora. The Russians entered Gross-Rosen on 5 May 1945. They found only a handful of survivors. The sick Jews of Gross-Rosen had all been liquidated after their sector was evacuated on 7 or 8 February 1945.

even worse. On the first night, Michel realises that his bread has been stolen. In the circumstances, it was, without exaggeration, a catastrophe; life or death hangs on a few calories.

We leave on the night of 31 January–1 February. For six days and five nights we remain locked up in the wagon with nothing to eat. But even worse than hunger is the thirst that tortures us. The SS didn't even make provision for water for us. Luckily, it snows. One after the other, the fitter among us put our hands through the rails of the window and scrape some snow from the roof. I doze, the days pass, the nights slip by in a long, feverish nightmare. We vegetate, we are delirious; we die. In the depth of my being, some minute corner of lucidity remains; the rumour circulates that we are on our way to Buchenwald. If this is true, I must try to survive until then, because Buchenwald is known as a 'good' camp.

About 500 kilometres of railway separates Gross-Rosen in Silesia from Weimar in Thuringe, in the heart of the Reich. Our convoy travels for six days. We enter Weimar station only on 6 February. On the rails next to us, a train with inmates stands motionless. It must have just preceded ours. It was bombed in the station with the inmates still inside.[25] It is totally smashed, and between the torn and blackened sheets of metal, parts of dead bodies can still be seen stacked inside the wagons. Our evacuated comrades have also reached their destination, but they are dead.

---

25. Marc Klein also saw that train in the Weimar freight station. Could it have been Klieger's, who reports that half of his train was bombed in the Weimar station, killing 300 (*Le chemin*, p. 135)? It is very difficult to reconstruct an exact chronology of those days. 'Some wagons were directed to sidings where they became a target for Allied bombings' (G. Perl, quoted in Hilberg, *La Destruction*, p. 852). In a more thorough investigation on the total lack of help for the prisoners of the death marches, Yehuda Bauer asks why the Allies didn't gather more information, to avoid bombing trains filled with prisoners. They did obtain information to locate Allied prisoner of war convoys and launched parachutists to help them. Nothing was done for the thousands of death convoys zigzagging through Germany, while a few brilliant rescue operations could have awakened public awareness, or even encouraged the German population to help and feed the prisoners. The priority was to pursue war ('The Death-Marches, January–May 1945', p. 508).

7 Buchenwald: The Agony

> The abyss is less deep between the tramp who shuffles along the
> streets of Paris and the reveller he meets on his way at night, than
> between the elegant sated figure of the *Lagerältester* crossing the
> Appelplatz in his elegant boots with their impeccable shine ... and
> the miserable shuffling skeleton of the Small Camp, covered in a
> few rags, and stumbling with weakness.
>
> Albert Kirrmann, 'Buchenwald: The Great Town',
> in Robert Waitz and Marc Klein,
> *De L'Université aux camps de concentration*

It is the beginning of February 1945.[1] After days and nights in a
stupor close to death, our convoy finally arrives in Thuringe:
frozen, exhausted, weak beyond imagination. We are in a state
of starvation well beyond hunger. Many have died. But can
those who are still breathing really be counted among the
living?

The order is given to leave the wagons. Of course, we are
immediately organised into columns of five and pushed
forward. Physically and mentally I could not be worse off. The
trip and hunger have totally numbed me. To say that I am weak

---

1. *The Buchenwald Report* mentions the mass arrival of 6,805 evacuees from Gross-
    Rosen (not only Jews) on 10 February, representing several convoys. Their regis-
    tration date, and not arrival date, was therefore 10 February. This group must
    have waited between one and four days before being registered and assigned to a
    Block. W.B. thinks that he remembers alighting from the train in Weimar and
    walking up to Ettersberg. It seems more likely that his convoy was transferred to
    Buchenwald in open flat wagons, using the Weimar–Buchenwald track (12
    kilometres, 200 metres of slope), which had been built by inmates, an incredible
    torture, to serve the Gustloff factories near the camp. (An order from Himmler on
    18 March specified that the line must be ready on 21 June of the same year, and it
    was only operational for one day, collapsing the day after its inauguration. The
    section was made operational again by the end of the summer of 1944; ibid., pp.
    94 and 300–1). For more information on this transfer, see P. Steinberg, *Chroniques*;
    and Klein, in Waitz and Klein, *Témoignages strasbourgeois*, p. 509).

1. *Hasmoneah*, Czernowitz, 1936–37. Willy is the third from right, on the bottom row.

2. Willy Berler at the Agricultural School, Mikveh Israel, Israel, 1937.

3. The agricultural research buildings at Rajsko.

4. Crematorium IV, Birkenau, in spring 1943, just closed. Picture taken by the SS in 1943.

5. *Kommandant* Arthur Liebehenschel.

6. *Rapportführer* Gerhard Palitzsch.

7. A view of the Buna factories, taken from a documentary film about the liberation of the camp by the Red Army in 1945.

8. Inspection of the building site at Buna by *SS-Reichsführer* Heinrich Himmler, 17–18 July 1942, accompanied by the engineer Max Faust of I.G. Farben and the *Kommandant* of the camp, Rudolf Hess. Picture taken by an unknown SS.

9. Men carrying a tree trunk. Drawing by an ex-prisoner, Mieczyslaw Koscielniak.

10. Carrying corpses to the crematorium. Drawing by Léon Delarbre.

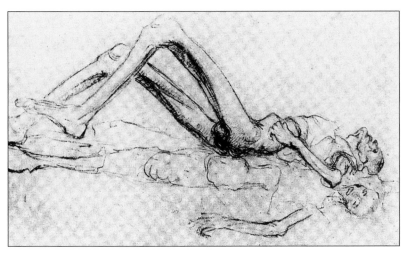

11 . Corpses of *musulmen*.

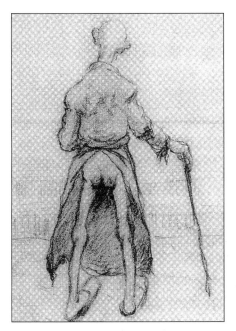

12. Dysentery in the Small Camp: drying the trousers. Drawing by Léon Delarbre.

13. The daily truckload of corpses being unloaded at the crematorium.

14. Executions at the Black Wall.

15. Standing at the *Appell* ground in a cold wind.
Drawing by Léon Delabre.

16. Ruth and Willy Berler, 1990.

is meaningless; I am in such an extreme state of exhaustion that I am bordering on lethargic. To walk at that moment requires a superhuman effort, the most horrible ordeal of all those I have endured throughout this long march of death since leaving Auschwitz. These last kilometres are really the most painful of all those forced on me for the last 22 months. This is my real death march, undoubtedly a walk to death. I am incapable of moving forward; my body refuses to respond any further, not to willpower, not to brutality. I have reached a state of exhaustion from which I cannot return. In a moment of lucidity, I ask myself if I will still be able to fight for my survival, and how. We move uphill. We arrive at the gate of the Buchenwald camp.

That is enough to raise my spirits a little. I am not dead and I don't have to walk anymore. With that slight arousal of consciousness, hunger also awakens and dominates everything while the convoy waits to be allocated to Blocks. The Buchenwald camp is seriously overcrowded, like Gross-Rosen. My group remains there two full days, waiting, without anybody paying any attention to us. Hunger gnaws painfully at my stomach, and I am freezing under the snow that has started to fall again.[2]

Finally, they remember our existence, and bring us a bowl of soup.

I eat the most delicious, the most nourishing, the most divine soup I have ever received in my life. It is even better; it is the best meal of my whole existence.[3] I know that until my last day on earth I will never forget that first soup in Buchenwald, even if I never suffer from hunger again. I haven't eaten anything for countless days and nights, but my wait is rewarded. I am served a soup so thick, so rich, so nourishing; far superior to anything that was ever poured into my mug in Auschwitz during the 22 months I was there. Suddenly, it dawns on me; there is life. It sinks in with the heat of the soup and the taste of lard, vegetables and potatoes.

---

2. Buchenwald was the last stop for many evacuees from Auschwitz, irreversibly exhausted by the effort of the death marches (Wiesel, *La Nuit*, p. 164; Klein, in Waitz and Klein, *Témoignages strasbourgeois*, p. 510).
3. For the same memories, described in similar terms, see Klieger, *Le chemin*, p. 136.

Surprised, I think: 'Maybe I am not yet at the gates of death. If there are such things to eat in this camp, we must be able to survive.'

There is an explanation for the quality of this soup: Buchenwald is administrated by political prisoners whose internal Resistance organization is very powerful and runs all the camp's domestic affairs. The inmate-officials therefore steal much less from the kitchens; while in Auschwitz, hunger was cleverly maintained by the corruption of the *kapos* and the *Stubendienst*, who became zealous accomplices in the Nazi system. The infamous brew of Auschwitz was in itself a crime against humanity.

Immediately after the soup, the SS put us through a body search. As if these human remnants leaving Auschwitz or the mines still carry gold or diamonds with them. The Germans can only reason like this, in the face of such obvious facts and circumstances, because of their absurd image of the Jew – born of hatred and fear – or because of obscene, exaggerated greed. We move forward in line, naked, and one after the other we are checked by two SS. Standing in front of the first, each *Häftling* must open his mouth wide. In front of the second one, he must step on a stool, and his rear opening is checked. I suddenly fear for Michel, knowing that he is still hiding his famous $100 bill in his anus.

But Michel passes the search triumphantly. Despite his exhaustion, he has retained some of his legendary flexibility: between the two searches he switched the bill, passing it quickly from one opening to the other ... I don't know if Michel is aware of his amazing feat, but he must have told himself at the second search that the bank note had a damn good taste, the taste of life, as we will find out a few days later.

We are taken to the showers. Some hundred naked men wait to get under the jet of water. Suddenly, a small, emaciated Jew points his finger at a fat inmate, a Ukrainian or a *Volksdeutscher*, and starts yelling at the top of his voice in Yiddish: 'This guy is a murderer! He murdered my brother! He killed him in Birkenau by hammering a nail into his head.'

Less than a second later, the fat guy is surrounded and

142

immobilized by a group of Jews who hurl themselves at him. Blows fly from all sides, aimed straight at their target. It is obvious that a lynching is about to take place. I look around me; all the actors and spectators of this drama are totally naked. The guy is strong, and tries desperately to defend himself as the fight continues. After a long struggle, four Ukrainians each seize a limb and send him flying into the air. He falls heavily onto the cement. I cannot help feeling some relief at seeing that it is the Ukrainians and not the Jews who are ending his life.

A raging madness then takes over, and the avengers finish him off just before the chief of showers, hearing the commotion, pushes open the door of the room. He is an old-timer from Buchenwald, and wears a red triangle. He immediately grasps the situation and yells: 'Where do you think you are? You are not in Auschwitz anymore! We are in Buchenwald here, and inmates don't fight each other, this is a political camp!'

People explain that this was a settling of scores with an old *kapo* from Birkenau.

'In that case, I saw nothing. I don't get involved in those things.' He leaves.

Naturally, I don't participate in this settling of scores, but naked, silent, shaken, I realise that I have just witnessed a murder.[4] It leaves me thoughtful: how difficult it is to kill somebody when one is naked.

Later, we are sent to be disinfected, and then to the store, the *Effektenkammer* [clothes store], where we are given wooden clogs and rags.[5] I get a pair of trousers much too small for me, which only come halfway down my leg, barely covering my knees. My neighbour, on the other hand, a Slovakian Jew, gets a superb pair of bricklayer's corduroy pants in excellent condition. He is in his forties – an old man – with whom I got on quite well in Auschwitz. His number is very old, as he arrived in 1942. I am astonished to hear him say: 'These pants are too

---

4. A long-time inmate, Stefan Heymann, confirms that lynchings were common on arrival in the Small Camp, and that all the murderous old *kapos* received their just deserts, even though *Kommandant* Pister ordered their isolation on arrival (*The Buchenwald Report*, pp. 321–2); see also Langbein, *Menschen in Auschwitz*, p. 219.
5. See Klieger, *Le chemin*, p. 136.

big for me, they will suit you far better. Can I exchange with yours?'

I agree, surprised but very satisfied, and proceed with the exchange. I slip on the wonderfully warm pants. I will understand the reason for his magnanimous gesture three days later, when the leeches covering the internal seams of the garment hatch into lice and start eating me up. Cleverer than I am, and with much greater camp experience, he had spotted them immediately.

Then we are sent to the administration office to be registered. Once that is done, we are taken to our assigned Blocks.

I am happy to be in the Block. The soup is good, those in charge relatively lenient, and I am washed and clothed. After what I experienced in Gross-Rosen, I must consider Buchenwald a luxury hotel. Alas, I will soon be disenchanted. Michel and I have been assigned to Block 12, but it is still under construction. The only components of the Block in place were cement foundations and walls. There was no roof, no windows; and with the cold weather, this could not be considered a shelter.[6] There is nothing to be done about it; we are penned up inside. I guess Buchenwald is so overcrowded by the endless arrivals of evacuees from the east that they must hastily build new barracks, and these fill up before they are completed. In addition to the cold, it rains and snows alternately, and the cement floor is covered in a thick layer of mud and water. How on earth are we going to lie down? Luckily, we find some wooden boards stored inside; these are the doorframes and the actual doors. We construct a sort of raft by laying the frames on the ground like piles. We settle down to sleep on our improvised structure.

Night comes. Never, in my whole internment, has it been so cold. I try to curl up, but nobody can fight the icy cold that spreads over our camp. It is going to be a night of

---

6. Otto Kip was a German inmate with a senior position in the Resistance. He remembers that some evacuees were placed in Block 12 and in the kitchen, both still under construction after the 24 August 1944 bombardment of the DAW factory. Each night, 60–80 people died in these Blocks, which echoed with the screams of the dying men. The organization then tried to arrange the Small Camp to house them there (*The Buchenwald Report*, pp. 316–17).

hallucinations. Our misery will never end. Indeed, the great SS machine is jammed, and the organization in charge of detention and death is no longer as oiled and efficient as our torturer's boots are shiny. No hope remains. They are going to complete their project after all; we are all going to die. Their camp commanders are no longer in any position to administer the influx of the cursed who keep arriving *en masse*, and yet there is no question of lessening our suffering or forgetting about us. We remain inmates, even if, like here, we have no roof over our heads. Can one sink lower than this? We are no longer driven to work with thrashings, we are not yet being killed, but we are also not given any shelter in which to cower.

I endure the night and the following day, totally frozen. On the second night, which promises to be as cold, I start talking in German with my neighbour on the raft. In the camps, nobody ever gives a name, but he does reveal that he is a musician and a composer from Vienna, that he was deported to Theresienstadt, and from there to Auschwitz. He was lucky to have escaped the gas chambers, a fate that awaited the majority of the transports from Theresienstadt. Under a frozen sky, he continues to talk in snatches, telling me about his life as a *Häftling*, until we both fall asleep, side-by-side, on our wooden frame, exhausted from the cold.

A few hours later, I wake with a start. The moon spreads a pallid light. Next to the raft, I spot the body of my companion on the ground, face down. He is dead. He must have fallen in his sleep, noiselessly, and drowned in the muddy water stagnating between the wooden boards.

Later, many years later, when works of Theresienstadt composers are rediscovered, I will try to find out more about the deported musicians. Who was this man, this artist who died that night by my side, absurdly drowned in ten centimetres of water, in the back of a Buchenwald barrack? What future music, never composed, has been denied us?

I am in a state of shock. The cruel, senseless death of my neighbour, added to the cold, drives me to temporary insanity. I get up to look for Michel, who is sleeping not far from me, and I wake him, delirious. I am agitated and shout: 'Look, Michel, they are giving us blankets; take one, cover yourself!'

The cold is unbearable and it is turning me into a madman. My glasses fall between two wooden frames; I cannot see anything, I stutter. Terrified, Michel understands that I am delirious, and on the verge of departing permanently ... He stands up and slaps me furiously. I return to my senses enough to realise that I should not remain where I am. Gathering what strength I still have, I leave the barracks. The moon has disappeared and I move in total darkness. Some instinct pushes me forward; I grope my way, moving ahead. It is madness, roaming Buchenwald at night. But by now, I am beyond any consideration of safety. In the total darkness, I go on and finally strike a wall. Unable to go further, I grope my way along the wall until I find a door. And there, miraculously, the door opens. I go inside the building, and suddenly I am no longer outside in the cold. Still groping, I explore what seems to be a narrow recess and come close to something glowing with warmth; I have found a heating duct. I fall there, stretched out for the rest of the night, without moving, glued tight to this miraculous source of heat. I am saved.

As dawn breaks, I try to see where I am. I realise then that I crossed the whole camp in the dark without attracting any attention and went straight to the disinfecting building, which is kept warm day and night. The next day, I tell Michel and a few others about my miraculous warm hiding place. We return there for the night. We sleep crammed on top of each other, but at least we are warm. Our sleeping there is vaguely tolerated. In truth, they don't know what to do with us.

My overwhelming memory of those first days in Buchenwald is of the cold, hunger, and scarcity.[7] But, in reality, I pass this whole last period of my deportation enveloped in a fog. Extreme exhaustion has finally conquered me and I am on

---

7. In Buchenwald, food rations reached their maximum in April 1938, then were continually diminished. On 1 March 1945, those inmates who worked received, on average, per week: 1,024 grams of bread; 3,500 grams of potatoes; 250 grams of meat (often rotten); 83 grams of fat; 375 grams of swede and other vegetables; 41 grams of yoghurt; 21 grams of white cheese; 33 grams of coffee substitute; and 250 grams of marmalade (or 125 grams of sugar). Inmates who didn't work – who made up one third of the camp population – received only 80 per cent of those quantities (*The Buchenwald Report*, p. 148).

the very edge of nothingness. I experience occasional moments of lucidity while floating in a sea of unconsciousness. There is not enough food, and we must keep a watchful eye on what we do get. Ukrainian prisoners snatch bread from your hands if you don't defend it fast enough. It is useless to try to snatch it back; they have swallowed it before you can blink. I am also sick, and this time my body is definitely giving up. I am suffering from dysentery, and together with the horrible diarrhoea comes general weakness. I can no longer differentiate between day and night. I lie prostrate in the box room of the disinfecting building, my only concern to keep warm enough to go on living.

After a few days, we are taken from our hole to Block 22, a Block of Jews. But that Block is incredibly overcrowded and living conditions are abominable. It soon becomes obvious that there is no place for us in this Block of Jews. We are then sent to the Small Camp. Miserable ghosts at the end of the road, evacuees like us from Auschwitz and other eastern camps, are penned up there.

It cannot even be called a camp. Nobody could 'live' here. The conditions are far from fit even for animals. The Blocks consist of stables overcrowded with human wrecks, with about 25 centimetres of sleeping space for each person to stretch out. The Small Camp is made up almost exclusively of Jews. We have ended up in the cesspool. This is where we are going to die, in total indifference, as those human worms who are still obstinately called *musulmen* die every day. This time, Michel and I have reached the end of our travels and our hopes for survival.[8] Not only has my body been emptied by dysentery,

---

8. Over 13,000 inmates died in Buchenwald during the first four months of 1945, the majority in the Small Camp. Block 61 – 'the most horrible cesspool imaginable' (Klein, in Waitz and Klein, *Témoignages strasbourgeois*, p. 121) – served not only as an infirmary for 500 patients with dysentery and tuberculosis, but also as an extermination station by lethal injection (of which Klein, like W.B., seems to have been unaware). The SS camp doctor, Waldemar Hoven, was first charged on those grounds in 1945, and the charges were then dropped. He was eventually sentenced to death at the Nuremberg physicians' trial. In January 1945, the SS doctor Schiedlausky decreed that Buchenwald must solve its overpopulation problem. From January to March, *SS-Hauptsturmführer* Wilhelm selected inmates to be killed by injection of phenol or sodium evipan (see testimony of *Blockältester* Louis Gimnich, *The Buchenwald Report*, pp. 319–21), and the number of dead per

but my head and my heart have been emptied too. We are not men anymore, we are only stinking empty shells with the tiniest spark of life still separating us from final rigidity. In Buchenwald, there are no gassings, but the crematorium works continuously, day and night.

After languishing for a few days in that cesspool, we recover a little. I guess we must still have some instinct for self-preservation that prevents us from simply waiting for death. I notice an impeccably dressed political inmate from the Large Camp moving about in the Small Camp, asking if there are any Buchenwald old-timers among the evacuees from the east. Apparently, some Jews who started their concentration camp journey in Buchenwald, and from there were sent to Auschwitz or elsewhere, have come back to Buchenwald on the evacuation route. A clique spirit operates here like anywhere else. There is an organization in this chaos that keeps an eye on its own.[9] I will later discover that these are members of the Resistance, essentially communists. Some of us, therefore, have the dubious honour of being considered Buchenwald old-timers, and an important official has been sent to look for them and transfer them from the Small Camp: to the Large Camp, from death to life.

What can we do to receive similar treatment? It is obvious that we have no chance of surviving the unbearable conditions of the Small Camp. In the Large Camp, however, if we are put in a Block where there is sufficient food, life will be bearable, and maybe all this will not last much longer.[10] I decide then that we must find a way to have ourselves transferred up there, at

---

day at the Small Camp rose from 15–20 to 60–200 (ibid.; Georges Greiner, in Waitz and Klein, *Tégmoignages strasbourgeois*, p. 107). Block 61 also served as a hiding place for the Resistance, where they had two 'privileged bunks' for inmates who were in danger, who were exchanged for dying prisoners or informers (Klein, ibid.; Langbein, *La Résistance dans les camps de concentration natio-naux-socialistes, 1928–1945* (Paris: Fayard, 1981), pp. 251–2).

9. Emil Carlebach, a German-Jewish inmate and member of the Resistance, proudly remembers the arrival of the convoy from Monowitz on 26 January, which, according to him, was perfectly organised and run by the old anti-fascist nucleus of Buchenwald from 1942 (*The Buchenwald Report*, p. 167). His optimism is probably exaggerated (see Wieviorka, *Déportation et génocide*, pp. 260–1).

10. Life also deteriorated in the Large Camp, although the differences between them remained. Food became more scarce and packages stopped arriving from liberated Western countries.

any cost. Since leaving Jaworzno, Michel has deteriorated badly, both physically and mentally. I am faring a little better, but everything is on the verge of falling apart.

Together, we discuss Michel's war treasure; the moment has come to try and use the famous $100 bill. This is our only chance, and we must not waste it. Then, I suddenly remember how, a very long time ago, in another life, my father had gone to a restaurant where a gypsy orchestra was playing. He tore a bank note in two and gave one half to the chief musician, promising to give him the second half if he liked the music.

The next day, I approach the inmate-official who has come to find the Buchenwald old-timers. He is Czech, and luckily we can communicate in German. I make my request: 'We are two in this Block, my friend and I, who want to get out of the Small Camp.'

He looks at me haughtily: 'But you are not old-timers of Buchenwald.'

'No, of course, but we have something interesting in our possession.'

He waits.

'We have $100.'

He looks at me disbelievingly. I take the bill out of my pocket, tear it in two, and give him half. 'You will get the other half the day we come to the Large Camp.'

Michel and I are transferred two days later. The Czech comes to receive the second half of the bill. I think ten dollars, or even one dollar, would have had the same effect ... One thing is certain, however; thanks to this famous bill that Michel stubbornly preserved through all the searches, this time, he has saved both our lives by allowing us to leave that place of death. We receive a temporary reprieve.

The month of March, which has just begun, finds us settled in Block 49 of the Large Camp. We both feel a little better, although we are in very poor physical condition. Dysentery confines me to bed. I have violent arguments with a gypsy *Stubendienste*, an anti-Semitic black triangle, because I cannot refrain from dirtying my bunk. I then remember an old remedy. I must eat charred wood. I get some pieces of wood, which I burn on the stove in the Block. As soon as I swallow it, the miracle remedy works. The dysentery stops. But I am still so weakened that I cannot stand up during the *Appell*.

As additional torture, my famous corduroy pants are full of lice. I managed to avoid lice in Auschwitz and elsewhere. Now I must suffer like everybody else. The vermin are all over my body, from head to toe, the itching unbearable, preventing me from sleeping.

During the whole period following my transfer to the Large Camp, I remain very weak and discouraged. If the Americans don't come soon, I am not sure we will survive until liberation. How long can this go on? By mid-March, we are transferred from Block 49 to Block 23, still in the Large Camp, but with Jews only.

In the Large Camp, I meet up again with my friend Robert Mandelbaum, the Belgian biologist who worked with us in Rajsko. He is now part of the international clandestine Resistance committee in Buchenwald in which, as a communist, he is starting to play a major role.

On 19 March, they put me to work. I can hardly stand, but I am assigned to a *kommando*. I am put in the Ettersberg *kommando*, which takes its name from the mountain where Goethe used to enjoy his walks, and on which the hell of Buchenwald has been built. We must build shelters. We prepare the ground, building site work. The *kapo*'s name is Peter. He is a Sarroy and behaves correctly. We even receive the additional rations normally given to forced labourers, and the soup is good. I am not really in any condition to work. Since the long transport from Auschwitz to Buchenwald, my legs have been swollen from hunger and cold, and I have sores on my feet. The *kommando* works deep in the mountain, and we have to walk quite a distance to and from the site which is, in itself, exhausting. Between these two exertions, it is hard to imagine that I could produce any kind of work.

I get weaker every day. I have no idea how I get through the day without dying. I keep repeating to myself that I must hold on, I must hold on. We don't actually work much. Air raid alerts, during which we cannot work, sound more and more often. Supervision of the *kommando* is ridiculous. We are guarded by *Landwehr* [old German soldiers] who only want to be left alone. During one of those alerts, while I lie still for a long time, I look down at what is growing on the ground around me. And in this clearing of Ettersberg where we are stationed, I discover wild garlic. I taste it. How delicious is that taste of garlic from another time! I am also aware of what this can mean as a vitamin supplement. During the alert, I then hurry to collect as much as I can and, back in the camp, I exchange it for a few pieces of bread. I am convinced that this increases our stamina a bit.

After three days of working in this *kommando*, I am called to the *Arbeitsstatistik*. It turns out that I have been spotted as an old member of the Hygiene Institute *kommando* in Rajsko. I find myself face to face with Dr Hans Münch, who announces to me and some other survivors of the *kommando* that he is forming a new lab *kommando*. This is only a few days before the liberation of Buchenwald. His chief, Weber, and he are regrouping the Hygiene-Institut der Waffen-SS in Dachau. What they probably have in mind is to prove to the Allies, after the defeat, the harmless nature of their activities in the camp.[11] 'Remember, in Rajsko, we always treated you well!'

He stresses that good treatment. Feeling the end of the war approaching, he is clearly trying to accumulate favourable testimonies. It is true that I cannot actually reproach Münch for anything in particular in the turmoil into which my life has sunk, except the undeniable fact that he is SS.

I jump ahead here: in 1995, while watching the celebration of the fiftieth anniversary of the liberation of Auschwitz, rebroadcast from the camp itself on German television, I will become emotional when I see Dr Hans Münch appear on the screen. So, the old SS doctor has the courage to return to the scene to take part in the celebrations and add his signature to a register kept there, testifying to the horrors in which he participated. This is not an insignificant testimony to counter the Negationists and Revisionists, even if, according to journalists, Münch has recently made some very distasteful statements.

---

11. See Lifton, *Le Médecins nazis*, p. 361.

As the month of March 1945 drags slowly by, every day I am a bit worse off, but I keep hoping that the end is near. I still want to be there on the morning of the great day. When the *kommandos* go to work, I mobilise the last of my strength, but I hardly manage to drag myself, because I can barely stand on my feet. The last days of March are atrocious.

On the 31st, the order is given not to leave the camp premises. I don't go to work, and this forced rest is welcome. Since the night before, rumours have been circulating that the Allies are approaching. There is talk of emptying Buchenwald of its Jews and sending them, once more, on a transport. Michel and I don't need to consult each other. We know what that 'transport' would mean; we would not survive another death march. If we are thrown into that final transport, it will be the end for us. We are both at the final stage of weakness, and our swollen legs are no longer responding. We will be shot in the back of our heads within the first kilometre.

That same day, the order is given to evacuate the 'Jewish' Blocks 22 and 23. We cannot be caught in this evacuation. No matter what, we must hide in the camp. I think feverishly of where to hide, and I suddenly remember the sewerage lid behind Block 12, which I noticed when we lived there, and which may be the beginning of a canal.

We run to it, lift the cover and slip inside. It is definitely a tunnel, not very wide, but luckily dry. Its diameter is not more than 60 centimetres, and we are forced to crawl, one behind the other. We grope along in total darkness. Suddenly, the first of us feels a half-buried object under his hands. Somebody was here before us, deeper in the tunnel. Maybe he is still there ahead of us. We stop. The object is a box. We open it. It is full of chocolate malt powder. What a find! Next to it, there are two enormous potatoes. A *Häftling* with foresight must have hidden supplies, meaning to take refuge in this tunnel at the last minute to escape the planned extermination in the camp.

Nobody knows, no more in Buchenwald than in Auschwitz, what to expect if we are not evacuated. The Americans might not arrive soon enough to liberate anything but corpses. In the meantime, crouching in our underground tunnel, we blindly swallow the contents of the box, more than a kilo of malted chocolate. We continue with the raw potatoes. For the moment, at least, we will not die of hunger.

For two nights, we stay in our underground tunnel, moving forward slowly in total darkness, not knowing where this tunnel is taking us. We also don't know what is happening outside. And we are hungry again: a hunger that tears at our insides. The end of the tunnel comes into sight; we reach a very solid, openwork oak door. From the outside, we cannot be seen in the dark where we lie, but we can see what is happening on the other side. Some men are peeling potatoes, mountains of potatoes. We are under the kitchens, in the *Kartoffelschäl- kommando* room, the potato-peeling *kommando*.

Only a few metres ahead of us, potatoes are piled as high as a mountain, which we cannot reach, and in front of which we salivate, like Tantalus did long before our time. Ten or fifteen men are busy peeling. Our hunger is becoming unbearable. We wait for one of the peelers to come by our door, and we discreetly signal to him. He has a purple triangle; he is a *Bibelforscher* [Jehova's Witness: lit., 'Bible scholar']. We whisper quickly that we are two Jews, hiding, on the verge of dying of hunger. He comes back after ten minutes with two piping hot bowls of delicious soup. Before he leaves, he promises to come back to feed us.

We wait a whole day and the whole following night, but our *Bibelforscher* doesn't come back. He may have left the *kommando*. Or become afraid. Or he may have been denounced. Desperate hunger takes over again, and we signal to another *Häftling*.

This one has a green triangle. Unfortunately, we have happened on a criminal, of whom there are few in Buchenwald. Too bad. We tell him our story, and he also comes back ten minutes later. But not with the promised soup: he arrives with the SS in charge of the *kommando*. He starts yelling at us, and orders the door – luckily very solid – to be broken, and those dirty Jews to be taken out of there. Then, tired of wasting his efforts on the door, he takes out his gun, puts his arm through the oak bars and aims at us. I am standing just in front of him. Michel, who is smaller, is safe behind me. Paralysed by the gun pointed at me, I don't retreat, I don't throw myself on the ground. I only hear myself shouting: 'Don't shoot! Don't shoot!'

And he doesn't shoot. After one or two infinite seconds, I turned around and see Michel, smaller and more agile than me, running towards the other end of the tunnel. I struggle after him, and we both leave the tunnel by the opening through which we came in. Just in time for the camp's internal police, the *Lagerschutz*,[12] to catch us. I don't know why the SS didn't shoot. Did his weapon jam? Or did he want to avoid reprisals, as he must have known that the Americans were about to take the camp?

We are in a strange situation; we are prisoners of the *Lagerschutz*, which consists exclusively of inmates. Our guards are almost all Yugoslavs, all members of the Resistance. And they put us in prison! They have a room in the barracks for use as a prison. My old friend, Robert Mandelbaum, comes to see us as soon as he hears, and brings us both a bar of chocolate from the Red Cross parcels. The Resistance committee of Buchenwald has seized the reserves accumulated by the SS,[13] and is distributing huge stocks of food and other goods – the Red Cross parcels which the Jews, always excluded from distributions, had never received. And so I eat my first piece of chocolate in two years.

Nevertheless, our situation is totally irregular, and poses a problem for Robert. All the other Jews must leave by transport,

---

12. The internal police of Buchenwald, the *Lagerschutz*, was created in June 1942 following an arm-wrestling match between the Resistance movement and the SS. In other camps, the internal police were generally in the service of the SS. In Buchenwald, it effectively protected the inmates, constituting a restraining influence on the camp and, on the whole, never let up. Consisting of 20–30 Germans at the beginning, it grew to 100 guards by August 1944, as the SS allowed foreigners to join because of 'linguistic problems'. Its *kapo*, Karl Keim, describes his assignment as being 'to enforce absolute discipline in the camp without resorting to SS methods; to stay in touch with all the inmates and to observe the SS' movements'. At night, as the *Lagerschutz* guarded the storerooms, the SS could allow themselves to leave the camp, which was to the inmates' advantage (Langbein, *Résistance*, pp. 397–400; Kogon, *L'État SS*, pp. 68–9; *The Buchenwald Report*, pp. 257–9).
13. The Belgian section of the Resistance distributed packages of shoes, clothes and food from the Belgian Red Cross to Belgian inmates in need (*The Buchenwald Report*, pp. 292–3).

or have already left; what will he do with us?

He finally finds a solution; he assigns Michel and me two numbers from two Belgian non-Jewish inmates who had died. This allows him to send us to Block 10, the Block of Belgians where he knows the *Blockältester*, a long-time communist called Grippa.[14]

Thanks to this subterfuge, we are temporarily safe with false identities. But hunger still gnaws at us. On 4 April, realising that we are probably still registered in our Jewish Block, we foolishly decide to go and get a second soup ration, the first with the Belgians and the second with the Jews. Boldly, we go to Block 23, and while we are queuing for our second ration, the Jewish Block is suddenly surrounded.

This time it is not the SS, who no longer set foot in the camp, but the *Lagerschutz*, who have joined forces with the *Vorarbeiter*, the *kapos*, and other important inmate-officials. We immediately understand the situation. They have united to organise the evacuation of the remaining Jews in Buchenwald. It is obvious they plan to sacrifice the Jews to save the other inmates. This time we are done for. There is no way out of this mess. Because of our stupid imprudence we are caught in the flood of the evacuation, and start slowly moving uphill towards the camp's exit. We are too weak to try to escape, and gradually, the human tide drags us along the steep climb of the Lagerstrasse. The camp's gate draws inexorably closer. Our fate has caught up with us, and it is our own fault, our hunger's fault.

As soon as we pass the camp's gate, it will be over for us. We will definitely not survive a transport. But as the crowd in which we are held prisoner approaches the exit, it passes Block 10, the Block of the Belgian Aryans. Grippa is on the doorstep and sees us. Pushing his way through the human chain containing the miserable flow of people on their way to evacuation, he yells with all his authority as *Blockältester*: 'But who is

---

14. Jacques Grippa, an engineer and chief of staff of the armed partisans of Belgium, was arrested at the beginning of 1943 and deported. He would become the undersecretary of state in the first post-war Belgian government (see Steinberg, *La Traque*, Vol. 2).

being taken in the transport? These two are Belgians and they belong to me. Give them back to me; I have to return them to my Block!'

He tears us away from the mass and succeeds in bringing us back to 'our' Block. When we tell him what we were doing in the Jewish Block, he slaps us with all his strength. That slap has the taste of life.

A few more days pass. On 9 April, a sense of uncertainty spread through the camp. Following the impetus of the *Lagerschutz*, more Resistance groups are forming in all the Blocks. Their mission is to surround the inmates in case of a general revolt. They will have to take control of the camp to avoid the final massacre. I am enlisted in one of these groups, as a *Laüfer* [a courier]. The irony of it! I will have to carry orders from one group to the other. With the flesh of my swollen feet raw and suppurating, I won't run very far.

The 11 April 1945. It is my birthday, I am 27 years old, but I have little hope left. That day, the Americans enter Buchenwald. At that moment, on 11 April, I cannot feel anything. I am in terrible physical shape. I am so exhausted that a few days earlier I fell against a burning oven and a horrible wound has developed on my arm, which, lacking care, has become infected, then gangrenous. The bone is showing through blackened flesh, and my arm reeks of gangrene.

But the worst is that my morale is at its lowest. This has lasted too long – the horror, the hunger, the desperation, the destruction of my person. I should feel joy at the news that it is finally over, that our SS torturers have no further power over us. But I feel nothing. I probably can't feel anything anymore. History has moved forward faster than my demise. If I am still alive, I cannot benefit from it spiritually, at least not for now.

I immediately regret this absence of joy, and I will regret it for a long time. We are free! How the Parisians must have exulted when their capital was liberated. And the people of Brussels. And now, Buchenwald is liberated. But me, I am trapped in the fog of my mind, not dead, not alive, not in prison, not free. The only thing I am still capable of doing is to follow a GI who is smoking a Lucky Strike, inhale, and satisfy myself as long as possible on the smoke from his cigarette. The Americans are horrified at what they see. They have no previous experience of this, Buchenwald being one of the first camps they liberate. They decide to feed us as soon as possible, and they give us the troops' soup, which is extremely rich. They don't realise that they are endangering[15] our lives with it. All over the camp, inmates are dying, although they are free and nobody should die anymore. I see men hallucinating; eating and defecating at the same time. In the course of a few days, hundreds and hundreds died.

The conditions that first week are appalling. When the Germans withdrew they blew up the water pump. It takes a whole week for the Americans to renew the water supply. Open latrines lie everywhere, with people suffering from dysentery perched on top. Everyone, especially the Russians, cooks whatever they can collect on small fires in front of the Blocks. The sewerage is blocked by excrement and the Americans requisition German crews to unclog it. Medically, however, I benefit considerably from the American presence. They give me sulphas, a whole new medical discovery. The horrible wound on my arm closes, and I avoid amputation.[16] It

---

15. Food was requisitioned from the Weimar, but clumsily administered. The diet of the chronically debilitated patients was not immediately controlled. They should have received only boiled food, milk and sugar in controlled quantities, preferably by transfusion (*The Buchenwald Report*, p. 7). Later, in Ebensee, for instance, the Americans – by then more experienced – gave the survivors meat stock every hour, and bread or corned beef in controlled quantities (Israel, *Le passage du témoin*, p. 272). There are many testimonies to the nutritional mistakes and many survivors owe their lives to their own weakness, which prevented them from overeating. Steinberg remembers a synthetic honey that wreaked havoc (*Chroniques*, p. 179). For more on these deaths in the final hour, see also Semprun, *L'Écriture ou la vie*, pp. 200–1.
16. On 15 April, the 120th semi-mobile American hospital arrived with 21 medical officers, 207 men and 40 female nurses. Two days later, it was operational and took care of 8,000–10,000 patients (half of the camp population), among them 5,000 patients who were seriously ill or chronically debilitated, mainly from the Small Camp. The SS barracks were transformed into quarantine quarters and the patients were grouped by disease and not by nationality. Mortality, originally nearing 150 per day, decreased rapidly. However, by 26 April, there were still 20–25 deaths a day (M. Overesch, *Buchenwald und die DDR, oder die Suche nach Selbstlegitimation* (Göttingen: Vandenhoeck & Ruprecht, 1995), p. 187). What did change, however, was the attitude towards death. From the first day of liberation, surviving inmates requested, and were given, permission to bury the dead in the Weimar cemetery.

is a small miracle. They also weigh me: I am over 1.80 metres tall and I weigh 42 kilos.

General Patton comes to visit Buchenwald. Mentally, his visit registers with me, although my mind is still a fog. He makes the dignitaries of Weimar visit the camp and forces them to look around and see everything. They walk in procession, well dressed and in silence. I cannot tell if they are disturbed by the sight of us. How many of them, I ask myself, would be able to recognise men like themselves in those corpses left outside, piled like dry wood along the road? How many of them see us as equals, plague stricken as we are, survivors by pure chance of this indescribable injustice? They probably still consider us enemies of the German people, those it would have been better to exterminate forever.

Yet, they cannot say that they didn't know about living conditions at Buchenwald. For eight years, the whole population of Weimar, Goethe's town, lived under the smoke of the crematorium, blown over them by whirling winds. They even glimpsed the inmates when they were sent to the town to clear away the bombed ruins. They could not have been ignorant of the state those 'striped ones' were in. They knew all right – they couldn't have not known – but it didn't affect them. For these people to become human again, 12 years of German indoctrination would have to be eradicated. Only after erasing those 12 years of the most ferocious and efficient political and racial propaganda that history has ever seen would it be possible to restore the universal notion of humanity in place of the notion of Aryan superiority. No, they are not affected, but they may be ashamed, I tell myself, not of having reduced us to what we have become, but of actually having been defeated by these ugly, deformed sub-humans, sick with vermin. They must have felt the injustice of it deeply.

In the meantime, the Americans capture a few SS who failed to escape. They put them straight to work, ordering them to bury the hundreds and thousands of bodies, piled along the camp roads, in communal graves dug by bulldozers. We go to watch them, and we, the liberated inmates, are tempted to justifiably reverse the situation and kick them, even a little, now and then. But the GIs keep a close eye; the SS are prisoners of war, and as such, untouchable. They are protected from any act of revenge.

Repatriation starts around 19 April, eight days after the Americans arrive.[17] My friend and companion in suffering, Michel Zechel, is lucky to be among the first. He is a Belgian citizen, which gives him the right to repatriation by plane. Nothing precise is yet scheduled for me, and I remain there. My wound is taken care of and my physical state is slowly improving, even though I am still very weak. As I was a nursing aide and a member of the Hygiene Institute *kommando*, they suggest I extend my stay in the camp for a while. I can be useful, helping to care for the countless sick. Typhus is still rampant.

I remain in Buchenwald for a whole month after its liberation, and it is only on 12 May that I start my return journey … in a cattle wagon. It takes me six days to return to Liège. In Erfurt, my first stop, I write my first letter as a free man to my parents (I kept a copy). What a strange sensation …

Erfurt, 14 May 1945

Dear parents,

First of all I would like to give you a sign that I am alive. I can well imagine that, without news from me now that the war has been over for a few days, you may think that I am no longer alive. I'm OK. If I'm writing, it means I am alive. I have even come out of this ordeal without too much damage to body and spirit. But it is definitely a miracle, because I am one of the rare survivors of four to five million men. I am aware that there is no special merit in having survived. I know that hundreds of thousands of human beings more capable, more intelligent and stronger

---

17. Unlike repatriation from Bergen-Belsen or Flossenbürg, repatriation from Buchenwald was swift, large-scale and efficient. The 3,000 French were evacuated by Priest Rodhain's mission – Rodhain was the chaplain for the war prisoners – who received absolute priority for transport. The first French inmates were already in Bourget by 18 April (Wieviorka, *Déportation et génocide*, p. 83 ff.). Six hundred Belgians were repatriated by plane. By 8 May 1945, all inmates had been repatriated, except Poles and Russians, who left in June. On 4 July, the Russians took control of the almost empty camp of Buchenwald, and from then on, it would hold other 'enemies of the nation'.

than me have not. It was due to chance and luck. I must also say that I was clever enough to extricate myself from all kinds of situations I fell into ... I am full of confidence in the future, because having successfully come out of what I have just lived through, no hardship that life may have in store for me could affect me. I no longer fear anything, not death, not the devil. I have had ample opportunity to look them both straight in the eye.

I go back to Liège after a short trip. In my small lodgings on Vertbois Street, everything is in its place, as if I had never left. Time here is a different time, and nothing in the world to which I return brings back the image of what I have lived through. But the world is not the same as before. I meet my girlfriend again, and we separate. I feel that I must retain what I have lived through, not let anything slip away. I must write everything down. I complete notebook after notebook.

Shortly after my return, all the accumulated suffering in my body suddenly erupts. I am hospitalised with double pleurisy. I have, in fact, brought tuberculosis back with me from my stay in the camps.[18] I remain in hospital for many months, where I am wonderfully cared for. I soon gain weight; in record time I go up from the 42 kilos I weighed when I was liberated, to 80 kilos. I am then transferred to a convalescence home for ex-political prisoners in Dahlem, one hour by tram from Liège. There, I have plenty of time to update my little notebooks, and try to reconstruct, day by day, everything that has happened since 1 April 1943.

Like most deportees, I suffer significant memory lapses. Every day, I walk with another camp survivor, a Jew called Kuranda. We feel the same need to rediscover our mental faculties and, every day, we play geography names, or celebrity names. Bit by bit, our memory starts to function, and with it, our personality from before.

---

18. According to Robert Waitz, tuberculosis raged in the camps of Upper Silesia and spread wildly in Buchenwald after the arrival of the evacuees (*Témoignages stras-bourgeois*, p. 492).

8 Epilogue

The turmoil of this story ended on 8 May 1945, but over five million Jews from across Europe, from east to west, had been engulfed in the process. I came within a hair's breath of never returning, which would have been consistent with Nazi thinking. In reality, the survivors constitute a twist in history. In a way, I am a miracle; of the 1,400 Jews of the 20th Belgian convoy that arrived in Auschwitz – excluding those who escaped – only 150 returned; and this convoy had an exceptional number of survivors.

I was also extraordinarily lucky, unlike so many of my companions of misfortune who came back from the camps without wives, parents, children, to a devastated community and a family hearth extinguished. My family was safe. I traced them thanks to cards circulated by the Red Cross. My brother had enlisted in the Czech Legion of the Red Army, and fought in the Allied ranks. My parents were able to remain in our house through most of the war, with the paid co-operation of the Romanians. They were only evacuated once, for a short forced stay in the ghetto.[1] At the end of the war, when the northern half of Bucovina and its capital, Czernowitz, passed over definitively to Soviet control, they ran away, taking with them only the key to their house. They took refuge in a small town in the southern part of the province, which had remained

---

1. The ghetto in Czernowitz was created on 9 October 1941. On 11 October, all Jews were ordered to move to it, and they went without resistance. In all, 50,000 Jews were crammed into an area intended for only 10,000. For payment, the mayor, Traina Popovici, exempted 20,000 potential deportees from lists drawn up by the Jewish community (Hilberg, *La Destruction*, p. 760), and 15,000 Jews were allowed to return to their homes (Reifer, 'Geschichte der Juden', p. 21). Of the 20,000 exempted, 5,000 were eventually deported to Transnistry in June 1942, among them, the parents of the poet, Paul Celan. In March 1943, the new governor of Bucovina, Dragalina, forbade violence against the Jews.

161

Romanian. For five years, my father bought his and my mother's safety with cash, carpets and silver. There were ways to get around the Romanian authorities' orders; the destruction of Jewish communities was only systematic where the Germans themselves had control.

Towards the end of 1945, I have already slightly recovered, physically. I join my brother and his wife, who notified me that they were in Paris. She is a doctor in the Czech Legion, with the rank of Major. I still have no papers, and I cross the French border illegally. We joyfully celebrate our reunion. Throughout this stay, my brother and sister-in-law, not yet demobilised, parade through Paris in their Red Army uniforms! My brother and I decide to go and see our parents in Romania as soon as possible. I return to Liège, where, thanks to my Romanian passport from before the war, the Belgian authorities issue a document certifying that I am stateless, residing in Belgium.

I arrive in Prague, where my brother is stationed, for New Year. It is my first stop on my way to Romania and back to my parents in that devastated, immediate post-war Europe. At the time, my brother is waiting to be demobilised. He welcomes me into his home, a grandiose apartment confiscated from a Sudeten German, a member of the Nazi party. One night, as I return from a walk, I am rounded – up having been mistaken for a black marketeer – and immediately sent to Pankracz, the sinister prison of Prague, and thrown in a cell. I protest loudly, and proclaim to whoever wants to listen that I am an ex-political prisoner … My tattooed number on my forearm is there to prove it. This pays off. My cell companions – who were all arrested for 'uncivic' acts, such as trafficking and black marketeering – give me the best bed! The ceiling of the cell is very high, and all night long, more enormous bugs than I have ever seen, even in the camps, fall from it. They land on our faces like bombs, although it is insignificant to me after Auschwitz and Buchenwald. They keep me in prison for another two days, after which I am released.

Finally, my brother is demobilised and we start our journey to Romania. The first town on our trip, which will be filled with adventures and danger, is Budapest. As the train reaches the border between Czechoslovakia and Hungary, it stops. The border is guarded by the Russian Army. A soldier approaches us and asks us what we are doing there. He is a small Kalmouk with the rank of lieutenant. My brother, although demobilised, is still in his Czech uniform, and as he speaks Russian quite well, he tries to negotiate with him. He explains that I am a survivor of the camps, and that he is accompanying me to Romania to find our parents. It is no use.

'You cannot go through. You need a *propuska*, a pass.'

'Where can we get that propuska?'

'In Budapest.'

'But that is exactly where we want to go, Budapest! You are the one stopping us!'

'In that case, there is nothing you can do. You have to take the next train back to Prague.'

Discouraged, we cross to the other platform and slowly walk to the train for Prague. My brother spots a Russian sergeant wearing the cap with the yellow band of the NKVD,[2] patrolling the station. He runs to him and explains our situation. The interaction between the two men in uniform is lively and my brother obviously gets through to him. The Russian is nearly crying: 'Your brother comes back from Auschwitz, he wants to see his *matka* [mother] and they don't let him pass! Wait, I am going to sort this out immediately!'

He takes us both by the arms and drags us briskly to the Kalmouk lieutenant – he himself is a simple sergeant, but a member of the NKVD! – and in a haughty tone tells his superior: 'I have just arrested these two. They are suspects! I am taking them to the *Kommandantur* of Budapest!'

And we get on the train to Budapest ...

There is a terrible commotion around the train, people rushing into wagons. On the platform, I see Russians kicking out Hungarian generals after tearing off their epaulettes.

---

2. The NKVD [*Narodnyi Komissariat Vnoutrennykh Del*: Official Board of the People for Internal Affairs] were the Soviet political police, created in 1934 to replace the Guepeou, which itself had succeeded the Tcheka. It was granted legal powers, police powers, and the administrative power to intern suspects in the system's camps. It was a powerful and much feared organisation. From 1938 to its dissolution in 1946, it was run by Lavrenti Beria.

However, my brother, the Russian sergeant and I still find an empty wagon. It is reserved for Russians. The sergeant has a bottle of vodka, and we have some sausage. The train starts its long journey, during which both my brother and the sergeant do justice to the vodka. They engage in a pastime that they probably learnt in the military. Their game involves shooting at telegraph poles with a Soviet regimental gun.

Our train arrives in one of the Budapest stations, which is still very impressive, even if partially destroyed by bombs. When we disembark, the station is bustling. We head for the exit, and there, as in peacetime, a ticket inspector asks us for our tickets. Needless to say, we don't have any! In response, our Russian friend takes out his gun. The effect is immediate and striking. The station empties in an instant. By the time we arrive outside and want to leave our protector, nobody remains around us. He has been of tremendous help and we want to reward him. We offer him a huge sac of *pengö*. (The Hungarian currency has just been devalued and we obtained a million or a billion *pengös* for one dollar.) But our big-hearted Russian sergeant protests loudly. He doesn't want to take anything from us.

Budapest: the women are beautiful, but we cannot stay forever. A day or two later, we leave for Romania. At the Romanian border, the train stops. We are next to the town of Arad, already on Romanian territory. Everybody disembarks to have their documents checked. As I know we are in Romania, I am proud to show off my Romanian citizenship. So I hide my Belgian pass and show the Romanian passport that remained in Liège throughout my detention. After all, I tell myself, nobody could forbid me to return to my own country! This is a big mistake: the passport is no longer valid.[3] We are told dryly that we must return to Budapest on the next train.

To fail so near to our destination is frustrating! It seems we will never reach the end of this journey.

---

3. In August 1944, King Mihai I ordered the arrest of the *conducator* Antonescu, then declared war on his ex-German ally, and signed an armistice with the USSR. From 1945 until the communists took over on 30 December 1947, Romania – excluding Bessarabia and northern Bucovina – was ruled by a nationalist, monarchist government.

However, once again, my brother saves the day. In this border-post, in the middle of nowhere, he spots an old school friend from Czernowitz who is half-Jewish. Recognition, joy, words ... they start recounting their latest adventures to each other. And it is our luck that this man is an inspector with the Arad political police! He makes us a tempting proposition: he can arrest us and take us, handcuffed, to the Arad prison. There, if we swear an oath that we will leave Romania after two weeks, we will be free to see our parents during that time. One strict condition applies: we must return to the Arad prison at the end of those two weeks to be expelled.

We readily accept that solution as it offers us an additional unexpected advantage. Not only can we enter Romania, but more importantly and no small matter, we will be able to leave.

A taxi is then called, two police officers from Security handcuff us, and we are taken to the Arad prison. My third arrest since the beginning of this trip. An ex-Colonel of the Romanian Army is governor of the prison. He welcomes us nicely. We swear our oath and our fingerprints are taken. But, instead of putting us in a cell for the night, the governor invites us to dine and sleep in his house! From then on, everything becomes easy. We reach Bucharest, then Suceava in the south of Bucovina, where our parents, who have been waiting impatiently, are delighted to see us and find us in good health. They tell us they wish to leave the country, and we plan their move to Belgium. The regime in Romania at the time is transitional. The king still resides there, and it is still possible to emigrate. My father quickly obtains all the necessary emigration documents, for which he only has to pay the fees. Then, at the end of two weeks, when everything is done, we just present ourselves at the Arad prison and we are accompanied to the Hungarian border.

I swear not to make any more mistakes, and from then on, present my Belgian pass at all border checks. But we are still not safely back. When the train reaches the border between Hungary and Czechoslovakia, on the bank of the Danube, it stops. All the passengers are ordered to get off and cross the bridge on foot with their luggage. On the Slovak side, *Hlinka*[4] guards stand watching. We are immediately arrested as black marketeers!

We remain in prison for a whole day before they decide to release us, and we can continue to Prague. Luckily, the *Hlinka* does not realise we are Jews. We will later discover that these *Hlinka* guards are old German collaborators, and are still fiercely anti-Semitic, killing any Jews they encounter. Again, we have a lucky escape.

Three stays in prison, just to visit my parents! However, everything sorts itself out when we arrive. I settle down quite quickly in Brussels, where my brother and his wife join me, and then our parents come to live with us.

Michel Zechel returned to Liège, and his dental clinic. For years, we saw each other regularly, either in Liège, where I went to see him, or in Brussels, when he came to visit me. He died in his nineties.

Robert Mandelbaum and his wife came back to Brussels, where they both made careers in biology at the university.

My Dutch friend, Dorus Wolf, settled in Brussels for a year or two after the war, and we saw a lot of each other before he returned to Holland. We remained friends.

Maurice Goldstein had a very interesting career.[5] He had always wanted to be a doctor. When he was repatriated, he didn't even have a high school degree. He was totally alone, having lost his family – his father, mother, wife and brothers – in the massacre of the Holocaust. He found himself destitute. He studied extremely hard to pass the jury central, one of the most difficult exams in Belgium, which allows a person without

---

4. After Germany annexed Bohemia-Moravia in March 1939, making it a 'protectorate', Slovakia became independent. Governed by a Catholic priest, Mgr Josef Tiso, Slovakia placed itself under Germany's 'protection', and, in aiming to please the Germans, pursued an anti-Jewish policy. This collaborating dictatorship was exceeded, on the right, by the extreme pro-Nazi movement of Prime Minister Vojtech Tuka, the '*Hlinka* Guard' (named after the nationalist dictator, the Slovak militant, Andrej Hlinka, who died in 1938). The *Hlinka* Guards, who were the equivalent of the SS, proceeded to round up Jews, who were deported between March 1942 and September 1944. From the end of the war to the beginning of 1948, the reunified Czechoslovakia was ruled jointly: by the former president, Benes, and the communist leader, Gottwald.
5. See the interview with Maurice Goldstein in Israel, *Le passage du témoin*, p. 238 ff.

a high school degree to go to university. He passed the exam quite easily, although he was still very rundown from his ordeal. He received a grant for his medical studies, which he could keep for six years, provided he completed each term with a distinction. He did it! Maurice became a brilliant surgeon, a head of department and a university professor. He also became president of the International Association of Auschwitz, and founder of the Auschwitz Foundation in Brussels, two organizations in which he was incredibly active, and to which he dedicated a great part of his life without ever neglecting his professional activities. In recognition, he was given the honour of guiding King Baudouin and Queen Fabiola during their visit to Auschwitz. He was honoured with a title in 1994, and died recently.

And me? Settled in Belgium, my brother and I started to work. Together we set up a small business. I didn't become a chemist, but a businessman.

During the first part of my return to ordinary life, neither I nor anyone else who had returned from the camps found it easy to communicate with 'normal' people, those who had never been there. We were convinced that those people either couldn't understand us, or didn't believe us. And we were not very talkative, either. We didn't like to speak of the horror we had lived through, and this lasted a long time. I think that we were most afraid of their pity. Whatever our reasons, we essentially kept to ourselves.

I regularly visited my friend, Maurice Goldstein, and his companion, Rosa,[6] also a survivor. Rosa was often visited by a young Jewish girl from Berlin. They had met in Birkenau, then in Bergen-Belsen, where they were liberated together. When still an adolescent, Ruth's parents had sent her to Belgium, to safety. Later, all her family was exterminated. She escaped to the unoccupied French zone, and joined the Resistance in Nice, until she was arrested and deported. When I met her, she was

---

6. Rosa Ehrlich, Goldstein's wife: see ibid., p. 280 ff., where she provides an incredible testimony.

still using her war name, Renée Denies.[7]

Maurice must once again have been destined to play a role in my life, and what a role! I met Ruth at his place. We were on the same wavelength, we had the same painful memories, I didn't need to explain anything to her. The day after we met, I asked her to marry me.

We had the same hunger for life, to build a future for ourselves, to finally succeed in life, the same need for love. Ruth had no family; nobody. We waited for my parents to arrive from Romania, and we celebrated our wedding in 1947. Neither of us has ever regretted, for even a moment, that we found each other. No doubt our experiences in the camps has contributed to our mutual understanding, and, paradoxically, to a happy life. More than many 'normal' people, we have both known how to appreciate every moment of happiness we had together.

We wanted to have children. After several courses of treatment and experimental sterility treatment available at the time, we twice knew hope, and twice sadness: two miscarriages when four months pregnant. Was it the thought of bringing children into such a cruel world, the thought of possibly exposing them, some day, to the same atrocities we had lived through? Or was it the sleepless nights in which Ruth continued to relive her experiences in her nightmares?

We lived with it. As a couple, we have appreciated every good moment life has brought us. There have been many, and there are many more to come: a few months ago, we had the great joy of celebrating 50 years of marriage, surrounded by many friends of all ages, from all generations. As I looked at the youth and the white heads around me, I told myself, what wonderful revenge on the Nazi extermination project! When I ask my wife what she feels, she answers: long live life, despite everything.

---

7. She appears under this name in the memoirs of Odette Abadi, *Terre de détresse Birkenau–Bergen-Belsen* (Paris: L'Harmatton, 1995), p. 18 ff.

Appendix 1: Bucovina

The Jewish Population of Bucovina

Located west of Dniestr, Bucovina was the centre of the ancient Romanian principality of Moldavia. Under Ottoman rule from 1554, Bucovina was given to Empress Marie-Therese of Austria in 1775, in appreciation for her support during the Turkish–Russian war of 1768–74. Its Jewish population, particularly in Czernowitz, grew quickly from 1848. When Franz-Joseph I proclaimed the Imperial Constitution of 1867, he granted his Jewish citizens equal rights and freedom to trade and settle. Loyalty and respect, even veneration, from the Jews for the emperor are widely acknowledged. In Yiddish, he was sometimes familiarly called *unzer Frojme-Yossel*. Conscious of the Jewish bourgeoisie's support, the emperor visited Czernowitz three times, even visiting the new synagogue in 1880.[1]

Cultural life in Czernowitz was rich. It was the Jewish bourgeoisie that lent the city its German cultural character, and the city remained 'an Austrian town until 1944'.[2] From the middle of the nineteenth century, the progressive Jews sent their children to the State *Gymnasium* [High School] and to the Franz-Joseph University, which was founded in 1875 and had two faculties: Law and Literature. The 'modern' synagogue was inaugurated in 1877. Part of the Jewish bourgeoisie – the most influential class in Czernowitz – was so assimilated that it considered itself 'German of the mosaic faith'. At the same time, a Hassidic ultra-religious culture remained very much alive in

1. H. Sternberg, *Zur Geschichte*, p. 43.
2. B. Helmut, *Rose Ausländer, Materialen zu Leben und Werk* (Frankfurt-am-Main: Fischer, 1992), p. 7.

the provinces, with major centres in Sadagora, Vischnitz and Bojan. The different ideological trends confronted each other, with no understanding of the other's point of view. Nevertheless, the rise of German anti-Semitism led some to return to Judaism, with the establishment of the Jewish National Party, and later, the Zionist movements. Jews were welcome in political life until 1918; they occupied 20 of the 50 seats on the Municipal Council, and two Mayors of Czernowitz were Jews.[3]

On Armistice Day in 1918, Romanian troops occupied the whole of Bucovina. The transfer of the province to Romania was confirmed on 10 September 1919 by the Saint-Germain treaty, one of the agreements dealing with the break-up of the Austro-Hungarian Empire. In 1918, the population of Bucovina was divided as follows: 40 per cent Ruthenians, 35 per cent Romanians, 10 per cent Jews, 6 per cent Germans, 5 per cent Hungarians, 4 per cent Poles and others. Proportions were slightly different in Czernowitz, as 50 per cent of the town was Jewish. In the new national states of the former empire, the Jews asked to be recognised as a national minority, and in 1919, sent delegates to the Commission of the New States and the Protection of Minorities based in Paris. In Romania, they tried to obtain and preserve Romanian nationality and establish a national Jewish party, while at the same time fighting discriminatory laws and violent anti-Semitic trends. Despite Romanization, the Jews of Bucovina regained some prosperity after the war. Trade and industry in Czernowitz remained essentially Jewish.[4]

On the eve of the Second World War, the Jews of Romania, including Bucovina and Bessarabia, numbered between 760,000 and 800,000, of whom about 156,000 were in Bucovina in 1940, and 49,932 in Czernowitz alone.[5]

---

3. H. Sternberg, *Zur Geschichte*, p. 27.
4. Ibid., p. 60.
5. Gilbert,*Endlösung*, Map 79.

The Jews of Bucovina, 1940–45

The Soviet Union annexed Bucovina and Bessarabia on 28 June 1940 without striking a blow and with Germany's approval, thanks to the German–Soviet non-aggression pact of 1939. Russian occupation led to pogroms. At the time, Romania, minus two of its provinces, was still ruled by King Carol II, who abdicated in 1940 in favour of his son, Mihai. On 23 November 1940, Marshall Antonescu, head of a government that included the Iron Guard, joined the Axis powers.

Antonescu declared war on the Soviet Union on 21 June 1941. Heading towards Russia, German and Romanian troops invaded Bucovina: Czernowitz was taken on 4 July. Jews were immediately massacred: 2,400 in June–July 1941.[6] *Einsatzgruppe* D and the Romanian police killed another 4,000 in August.[7] The Gestapo arrived with the *Wehrmacht* luggage, and even before the Germans were ready, the zealous Antonescu started organising the deportation of the 'non-Rumanised' Jews of Bucovina and Bessarabia to Transnistry, a military zone between Dniestr and Boug,[8] intended to be handed over to Romanian control. The Jews were crowded into the 'colonies' of Moghilev, Shargorod and Bershad, and into the concentration camps of Piciora and Vapniarca, without food, and in terrible sanitary conditions. In 1942, only 14,000 Jews remained in the whole territory of Bucovina and Bessarabia.[9] The deportation to Transnistry lasted a whole year and led to 124,000 deaths among the 150,000 deportees from Bucovina, and the deaths of 148,000 Bessarabians.[10] Marrus recorded a slightly more optimistic number for Bucovina: up to 50,000 Jews (about a third) may have survived.[11]

The blow to the Jews of Romania proper was less severe: 40,000 dead and 430,000 survivors.[12]

---

6. Ibid., Map 73.
7. Hilberg, *La Destruction*, p. 265.
8. Ibid., p. 666.
9. Ibid., p. 668.
10. Gilbert, *Endlösung*, Map 80.
11. Marrus, *L'Holocauste dans l'Histoire*, p. 117.
12. Gilbert, *Endlösung*, Map 315.

At the end of June 1944, the Russian Army took back Czernowitz and northern Bucovina; both would be handed over to the USSR under the peace treaty of February 1947.

Appendix 2: Belgian Jews

The Jews in Belgium, 1940–45

Before autumn 1940, the situation of the Jews in Belgium did not seem particularly dangerous.[1] The German *Militärbefehlshaber* [commander] refrained from openly discussing the Jewish problem to avoid ideas of annexation (Belgium was considered a conquered country, not an annexed country). On 28 October 1940, however, the 'Decree Concerning Measures to be taken against Jews' was issued, ordering the census of Jews and limiting their right to dispose of their own property. Dispossession and 'Aryanization' had started. In November 1940, the military authority, wishing to be rid of the Jews, expelled 8,000, mainly refugees from the Reich, to the Free French Zone.[2] By the end of 1940, only 52,000 Jews remained in Belgium (of whom fewer than ten per cent were Belgian citizens). Half of them, well hidden in the heart of the country, escaped deportation, under the nose of the occupying forces, who estimated in June 1944 that 80 per cent of the Jews still present in Belgium had false papers.[3] In June 1941, communist Jews were arrested during the coal miners' strikes, and later, during the invasion of the USSR.

The Final Solution for Belgium began in 1942. The Germans set up the local *Judenräte*, the Jewish Association of Belgium (AJB: *Association des Juifs Belges*), which consisted of high-ranking, 'second-rate' personalities. The Gestapo expropriated the building at 56 Boulevard du Midi in Brussels. The AJB

---

1. See Steinberg, *La Question juive*.
2. Hilberg, *La Destruction*, p. 515.
3. Ibid., p. 520.

distributed the Yellow Stars following the refusal of the Belgian civil authorities to do so. On 11 June 1942, Eichmann's department fixed a quota of 10,000 Jews to be deported. At the same time, several thousand young Jews from Belgium were designated for forced labour in the French departments of the North and Pas-de-Calais. The AJB prepared the lists for the deportation, but partisans burned the file on 25 July, making the task more difficult. Robert Holzinger from the AJB was murdered on 29 August by MOI (Main-d'Oeuvre Immigrée) Resistance fighters. He had been in charge of the deportations and had to ensure a train of 1,000 people would be 'available' once a week. First, Polish Jews were deported, then Czechs, then Russians and 'others'.[4] Naturally, the purpose of these deportations was concealed. There was talk of paid forced labour.[5] On 4 August 1942, a first convoy of 998 deportees, 140 of them children under six, left Mechelen for Auschwitz. Two thirds of the deportees from Belgium were transferred before the end of 1942, in a period of 100 days. It took another two years to transfer the last third.[6] Rumours of genocide spread very quickly. In December 1942, Deputy Foreign Affairs Minister Luther asked his representative in Belgium, von Bargen, to also organise the deportation of Jews with Belgian citizenship, because they were becoming nervous, and 'sooner or later' it was bound to happen anyway.[7] The Belgian nationals were temporarily protected by the Queen Mother, Elisabeth, who intervened with Hitler. Unfortunately, it was ultimately to no avail, as they were rounded up in September 1943. Twenty-seven convoys of Jews and one of gypsies left Mechelen: in total, 25,257 racial deportees. The last convoy left on 31 July 1944, a few weeks before the liberation in September. On 8 May, only 1,207, or 4.8 per cent, of those deported remained alive.[8]

---

4. Ibid., p. 521.
5. See Steinberg, *La Révolte des Justes*, p. 257.
6. See Steinberg, *Les cents jours de la déportation des juifs de Belgique* (Brussels: Vie ouvrière, 1984).
7. Hilberg, *La Destruction*, p. 522.
8. See S. Klarsfeld and M. Steinberg, *Memorial de la déportation des juifs de Belgique* (Brussels: Union des déportés juifs en Belgique/New York: Beate Klarsfeld Foundation, 1982), p. 14.

Attack on the 20th Belgian Convoy[9]

As the trains for the Final Solution carried the deportees to their deaths, only a few people were convinced that they would not return. The better-informed feared the worst from this deportation, especially for the elderly and the children. From the end of 1942, the *Comité de Défense des Juifs* (CDJ) was secretly established to help Jews hide among a population that was very sympathetic to those persecuted by the German occupiers.

In spring 1943, the imminent departure of a 20th convoy from the camp of Mechelen, where Jews were gathered, was announced. The CDJ had the idea of intercepting the train before the Belgian–German border and freeing the deportees. The motion under consideration was different from anything the armed Resistance had ever done before. Nowhere in the Europe of the Final Solution had such an act ever been attempted; even the Allies themselves had avoided shelling rail tracks that led to the extermination centres in Poland. The armed forces organizations, to which the CDJ turned, were not prepared to risk such a reckless raid.

A young Jewish doctor, Youra Livschitz – who was unaccountable to any organization – decided to carry out this crazy act himself. Shot in 1944 as a 'terrorist hostage' for his participation, on 19 April 1943, in the attack against the convoy of Jews being transported by train, the young man was not 'the chief of a terrorist gang' that the SS police believed they had caught! His 'gang' consisted of two non-Jewish high school mates, Robert Maistriau and Jean Franklemon. The daring trio had carried only the one handgun, which the young Jew used 'after his flight', as he would admit to Nazi police officers, to 'shoot the soldiers who pursued him'.

Unexpectedly, the German escort had also positioned themselves behind the last wagon. Their shots took the young people by surprise; who – with the help of a flashlight – had forced the train to stop between Boortmeerbeek and

---

9. See Steinberg, *La Traque*, Vol. 1, Chs 3 and 4.

Westpelaer, before Leuven. Nonetheless, under heavy gunfire, they still managed to open one wagon, from which 17 deportees escaped.

The total number of fugitives from the 20th convoy was quite remarkable. The convoy had left Mechelen on the very day that, over 1,000 kilometres away, the revolt of the last survivors of the Warsaw ghetto had begun. The 1,631 deportees from the 'Belgian' convoy consisted of many rebels. From almost every wagon, all the way to the border, people kept jumping out of the moving train. The German escort shot 23 of them. On crossing the border, the convoy of escapees had lost 231 deportees, including the 17 who were freed by the raid. Unfortunately, a tenth of them died. After this 20th convoy, the SS took extra precautions to ensure delivery of the expected quota to Auschwitz.

Youra Livschitz was later denounced by a Gestapo agent who had infiltrated the Resistance. Arrested on 14 May 1943, he escaped, was recaptured on 2 June, and sentenced to death in Breendonck on 17 February 1944. A plaque in his honour has been erected in the Auschwitz Museum.

Appendix 3: Auschwitz I–III

Arrival in Auschwitz of the 20th Convoy from Mechelen

The 20th Belgian convoy left Mechelen on the night of 19–20 April 1943 with 1,631 Jews, of whom 231 escaped in Belgium. Thus, 1,400 arrived in Auschwitz on 22 April: 507 men, 631 women, 121 boys, 141 girls and young women, including Belgium's youngest deportee, Suzanne Kaminski, who was only 39 days old on the day the convoy left.[1]

After the selection, 879 men and women, comprising the old people (the age limit, not known for certain, fluctuated around 50), the children, and mothers with children, were killed in the gas chambers. The 276 men selected for work received numbers from 117,455 to 117,730, and the 245 women received numbers from 42,451 to 42,695; they were registered in the camps of the Auschwitz complex. Sixty-three per cent of the deportees were gassed on arrival, and 37 per cent put to work, which was a relatively high proportion.

In comparison, on that same day, in a convoy of 2,800 Greek Jews from the Salonika ghetto, 255 men and 413 women were selected for work; the other 2,132 men, women and children – 76 per cent of the convoy – were sent straight to their deaths.[2]

The 20th Belgian convoy actually had a 'high' survival rate (150 out of 1,400). One of the reasons for this survival rate of 10.7 per cent – not counting the escapees – was that many women were selected for medical experiments.[3]

In April 1943, two of the four large crematorium-gas chamber complexes (II and IV) had just been put into service in

---

1. Czech, *Kalendarium*, p. 474; Klarsfeld and Steinberg, *Memorial*, p. 30.
2. Czech, *Kalendarium*, p. 475.
3. Klarsfeld and Steinberg, *Memorial*, p. 31.

Birkenau, with a daily capacity of 3,000 and 1,500 bodies, respectively. The month of April 1943 witnessed the arrival in Auschwitz of 27,321 Jews, mainly Greeks, of whom 20,444, or 74.8 per cent, were sent directly to their deaths on arrival.[4] Three deportees out of four could therefore be considered sentenced to death from the moment they climbed into the wagons. On 22 April 1943 in particular, 3,011 Jews were killed in the extermination centre of Auschwitz-Birkenau, not counting those who succumbed to abuse and disease in the various camps of the concentration camp complex.

Selection of Jewish Deportees on Alighting from the Train

The SS doctor in charge, Eduard Wirths, had imposed the following rule in Auschwitz: the entry selection was each SS doctor's responsibility when he was on duty. This rule applied to all doctors, including himself.[5] Only Hans Münch obtained a dispensation (see Chapter 5). Like many Auschwitz survivors, W.B. believes that Doctor Mengele was in charge of the selection on that day. However, Josef Mengele started his service in Auschwitz only a month later, on 30 May 1943, as chief doctor of the gypsy camp.

In April 1943, it was essentially the SS doctors Thilo and Entress who performed selections when the trains arrived. Heinz Thilo, born, like Mengele, in 1911, practised in Auschwitz from October 1942. He appeared to be totally detached at the train selections, and sadistic during the internal selections at the hospital.[6] He coined the phrase *'anus mundi'* to describe Auschwitz, which was, in his eyes, a positive metaphor: the camp was the excretory organ of harmful physiological material. Thilo died in 1945 in unclear circumstances.

Friedriech Entress, an ethnic German born in Posnan in 1914, was moved from the Gross-Rosen camp to Auschwitz in

---

4. Czech, *Kalendarium*, pp. 456–82.
5. On the doctor-executioner, Wirths, and his dual loyalty to his Nazi duty and his ethical responsibilities as a doctor, see Lifton, *Les Médecins nazis*, pp. 432 ff.
6. Ibid., pp. 197 and 221; also *Contribution à l'histoire du KL Auschwitz*, Vol. 2, pp. 256 ff.

December 1941. Before he had even finished his studies, he was exempted from presenting his thesis and qualified as a doctor in 1942, under a special provision for the *Volksdeutsche*. Without hesitation, he can be classified among the worst SS murderers:[7] he wasn't satisfied with executing orders, he needed to exceed them, interpreting them as a *carte blanche* for killing. Entress initiated murder by phenol injection, the execution of which he delegated to SS nurses. He used inmates as guinea pigs to study tuberculosis, and would send them to be killed at the end of the experiment. Wirths, who respected his ethical duties regarding camp inmates, sent Entress away from Auschwitz by moving him to Monowitz in May 1943, dismissing him definitively on 20 October 1943. Entress was then transferred to Mauthausen until July 1944, and finished his career in Gross-Rosen with the title of *Lagerarzt* [camp doctor]. At the beginning of 1945, he was evacuated to Dachau. Sentenced to death by an American court in the 'Mauthausen' proceedings, he was executed on 28 May 1947.[8]

In court, Entress described the selection procedure at the ramp as follows:

> The inmates were taken on by the chief of the Political Section. The head of the camp or his substitute, a doctor of the camp and the chief of labour performed the actual selection on the spot. Young people under 16, all mothers with children, all the sick and handicapped were loaded onto trucks and sent to the gas chambers. The others were taken on by the chief of labour and brought to the camp.[9]

Extermination or Exploitation?

The debate is inconclusive: was the economic importance of racial inmates employed in the war economy stronger than the

---

7. Langbein, *Menschen in Auschwitz*, pp. 377–9.
8. *Contribution à l'histoire du KL Auschwitz*, Vol. 2, p. 16; Lifton, *Les Médecins nazis*, p. 291; Langbein, *Menschen in Auschwitz*, p. 251.
9. Deposition in Nuremberg, 14 April 1947, cited in E. Kogon, H. Langbein and A. Rückerl, *Les chambres à gaz: secret d'État* (Paris: Seuil/Points Histoire, 1987), p. 194.

wish to exterminate them; was the desire to exploit their energy stronger than the wish to kill them all – work being the instrument of death?[10] Pohl wrote the following to Himmler on 16 September 1942: 'The usable Jews who emigrate to the east will have to interrupt their journey and work for the war effort.'[11] Annette Wieviorka suggests that rather than talking of 'extermination', a concept too closely linked to the recognised goal of killing a whole group of people, it would be better to apply the term 'elimination' to the process that the inmates who were selected for work underwent. This comes back to the original Nazi concept of *Vernichtung durch Arbeit* [destruction through work]. Nevertheless, survivors of the concentration camps unanimously 'feel that they were all doomed to extermination'.[12] Marrus states that, in general, 'even for the most optimistic [Nazi leaders], deportation of the Jews was to include "elimination through wear"'.[13] Still, even at the height of the war, selections on arrival continued, and potentially useful workers were sent to be gassed.[14]

The contradiction between elimination and exploitation provoked violent disagreements bewtween the SS Economic-Administration Main Office, the WVHA, and the Reich Security Main Office, the RSHA. The WVHA, run by Gerhard Maurer and Oswald Pohl, was responsible for administering the camps and organising the industrial effort. Heinrich Müller ran the RSHA, whose Jewish Affairs Section was headed by Adolph Eichmann, who was responsible for implementing the Final Solution. Auschwitz commander, Höss, mentioned these fights in the autobiographical notes he wrote in prison before his trial:

The RHSA and the WVHA had totally opposing aims. Pohl seemed to have been in a stronger position, because the *Reichsführer-SS* [Himmler] was behind him, demanding

---

10. For Auschwitz in particular, see Piper, *Arbeitseinsatz*, p. 9. ff.
11. Cited in Hilberg, *La Destruction*, p. 795.
12. See Wieviorka, *Déportation et génocide*, pp. 203–4.
13. See Marrus, *L'Holocauste dans l'Histoire*, p. 96.
14. For example, in March 1943, with the liquidation of the Jews in Berlin. See Hilberg, *La Destruction*, p. 795 ff.

180

with greater and greater urgency inmates for the arms industry, bound as he was by the promises he has made to the *Führer*. At the same time, the *Reichsführer-SS* also wanted as many Jews as possible destroyed.[15]

In reality, the economic exploitation was not very successful; the inmates' miserable condition was clearly reflected in the number of people in *kommandos*, compared to the total number of inmates.[16] About six out of seven inmates registered in the Auschwitz-Birkenau complex died in the elimination process.

The Monowitz Arbeitslager

As Hilberg says: 'I.G. Farben was not just any factory, but a bureaucratic empire and a very important component of the destruction machine.'[17] Sadly enough, the consortium was quite representative of what prisoner exploitation was about: combined enslavement by the SS and the factory foremen. They starved the inmates to death and made them work at an inhuman pace.

In the summer of 1942, the I.G. Farben administrators decided to build a camp near the site to reduce delays and costs, and to isolate the Buna workers from the typhus in Auschwitz and Birkenau.[18] Before that, the prisoners walked 14 kilometres every day (round trip), and were then put on the Reichsbahn train. The Monowitz concentration camp was a private institution, financed by I.G. Farben.[19] The Buna was surrounded by a crown of various camps: one for British prisoners of war and one for Ukrainian women, an STO (Service du Travail Obligatoire) camp. But the largest of all was the 'KZ', the labour camp, usually called 'the Jews' camp'. From the end of 1942, most of the Jews selected for work on arrival at

---

15. See R. Höss, *Kommandant in Auschwitz: Autobiographische Aufzeichnungen*, 2nd edn, Martin Broszat (ed.) (Munich: dtv, 1963), p. 208; also, Czech, *Kalendarium*, pp. 427–30.
16. See Piper, *Arbeitseinsatz*, pp. 71 and 81.
17. Hilberg, *La Destruction*, pp. 799 ff.
18. J. Borkin, *L'I.G. Farben, ou la puissance, les crimes et la chute d'une enterprise multinationale et nationalist* (Paris: Alta, 1979), p. 191; Hilberg, *La Destruction*, p. 805.
19. Borkin, *L'I.G. Farben*, p. 192.

Auschwitz were sent to Monowitz. Among the first residents was a very organised group of communists, who had acquired enormous experience in Buchenwald.[20] German-speaking Jews were favoured and got clerical positions. On average, 10,000 inmates were employed on the site at any one time. Between setting up the camp and evacuating it in January 1945, 35,000 inmates, mainly Jews, passed through Buna-Monowitz, of whom at least 25,000 died of exhaustion, hunger, or from beatings. The whole site was seriously damaged by the 1944 summer/autumn bombardments. From 25 August 1944 onwards, the factory no longer produced acetylene.[21]

Only some 15 SS (armed forces not included) managed the Monowitz camp.[22] The *kapos* and all the inmate administration, mainly criminals, took over: to the great satisfaction of the Germans. Primo Levi[23] notes that in Monowitz, although there were no real political prisoners, almost all the non-Jewish inmates (and some Jewish ones) had some responsibility, even if minimal. The first *Lagerführer* was the *SS-Obersturmführer* Vincent Schöttl, a Bavarian who, according to Robert Waitz, was happy enough just to carry out orders, and who sometimes talked about 'his' inmates with affection. He was sentenced to death in 1946 by an American court and was subsequently executed. In November 1943, during the reorganisation of the Auschwitz complex, the bloodthirsty Heinrich Schwarz was promoted to commander of all annexed camps and *kommando*s outside the Auschwitz-Birkenau complex. He had been chief of labour organization in Auschwitz I, and was sentenced and executed in 1947 by the French for being the last commander of Natzweiler-Struthof. The complex was renamed Auschwitz III, with Monowitz as its centre.[24] The SS at Monowitz also included *Rapportführer* Goering and *Arbeitsdienstführer* Stoelte.

---

20. Langbein, *Menschen in Auschwitz*, p. 45.
21. Czech, *Kalendarium*, p. 869.
22. Waitz and Klein, *Témoignages strasbourgeois*, p. 477.
23. P. Levi, *Se questo è un uomo*, p.97.
24. Langbein, *Menschen in Auschwitz*, p. 363.

I.G. Farben's Buna Factory in Auschwitz

At the beginning of the war, the industrial empire of I.G. Farben, which became 'Aryanized' and 'Nazified' in 1937, comprised 56 factories active in the pharmaceutical (Bayer), photographic (Agfa) and chemical (BASF, Degesch, producer of Zyklon B, etc.) industries. The enterprise had the monopoly on the production of rubber, nitrates, and synthetic petrol. As proof of the coalition of powers in the Nazi Reich, the consortium's main decision-making centre was not within the enterprise – whose administrators had been effectively stripped of their power – but resided in the State. The management of the four-yearly plan was headed by the all-powerful Carl Krauch, who conducted the German chemical industry's expansion policy. Early on, Hitler had insisted on the need, in case of war, to replace imported rubber, which was a strategic raw material second only to petrol and indispensable for military vehicles' tyres. Two 'Buna' factories began operating in Germany in 1936 and 1938. However, in view of the Soviet invasion, production had to be increased to 150,000 tonnes a year.

In February 1941, the Dwory site, next to the village of Monowitz, seven kilometres from Auschwitz, was chosen over Norway to build a giant factory because coal, water and lime were available there in quantities, and also because it was connected by rail to the rest of the expanded Reich. As German workers were unwilling to go to Upper Silesia to work, the idea was to exploit the inmates of Auschwitz.[25] Himmler was in favour of the project, and on 1 March 1941, he came for a first in-depth visit to the Auschwitz 'efficiency site' (*Interressengebiet*: an area around the camp of about 40 square kilometres), accompanied by Commandant Höss; his second visit took place in 1942. Himmler gave orders to expand and develop the concentration camp and, following the decisions of the large Nazi industry, made 10,000 inmates available to I.G. Farben to build the factories. The site was enclosed by a wide belt of *grosse Postenkette* [armed guards] of Auschwitz-Birkenau. The town of

---

25. Borkin, *L'I.G. Farben*, pp. 176 and 183 ff.

Oswiecim was emptied of its residents, and two workers' cities were built to accommodate workers and civilian staff. On 27 March, the contract between I.G. Farben and an enthusiastic Himmler ensured that all Auschwitz inmates in 'reserve' would be made available to the new enterprise, namely 30,000 men. Criminal *kapos* were brought in from other camps. The inmates worked ten to eleven hours a day in the summer, and nine hours in the winter. I.G. Farben paid the SS four reichsmark a day per skilled worker, and three reichsmark a day for an unskilled one. Not one pfennig was given to the inmates. These sums went through the camp's *Kommandantur* coffers and were transferred to the Reich's account, either by the camp administration, or by the WVHA. Two production units were planned for the site: synthetic rubber (a Buna process), and gas from hydrogenated coal (a Bergius process). The factory was slated to be the largest of the I.G. Farben group, and attracted considerable investment. However, because of delays and the inmates' low productivity, no rubber, and only a small yield of gas, was ever produced.[26] Primo Levi remembers tanks of methanol and acetylene gas metres, as well as an electricity factory.

Rations for Auschwitz Inmates

According to Polish prosecutor Jan Sehn, who conducted the Auschwitz court proceedings after liberation, the daily food rations for a normal inmate – he didn't distinguish between the three camps – was between 1,300 calories and 1,700 calories for a forced labourer.[27] Sehn's numbers were based on the study by Dr Hans Münch, of Rajsko's Hygiene Institute, carried out during his investigation, *Hunger und Lebenserwartung in Auschwitz*, which was published in 1947.[28] The planned ration

---

26. Ibid., pp. 190 and 201.
27. Sehn, *Konzentratinslager Ozwiecim-Brzezinka*, ch. 5.
28. Reproduced in French in L. Poliakov, *Auschwitz* (Paris: Juillard/Archives, 1964), p. 197 ff.

was 1,750 calories per person (2,150 calories for forced labourers), but repeated thefts in the kitchen, and while rations were being allocated (by the people in charge of the Blocks and the rooms), routinely reduced this ration. In comparison, Münch estimated that a worker needed 3,600 calories a day, and a forced labourer needed 4,800 calories. According to Dr Robert Levy, who was an inmate-doctor at the Birkenau hospital, the average rations there were 900–1,000 calories. Conditions in Birkenau on the whole were the worst of the complex.[29] According to Marc Klein, who held a similar position in Auschwitz I, the inmates' food rations were 1,500–1,800 calories.[30] Robert Waitz specified the following rations for the Monowitz camp, at which he arrived in October 1943: 350 grams of bread (rich in bran and wood dust) daily; 25 grams of margarine five times a week; 75 grams of semi-vegetable sausage weekly; 20 grams of marmalade weekly; from time to time, two teaspoons of cheese made with skimmed milk (30–40 grams); all of this equivalent to 1,000–1,100 calories a day. The water was undrinkable. In addition to the very liquid midday soup and the evening soup, half a litre of coffee substitute (with almost no sugar) was given in the morning.[31]

The Inmates' Hospital in Monowitz[32]

In the northeast corner of the Monowitz camp, the *Häftlingskrankenbau* (HKB) occupied Blocks 14–20, which were separated from the rest by a wall. Its administration was separate from that of the camp, and was directly answerable to the *SS-Standortarzt* [SS chief-doctor], and the *Sanitätsdienstgrade* nurses [SDG: health officers]. The inmate-doctors tried their best to genuinely treat the sick.[33] The first *Lagerältester* of

---

29. Waitz and Klein, *Témoignages strasbourgeois*, p. 461.
30. Ibid., p. 422.
31. Ibid., p. 485
32. See R. Waitz, 'La relation', in Waitz and Klein, *Témoignages strasbourgeois*, p. 482 ff.
33. *Contribution à l'histoire du KL Auschwitz*, Vol. 2, p. 127 ff.

the hospital was the Austrian communist Ludwig Wörl, promoted in March 1943 to the same position at the HKB in Auschwitz. He contributed greatly to ensuring that inmates were treated properly – as far as it was possible – in the camp. Soon after he took up his position, the Monowitz hospital acquired excellent equipment, with an operating theatre, laboratories, radio equipment, and even an electroshock installation. Most of these machines had been 'organized' on the I.G. Farben site by inmates, and the SS were well aware of all this; they were actually proud of their hospital.[34] Probably the most useful acquisition was the steam boiler, which served as a heater and a disinfecting device, and helped prevent epidemics, at least until the winter of 1944, when the *Erziehungshäftlinge* [political inmates] introduced yellow fever, diphtheria and typhus, which raged until evacuation.[35]

The percentage of admissions was regulated. According to Entress' testimony, I.G. Farben had demanded that the hospital remain small, so that only a minimum number of days would have to be paid for sick workers. The maximum stay allowed was three to four weeks, and selections were frequent.[36] As soon as the hospitalized inmates reached five per cent of the total inmate population (ten per cent in the winter and six per cent in the summer, including the *Blockschonung*, according to Robert Waitz), a selection would take place, and some of the sick would be transported to Birkenau and gassed. From March to October 1943, the *Lagerarzt* was the feared Friedrich Entress.

The other SS doctors were Hans Wilhelm König (who performed unnecessary amputations on sick people suffering from inflammation of the limbs)[37] and Horst Fischer (who was in charge of all the external camps). According to Waitz, Fischer was the only doctor who showed any humanity.[38] The SS nurse in charge was SDG Neubert. The inmate-doctors could practise

---

34. Langbein, *Menschen in Auschwitz*, p. 168.
35. Levi, *Se questo è un uomo*, p. 144.
36. Ibid., p. 507.
37. Ibid., p. 399.
38. Waitz and Klein, *Témoignages strasbourgeois*, p. 478.

(permitted in the Auschwitz complex only from 1942), but most ailments could not be treated.[39]

German Industry and the Labour Camps

In his 1947 testimony, Höss confirmed that the civilians working in the industries abused the inmates. Was this cruelty imposed or spontaneous? After the war, industry managers pleaded that they had been instructed to be very strict with the inmates and that they had been acting under duress.[40] However, they didn't seem to have needed to make a great effort. Many industrialists had absorbed Nazi ideology, and there was an extraordinary convergence of interests between the repressive policies of the labour camp and industry's outrageous exploitation. Not only was the inmate's labour free of any social security payments, it also advantageously replaced costly investments in machinery. Even if profitability was lower, the cost was also extremely low. Sometimes, to preserve the labour force, inmates were trained, and in some *kommandos* and workshops, their living conditions were even improved.

The I.G. Farben managers were indicted by an American military court in Nuremberg from 27 August 1947 to 12 May 1948, and received light sentences of a year and a half to eight years' imprisonment.[41] Gustav Murr, site overseer, declared for example that, when the industry complained of low productivity from inmates, which happened often, the SS would replace them with stronger inmates. However, they claimed that they had no idea what happened to the inmates sacked for their weakness. They also claimed that they didn't know what the crematorium chimneys were for.[42] The engineer, Max Faust, who can be seen on photos from 1942 next to Himmler during

---

39. On the relative haven of the Monowitz hospital for doctors and nurses, see also the memoirs of Georges Wellers, who was a nursing aide there (Wellers, *Un Juif sous Vichy*, p. 241 ff.).
40. Langbein, *Menschen in Auschwitz*, p. 506–112; Hilberg, *La Destruction*, p. 798 ff.
41. Borkin, *L'I.G. Farben*, p. 211 ff.
42. Langbein, *Menschen in Auschwitz*, p. 507.

Himmler's second visit to the Buna,[43] was assistant manager in the Walter Dürrfeld factory. He wrote, in a weekly report of October 1943: 'I have always been against the inmates being shot on the sites or beaten half to death. However, I believe that punishment in a moderate form is absolutely necessary to preserve working discipline among the inmates.'[44] Other I.G. Farben managers remember the chimneys of Birkenau and their smell, of which they complained. No one seems to have been genuinely unaware of what went on there.

An Insight into Auschwitz

Consisting of former Polish barracks, the camp of Auschwitz was zealously developed by its commander, Rudolph Höss, from its foundation on 4 May 1940. Four *Lagerführer* [camp commanders] managed the camp under Höss' orders. Auschwitz remained a small disciplinarian camp of 10,000 inmates until 1942. It also served as an internment camp for prisoners of war: first Poles, and then Russians. Only during the spring of 1942 did Auschwitz develop into a gigantic extermination and exploitation complex. From March 1942, it held women; from January 1943, gypsies (whose internment order dated only from 1942). In March 1941, Himmler ordered the construction of a gigantic extension to hold 200,000 prisoners: this was to become Birkenau, of which only sections B I and B II were ever built, and which would hold up to 140,000 inmates in 1943. Over 200 factories for the war effort were progressively installed in the vicinity (the *Interessengebiet*) of Auschwitz: including I.G. Farben, Deutsche Ausrüstungs-Werke, Krupp, Weichsel-Union and Siemens.

Höss asserted that he had been informed by Himmler, in June 1941, that his camp had been chosen for carrying out the Final Solution to the Jewish problem.[45] In August 1941, in the

---

43. Czech, *Kalendarium*, p. 79. Himmler would visit for the third time in the summer of 1943.
44. Langbein, *Menschen in Auschwitz*, p. 510.
45. Höss, *Kommandant in Auschwitz*, p. 237.

basement of Block 11, the first collective murder using Zyklon B gas was carried out on a group of Russian prisoners. In view of the experiment's success, Höss set up sealed gas chambers in two small farms next to Birkenau, the 'little red house' and the 'little white house', also called *Bunkers* 1 and 2. On 15 February 1942, a first convoy of Jews from Silesia was gassed in the basement of the main camp crematorium; the bodies were buried in pits. The Auschwitz crematorium received only the bodies of those who died in the camp. The first convoy, sent by order of the RSHA (Department IVb4, Eichmann), arrived on 26 March 1942: 999 Slovakian Jewish women who were interned. It was only from 4 July 1942 that deportees faced selection on arrival: the first time, 372 people were preserved for work, the rest (possibly 1,000) were gassed.[46] In spring 1942, internal selections began in the camp and at the hospital. At the end of the summer of 1942, as part of secret operation '1005', the SS reopened all the ovens to burn the bodies.

For mass extermination, a new type of death factory had to be improvised; four large crematorium-gas chambers were built in Birkenau during the first half of 1943, of which two had a daily capacity of 3,000 bodies, and the other two, 1,500 bodies each. Auschwitz-Birkenau became the main extermination centre for Jews after the closing of Chelmno, Belzec, Sobibor and Treblinka.

Throughout the war, next to the extermination camp, was a labour camp run by the SS Economic-Administrative Main Office, the WVHA, administered by Oswald Pohl. Auschwitz-Birkenau was also the site for criminal medical experiments: performed by Mengele on invalids and twins, by Clauberg on the sterilization of women, by Schumann on the sterilization of men, and by others.[47] The *Kalendarium*, published by Danuba Czech, carefully retraces the events that took place in the camp day by day, according to available sources.

---

46. Czech, *Kalendarium*, p. 241.
47. See Lifton, *Les Médecins nazis*.

The Inmates' Hospital in Auschwitz.

The HKB of Auschwitz[48] comprised Blocks 9, 19, 20, 21 and 28, 'whose internal arrangement met most of the requirements of modern hospital technique';[49] however, as far as the inmates were concerned, until 1943, this was mainly an antechamber of death.[50] Internal selections took place until November 1944. The first *Lagerältester* of the hospital (whose administration was separate from the camp administration) was the criminal Hans Bock, a morphine-addicted homosexual. He was a soft man, but he still agreed to give the lethal injections. Bock was replaced in March 1943 by the political prisoner, Ludwig Wörl. In August 1943, Wörl was sent to prison and the job fell first to the Polish surgeon Dering;[51] then, in January 1944, it fell to the Polish doctor Wladislaw Fejkiel, who was to later write his memoirs.[52] Only Dering drifted quickly towards collaboration; the other hospital chiefs, even Bock, had a sense of duty to protect the sick. From 1941, the SS chief-doctor Entress gave lethal injections to people sick with tuberculosis, and in May 1942, instigated euthanasia by order of his superior, Enno Lolling, who that year had become *Amt D III für Sanitätswesen und Lagerhygiene* [chief of medical services of the WVHA camps]. When indicted in 1945, Enno Lolling committed suicide. Those who were liquidated were the mentally ill, people with tuberculosis, and inmates unable to work for lengthy periods, as convalescence was not to exceed four weeks.[53] Any prisoner aware of what was going on became terrified at the mere mention of hospital.

Beginning in August 1942, political prisoners took over the internal running of Auschwitz, and this movement started at the HKB. In September 1942, the new *Standortarzt* [chief doctor], Eduard Wirths, arrived.[54] He was to remain in

---

48. On the HKB, see *Die Auschwitz-Hefte*, Vol. 1, p. 159 ff.
49. Klein, in Waitz and Klein, *Témoignages strasbourgeois*, p. 445.
50. See Czech, *Kalendarium*, p. 200; Langbein, *Menschen in Auschwitz*, p. 239.
51. Ibid.
52. See Langbein, *Menschen in Auschwitz*, p. 583.
53. Ibid., pp. 47–8.
54. Ibid. On Wirths, see Lifton, *Les Médecins nazis*, ch. 18.

Auschwitz until the evacuation, and he took the political inmate Hermann Langbein as his secretary. The situation at the HKB improved for the inmates.[55] Langbein draws a poised, fair, even warm, portrait of Wirths, 'the most interesting SS personality of Auschwitz', of which he saw only one side: the one of the doctor who was there to treat and not to kill, who proceeded with the selections against his will,[56] who favoured political inmates and relied on inmate-doctors to provide care.[57] Wirths fought to eliminate typhus, blocked executions, tried to recall the sick who were sent to outdoor *kommandos*, and censured Entress and Klehr and had them transferred, in autumn 1943, for having exceeded the euthanasia directives. He sent his superiors honest reports on the situation in Auschwitz, which were effective because of the fear of public opinion. He also seems to have succeeded in getting approval for abandoning the sick at the time of evacuation instead of killing them.[58] In the words of the inmate-doctor Stanislav Klodzinski, a 'normalization, in the positive sense of the word, occurred in the life of the quarantined in 1943 and 1944'.[59] Notwithstanding, Wirths never refused his responsibility in the extermination; he organized medicalization of the selection. Taken prisoner by the British, he hanged himself during the first night of his detention.[60]

Executions at the Black Wall

From 22 November 1940, collective executions by shooting occurred in Auschwitz. They were later replaced by liquidation by gassing or by phenol injections (the codes in the morgue register are difficult to decipher). In October 1941, there began a series of mass executions of political prisoners, mainly Poles and Russians.[61] For reasons of discretion, they no longer took

55. Langbein, *Menschen in Auschwitz*, p. 416.
56. Ibid., pp. 414 and 427.
57. Klein, in Waitz and Klein, *Témoignages strasbourgeois*, p. 446.
58. Langbein, *Menschen in Auschwitz*, pp. 419, 421–2 and 431.
59. Ibid., p. 52.
60. On the fundamental schizophrenia of the Auschwitz doctors, see Lifton, *Les Médecins nazis*, p. 234 ff.
61. See Kielar, *Anus Mundi*, ch. 21.

place in the quarry opposite the camp, but against a breeze-block wall, built in the yard between Blocks 10 and 11, and painted black to dampen the noise from shooting. The first execution by the Black Wall took place on 11 November 1941, a Polish national holiday. The condemned were shot in the back of the neck with a weapon equipped with a silencer. These executions continued until October 1943.

It was often *Rapportführer* Gerhard Palitzsch who carried out the shootings. It is possible that *SS-Rottenführer* Perry Broad, employed in the Political Section and heard as a witness after liberation, also participated in the killings, despite his denials.[62] According to witnesses, Palitzsch – a Saxon, and one of the rare SS to correspond physically to the Aryan prototype – was capable of committing an infinite number of executions without showing the least emotion, whistling and chatting with his assistants between shots. Höss confirmed that Palitzsch displayed no sign of having second thoughts about his job.[63] In addition to Poles, the executed included Germans, Frenchmen, Russians, gypsies, Jews, and other nationalities; some were hostages of the Gestapo, with no idea that they were considered such.[64] Finally, there were those who had escaped and been recaptured. The names of those executed were found in the *Bunkerbuch* [the *Bunker* register], which has been preserved.

In autumn 1943, *SS-Obersturmbannführer* Mildner, the mobile court president, and Grabner, the chief of the Political Section of Auschwitz, were indicted by SS Judge Morgen, head of the SS investigating commission dealing with corruption.[65] The regime didn't permit collective executions of political prisoners like those perpetrated in Auschwitz, and Morgen therefore concluded that they had to be considered murders! Accused of 2,000 arbitrary murders, Grabner was dismissed in October 1943 and sentenced in October 1944 to 12 years in prison. Protected by the head of the RSHA, Heinrich Müller, he

---

62. Langbein, *Menschen in Auschwitz*, p. 436; *Der Auschwitz-Prozess*, p. 509 ff.
63. Langbein, *Menschen in Auschwitz*, p. 439, relies on the ambiguous testimony of Perry Broad.
64. Höss, *Kommandant in Auschwitz*, p. 154.
65. Langbein, *Menschen in Auschwitz*, p. 56 ff.

avoided prison and melted into the crowd, but was caught and executed in Krakow in 1947. According to Broad, Mildner managed to find refuge in Denmark. The scandal following the trial against the Political Section seems to have played a part in the dismissal of Höss in November 1943. Broad confirmed that the investigation against Grabner had been ordered by Himmler himself, after rumours of the executions had filtered through to the Allies via the Polish Resistance, and had been mentioned by the BBC.[66]

No further executions occurred in Auschwitz under the new commander, Liebehenschel, who headed the Auschwitz-Birkenau complex from November 1943 (but they would still occur inside the crematoria of Birkenau). It appears that the Black Wall was destroyed on 5 May 1944.[67]

Like Sheep to the Slaughter?

Resistance in the *Lager* did not end with armed underground organization, which was primarily found in political camps like Buchenwald or Sachsenhausen. For the anonymous inmate, it just meant finding a way to survive without compromising oneself, or to die with dignity. The French women in Birkenau, when transported from Block 25 to the crematorium, sang the *Marseillaise* on the truck taking them to their deaths.[68] Of those executed at the Black Wall, testimonies on their final moments vary. Perry Broad states that many died yelling: 'Long live Poland!' or 'Long live Freedom!'[69] Filip Müller, a member of the crematorium *kommando* and, as such, a member of Block 11, tells that he heard 'Supplications and cries, prayers to God, but also patriotic proclamations, in Russian and in Polish: "Long live Free Poland!" or "Long live Stalin!"'[70]

Comparative judgements are delicate and emotional. When the Nazis took over Europe, the Jews as a whole, as a civilian

---

66. *Auschwitz in den Augen der SS*, p. 138.
67. Czech, *Kalendarium*, p. 767.
68. Langbein, *Menschen in Auschwitz*, p. 113.
69. *Auschwitz in den Augen der SS*, p. 102.
70. Müller, *Trois ans*, p. 61.

population, had no idea that they were fated to die in the Final Solution. Their long history of enduring pogroms was probably their downfall; they were used to suffering violence and waiting for it to pass. Nevertheless, one should not forget that they did revolt: the uprising in the Warsaw ghetto, of course; but also in the Treblinka camp on 2 August 1943; and the uprising that closed Sobibor on 14 October 1943; as well as the one of the crematorium IV *Sonderkommando* at Auschwitz on 7 October 1944. According to Yehuda Bauer, armed opposition occurred in 24 ghettos in central and western Poland, and thousands of Jews joined the Resistance fighters. In comparison, 3,300,000 of 5,700,000 Soviet prisoners of war died in the course of their imprisonment without any noticeable revolt before the end of the war, although the men were of the right age and in the right physical condition to fight.[71] It is true that in Auschwitz, no revolt is known to have occurred after an internal selection. The non-Jewish *musulmen*, however, behaved no differently from the Jews; the Jews were simply selected more often for the crematorium.[72]

A Wind of Improvement in Auschwitz

From late 1942 to early 1943, some changes were felt in the organization of inmates' labour. For instance, on 26 October 1943, Pohl sent a secret letter to all the camp's commanders, ordering them to improve inmates' conditions in order to increase their profitability: to feed and dress them properly, to use all 'natural' means at their disposal to improve their health, to spare them all superfluous efforts, and to distribute work bonuses. The great economist of the Reich distributed recipes on how to better peel and conserve potatoes, which were far too often rotten. This circular had no effect in Auschwitz, unless the shortening of *Appells*[73] could be seen as a reaction. Nevertheless, even before the reform of the camp, initiated in

---

71. Marrus, *L'Holocauste dans l'Histoire*, p. 195.
72. See Langbein, *Résistance*, p. 338 ff.
73. Czech, *Kalendarium*, pp. 478 and 639.

November 1943 by its second commander, Arthur Liebehenschel, a change of attitude occurred which led to greater respect for the labour force, and which could be summarized in the ironic slogan that circulated: 'What used to be crematorium, is now sanatorium.' This new attitude coincided, of course, with the German reversal on the Eastern Front and the increased need for labour in the arms industry. However, only:

> ... the increase in horrors which oppressed inmates day after day and which was difficult to face in the first few years, slowly disappeared. What was left was the 'normal' harshness of living ... in conditions that were still inhuman, even if they were no longer aggravated by devilish inventions of the mind.[74]

However, in Auschwitz, and for Jews in particular, the change was felt less than elsewhere. Improvement affected, almost exclusively, non-Jewish inmates (for example, the authorisation to receive parcels from October 1942), although at the time, Jews were in the majority in Auschwitz. Worse, even, the internal selections of the Jews in the camp and HKB didn't completely stop until gassing stopped, after the last selection at the ramp on 3 November 1944. Piper thinks that, in Auschwitz, the change of attitude towards inmates was more theoretical than real.[75] For them, the aim clearly remained elimination through work; the worker was not intended to survive the process. Höss himself concluded:

> If, in Auschwitz, Jews had been taken straight to the gas chambers, they would have been spared a lot of suffering. They would have died fast, without having accomplished anything important, and often without having done anything for the country's war effort.[76]

---

74. Kogon, *L'État SS*, pp. 306–7.
75. Piper, *Arbeitseinsatz*, pp. 15 and 231.
76. Höss, *Kommandant in Auschwitz*, p. 205.

SS Doctor Bruno Weber, Director of the Hygiene Institute

The Hygiene Institute constituted, in Auschwitz, a kind of extraterritorial zone: everything in it was answerable to the medical administration of the SS State and not to the camp management. Paradoxically – although this was due partly to the personalities of the three doctors in charge – no criminal experiments *per se* were ever performed there.

Its director, Bruno Nikolaus Weber, born in 1915, was a specialist in microbiology, and was eager to develop his institute, above all in the research of serology. He himself made observations on the noma of gypsy children, an ulcerating, degenerative disease whose infectious agent he tried to discover post-mortem. However, he never offered an improved diet, which could have saved those children.[77] He collaborated in 'brain-washing' experiments performed on Polish inmates, which led to the death of two human guinea pigs. He proceeded with serum injections of different types to study malignant clotting; blood samples were sometimes taken from the carotid, and sometimes 700–1,000 cc. of blood was taken in one go from a patient already weakened by hunger.[78] As the animal meat intended for cultures disappeared, stolen by the SS, the doctors, Weber and Kitt, took samples of human flesh from executed inmates whom they had palpated before the executions.[79] Like all Auschwitz doctors – except Münch – Weber selected deportees as they alighted from the trains. According to Langbein, he executed orders to the letter, unthinkingly, without excessive zeal, but also without looking for ways to help the inmates.[80]

The day he welcomed his future assistant, Münch, he showed him the chimneys of Birkenau through the window, saying, 'almost ironically', that 'The normal production of this machine [is] 1,000 men per 24 hours', adding, however, that the institute was totally autonomous and had no link with the

---

77. Lifton, *Les Médecins nazis*, p. 333.
78. Ibid., p. 325.
79. Broad, in *Auschwitz in den Augen der SS*, p. 111; Müller, *Trois ans*, p. 83.
80. Langbein, *Menschen in Auschwitz*, p. 398.

extermination machine, and that this state of affairs allowed them to keep their hands clean.[81] Münch admired and defended Weber,[82] and Lifton himself thought that the Auschwitz Hygiene Institute would not have been what it was without the rather humanitarian attitude of its chief. Weber also seemed to have intervened to save the French female doctor, Adélaïde Hautval, a figure with one of the highest moral codes in the concentration camp environment.[83] Weber was not indicted after the war, and died at home in 1956.

The Exception: Doctor Hans Münch

SS-Untersturmführer Hans Münch was probably the most upright figure of all the concentration camp medical staff: 'A human being in SS uniform'.[84] Born in Bavaria in 1911, he was not raised with the nationalistic ideology, and his mother was a fervent anti-Nazi. In 1939, he nonetheless wished to enlist for his country. As a young doctor, he won a chemistry competition, and through it, obtained the official support of the Nazi party. When he had to choose in which unit to serve, he opted for the SS, considered the most prestigious corps of the *Wehrmacht*. His career was well launched. He dealt with bacteriology and was sent to one of the Hygiene Institutes that the Waffen-SS maintained in the camps.

In this way, he arrived in Auschwitz in the middle of 1943, accompanied by his wife – whom Weber very soon sent home. Münch accepted the position, but refused, out of personal conviction, to perform any act contrary to medical ethics. Alone among all the SS doctors sent to serve in Auschwitz, he categorically refused to perform selections of the convoys at the ramp.[85] Weber understood him and covered for him until the summer of 1944. With the influx of Hungarian-Jewish convoys, Münch

---

81. Lifton, *Les Médecins nazis*, p. 341.
82. Ibid., p. 355.
83. Langbein, *Menschen in Auschwitz*, p. 265. A. Hautval is the author of the excellent work *Médecin et crimes contre l'Humanité: Témoignage* (Paris: Actes Sud, 1991).
84. Lifton, *Les Médecins nazis*, p. 339.
85. Langbein, *Menschen in Auschwitz*, p. 404.

was seconded by the then chief-doctor, Wirths, as were all the Hygiene Institute's medical staff. Münch didn't know what to do and how to resist. So he took the night train to Berlin and went to see his superior, Mrugowsky. According to Münch himself, Mrugowsky expressed horror at what was happening in Auschwitz[86] and called on his colleague, Wirths, to sort things out. Münch was only associated with the Hygiene Institute and was under no obligation to the camp administration. He was successful and did not perform selections.

Hans Münch was indicted in 1947 during the trial in Krakow of the 'Auschwitz staff'. He obtained numerous testimonies in his favour from survivors, and was the only accused to be acquitted. He returned to Bavaria to work as a general doctor. In a series of talks with historian R.J. Lifton,[87] he revealed a personality that was both strong and ambiguous. He never turned his back on his old colleagues, praising Mengele, for instance. He discussed the psychological pressure that affected all those in charge in Auschwitz. According to him, they were all plagued by doubts and either drowned their remorse in alcohol, or became overzealous in their work.

The Fight against Typhus

In autumn 1941, the Germans were already researching a vaccine against typhus. In 1942, a trial station was opened in Isolation Block 46 at Buchenwald, under the management of the *SS-Obersturmführer* Dr Erwin Ding (who called himself Schuler). Mrugowsky had fought long and hard for this project. The Austrian political inmate Eugen Kogon, as Ding-Schuler's secretary, attended 24 series of trials of several vaccines, on groups of (on average) 50 inmates. The Hygiene Institute was also doing research on yellow fever, diphtheria, cholera, typhoid and paratyphoid fever, as well as on toxic materials and poisons. Sometimes, patients were inoculated intravenously with such high doses of pathogenic agents that

---

86. Lifton, *Les Médecins nazis*, p. 344.
87. He appears under the pseudonym of Ernst B. (see ibid., ch. 16).

the trial lost all scientific value, because nature never proceeds in this way. These experiments were carried out with total contempt for the human subjects, and caused many deaths, without counting the guinea-pig 'transmitters' (three to five times a month) who were voluntarily infected so that the original typhus virus would preserve its full virulence.[88]

On 7 February 1943, the:

> ... wise men of the Weigl Institute of Lemberg [Lvov] ... arrived in Auschwitz, including the doctor and microbiologist Dr Ludwik Fleck,[89] Dr Jakob Seeman, Dr Bernard Umschweif and Dr Oswiej Abramowicz. With their wives and children, they were housed in Block 20 of the HKB of the main camp, and had to work in the newly created SS Hygiene Institute, which was temporarily in Block 10 of the main camp.[90]

The wives, Anna Seeman, Natalia Umschweif and Ernesztyna Fleck, were duly registered and also tattooed. Mrs Fleck and Mrs Umschweif were trained biologists.[91] Fleck himself would not stay long in Auschwitz. In August 1943, Ding-Schuler requested from the WVHA his transfer to Buchenwald, where he installed, in Block 50, a section of the Hygiene Institute for the study of typhus and viruses.[92] An atypical vaccine was being prepared following the procedure of Professor Giroud from Paris, using mice and rabbit lungs. This *kommando* gathered the best specialists of the camp: doctors, bacteriologists, serologists and chemists, and was named by Ding-Schuler himself *'Ultimum refugium judaeorum'* [The last refuge of the Jews].[93]

---

88. Kogon, *L'État SS*, p. 193 ff.
89. Fleck survived the deportation, wrote his memoirs and pursued his scientific career in the USA (see R.S. Cohen and T. Schnelle (eds), *Cognition and Fact: Materials on Ludwik Fleck* (Boston: D. Reidel Publishing Company, 1986)).
90. See Czech, *Kalendarium*, p. 407. On 11 February, they received the numbers 100,965 to 100,969. The child Ryszard Fleck got the number 100,966; the child Karol Umschweif, the number 100,796; and the child Bronek Seeman, the number 103,797.
91. *Die Auschwitz-Hefte*, Vol. 1, p. 215.
92. Kogon, *L'État SS*, p. 198 ff.

Like the Rajsko Institute, this Block enjoyed a kind of extraterritoriality and offered quite exceptional living conditions, namely food supplements, fat and sugar, leftovers from rabbits cooked at 120°. The vaccine produced there was of excellent quality: no inmate vaccinated from that stock became infected with the disease. Unknown to Ding-Schuler, they kept aside a good portion for the inmates particularly exposed (all the inmate-officials of Buchenwald were vaccinated from 1944), and a placebo was produced in large quantities for the SS. In Auschwitz, some inmates were vaccinated.[94]

The Hygiene Institute of Rajsko

The *Hygiene-Institut der Waffen-SS*, an institution of the Nazi State with its main office in Berlin – at Zehlendorf 6, Spanische Allee 10 – was the equivalent of a sanitary service for the army: for the prevention of epidemics, development of vaccines, laboratory analyses for the SS, especially in the camps. It was run by Dr Yoachim Mrugowsky, who carried the title of *Oberster Hygieniker* [Head Hygienist], and was sentenced at the doctors' trial at Nuremberg and hanged on 30 August 1947. He was held responsible for: lethal experiments, generally following the request of pharmaceutical firms, performed on criminals, homosexuals and political inmates; injecting typhus in Buchenwald; causing gas oedemas; causing infectious diseases in Ravensbrück; and experimenting with poisoned bullets in Sachsenhausen.[95] The Hygiene Institute of Berlin also stocked boxes of Zyklon B intended for the SS to use against vermin. Auschwitz ordered at least ten times more than normal, which was bound to awaken suspicion.[96]

In Auschwitz, the institute with the name *Hygiene-Insitut der Waffen-SS und Polizei Süd-Ost* was founded at the beginning of 1943 in Block 10, near Clauberg's gynaecological unit, then

93. Kirmann, in Waitz and Klein, *Témoignages strasbourgeois*, pp. 115–18.
94. Haffner, *Aspects pathologiques*, p. 38.
95. Lifton, *Les Médecins nazis*, p. 326.
96. Ibid., p. 196.

moved to Rajsko during May 1943, to one of the large buildings in the middle of a triangular block of land surrounded by barbed wires and watchtowers with views in three directions. Two floors were taken over and converted. Next to it was a villa with the SS offices, a library,[97] and the living quarters of Weber and Münch. In Block 10, meaningless experiments continued to be performed. W.B., André Lettich, Marc Klein and Mieczyslaw Kieta recalled precisely the layout of the Rajsko Institute. The ground floor comprised one very large bacteriology lab, with labs for biology, histology, pathological anatomy, parasitology and water analyses, as well as a kitchen for growing cultures. On the first floor was a chemistry lab which ran the whole length of the building, a lab for research into infectious diseases and detection of syphilis (Wassermann tests) run by Fleck, and later, after he left, by his wife, and another lab where the SS doctors Weber and Delmotte worked. The second floor contained the serology lab where W.B. worked, a lab for research on blood groups, and a tailor's workshop. Finally, the annexed buildings housed the bursar's office, a meteorology lab, and an animal house for lab animals.[98] Famous doctors worked in these labs: Professor Tomasek of Brno, a student of Calmette and Roux; Professor Lewin, assistant to Baudouin, a well-known researcher in France; Professors Jakubski and Slebodzinski from Posnan; Professor Mansfeld from Pecs; Professor Levy-Coblenz from Paris; and many others, some of whom were arrested for the specific purpose of giving the institute[99] scientific recognition. The histologists examined samples from dogs, sausages and plants in the neighbouring *Pflanzenzucht*, but not human material.[100]

The building was destroyed at the end of the war, but its archives were not burned by the SS (who perhaps intended to use them to clear themselves) and have been preserved in their entirety at the Auschwitz museum.

---

97. *Die Auschwitz-Hefte*, Vol. 1, pp. 213–16.
98. Ibid., pp. 216–17.
99. Czech, in *Contribution à l'histoire du KL Auschwitz*, Vol. 2, pp. 48–9.
100. Lettich, *Trente-quatre mois*, p. 32 ff.; Waitz and Klein, *Témoignages strasbourgeois*, p. 447 ff.

The Horticulture Kommandos of Rajsko

The horticulture centre of Rajsko – born from the 1941 plans of Himmler, who wanted to transform the Auschwitz domain into a model of agricultural exploitation – was run by *SS-Obersturmbannführer* Joachim Caesar. He was born in 1901, had a PhD in agronomy, and was chief of agriculture in Auschwitz. He employed two women's *kommandos*, the *Gärtnerei* for agricultural work and the *Pflanzenzucht* for biological and chemical research. According to Louise Alcan, the *Gärtnerei* women were considered the most important battalion; about 250 went through it.[101] They grew *taraxacum kok-saghyz*, the only rubber plant that could be cultivated in Europe, which was supposed to replace South American latex. (England and Sweden did similar trials during the war.)

The *Pflanzenzucht* employed agronomists, biologists and chemists, all highly qualified; 150 women went through this *kommando*, which was comprised of 25 women at any one time. The survivors testified that Caesar treated 'his' women inmates correctly and humanely, and protected them from typhus in reserved Blocks. This *kommando* contained many French Resistance women fighters, at least 17 in the month of August 1943, and several survived. They included Berta Falk, who wrote her doctoral thesis on Caesar's second wife, who was herself a *kommando* chief. Berta also secretly wrote a novel entitled *July 44* (in which she describes the liberation of Paris[102]) and Louise Alcan and Charlotte Delbo.[103] For the women of Birkenau, to be sent to Rajsko represented 'the most extraordinary luck of all in camp life'.[104] The women were housed on the site from 13 June 1943:[105] two Blocks for living quarters, one for work, and one infirmary with eight beds. The contrast with Birkenau seemed to Louise Alcan 'monstrous, incomprehensible': the *kapos* and the SS were lenient, the *Appell* lasted five

---

101. L. Alcan, *Sans armes et sans bagages* (Limoges: Les imprimés d'art, 1947).
102. Czech, *Kalendarium*, p. 813.
103. Wieviorka, *Déportation et génocide*, p. 246.
104. Zywuldak, *Tanz, Mädchen*, p. 214.
105. Czech, *Kalendarium*, p. 519.

minutes, and food was abundant – crops from the garden, which also produced vegetables. The women slept in night-dresses in real beds. They had to be properly dressed: Louise Alcan had first to 'buy' a dress in Birkenau with her bread rations. They were allowed to read, write and receive parcels.[106]

At the *Pflanzenzucht*, Louise Alcan performed a function similar to that of W.B. at the serology section: she had to count the grains of the *kok-saghyz* dandelion to determine the amount of latex it contained. She and her comrades counted some and threw the rest on the ground: 'I understand now what the work in Rajsko was all about: to watch those who watch us, so that they shouldn't watch us.'[107] The SS wanted, first of all, to create the right impression; then, that the 'mass of deportees glued to test tubes, to microscopes, to the selection of grains, make a positive impression on important visitors: they had neither the time nor the competence to review the experiments'.[108]

The Four Large Crematoria of Birkenau

By mid-August 1942, the SS had approved and installed four large crematoria, whose basements would serve as gas chambers, being airtight and with a device to prevent ventilation. They were built on the east side of sectors BI, BII and BIII of Birkenau. At the same time, the *Bauleitung* [chief of Construction Services], *SS-Sturmbannführer* Bischoff, approved the new expansion plan of Birkenau, increasing its capacity to 200,000. In the *SS-Reichsführer* and the RSHA directives, Auschwitz-Birkenau was considered both a place for mass extermination of Jews, and a potential reserve of workers needed for the war industry. Its expansion was supposed to serve both needs. The crematoria were used to burn the corpses from the giant work camps and those gassed in the two *Bunker*s, and also served for 'special operations'. The civil

106. Alcan, *Sans armes et sans bagages*, p. 60.
107. Ibid., p. 62.
108. O. Wormser-Migot, *Quand les alliés ouvrirent les portes: Le dernier acte de la tragédie de la déportation* (Paris: Laffont, 1965), p. 115.

engineering firm, Huta of Katowice, set up the project. The ovens were ordered from the firm of Topf and Sons in Erfurt,[109] which had delivered the Buchenwald ovens, and would patent all five three-furnace crematorium ovens II and III of Birkenau, which it considered a technical innovation. Engineer Kurt Prüfer[110] was put specifically in charge of the technical supervision of Birkenau's ovens. The Nazi authorities had agreed to use the term *Leichenkeller* [morgue] in their correspondence to refer to underground gas chambers. The term *Gaskammer* [gas chamber] sometimes appeared, notably in a letter of 29 January 1943 from Construction Management;[111] evidence that it was not a secret for any of those connected with its building.

Crematorium IV was delivered on 22 March 1943, II, officially on 31 March, III, on 14 June, and V, on 4 April, but they were not yet operational. On delivery, they cost 554,500 reichsmark for each of the two large ones, and 203,000 for each of the two small ones.[112] However, by the night of 13–14 March, 1,492 Jews from the Krakow ghetto (out of a convoy of about 2,000) were gassed with six kilos of Zyklon B in the crematorium II basement and incinerated in its ovens, thus inaugurating the era of large crematoria.[113]

On 28 June 1943, the Construction Service of Auschwitz assessed, for the WVHA, the incinerator's real daily yield, which was 1,000 bodies (against the 1,400 expected) for the two large ones with five-furnace ovens, and 500 bodies (against the 786 expected) for the two small ones (an oven with eight furnaces). In addition, various failures prevented, for long periods, the installations' proper functioning.

---

109. The firm was found guilty of having profited, in large part, from the extermination of human beings in the KZ, which is not exact according to Pressac, the firm's profits being mainly due to the manufacture of shells for the Wehrmacht, and the ovens contributing to only two per cent of its turnover (see J.-C. Pressac, *Les Crématoires d'Auschwitz: La machinerie du meurtre de masse* (Paris: CNRS – Éditions, 1993), p. 124). The firm existed until 1963.
110. He would be arrested after the war by the Americans, released, and then arrested by the Soviets and sentenced to 25 years forced labour in the USSR, where he died in 1952 (Pressac, ibid.).
111. Sehn, *Konzentrationslager Oswiecim-Brzezinka*, p. 165.
112. Pressac, Crématoires, pp. 76 ff. and 120.
113. Ibid., p. 119; Czech, *Kalendarium*, p. 440.

The *Sonderkommando* of crematorium IV rebelled on 7 October 1944 and burned down the building. On 6 September, Höss had already asked Moll for a report on the total destruction and the levelling of the Auschwitz-Birkenau complex. The report was published by the Polish Resistance.[114] Crematoria II and III were dismantled in December 1944 and blown up at the time of evacuation; V being blown up last.

The End of Auschwitz

Water and electricity were cut in Auschwitz on 19 January, when the last Allied shells fell on the factories. On the 25th, the *Sicherheitsdienst* (SD) tried one last time to empty the camp, and ordered the sick Jews in the hospital to join a column; it was the last 'separate' treatment of Jews. The column of 350 inmates met some motorized SS who sent them back to the camp; however, it was too late, the front had caught up with them, and the last SS and SD escaped from Auschwitz-Birkenau in trucks.

In Monowitz, 850 of those sick and unable to walk were abandoned with 18 doctors, and they organized their survival; at least 200 of them died before liberation on 27 January.[115]

In Birkenau, before their departure, the SS had ordered the sick of the HKB to carry the corpses to crematorium V, collect precious objects for them from the warehouses, and set the dynamite in crematoria II and III, whose structures had already been dismantled. They then blew everything up. Although they had received their order to march, an SS division returned to Birkenau and killed 200 women of the BIIe camp who had tried to escape. On 21 January, a few SS and SD still patrolled and killed many inmates who were wandering in the camp or were trying to get out of it. On 26 January, at 1 a.m., their last act was to blow up crematorium V, the only one still functioning.

---

114. Czech, *Kalendarium*, p. 869.
115. Levi, *Se questo è un uomo*, p. 162 ff.

The first Russian soldier to enter the concentration complex of Auschwitz arrived at the hospital zone of Monowitz on Saturday, 27 January, at 9 a.m. He was a scout of the 100th infantry division of the 106th corps of the 60th army of the first Ukrainian Front. Three infantry divisions circled the *Lager* zone and the town of Oswiecim; they were greeted by Poles stepping out of ruins and hiding places. They fought the *Wehrmacht* at the entrance to the main camp, and the Russians lost 231 men liberating the Auschwitz-Birkenau complex.

Evacuation from Auschwitz: Forced March or Liquidation?

From April 1944, the camp population of Silesia was highly mobile. The SS were aware of the need to evacuate the camps (potential Auschwitz survivors were thus more numerous, since the number given was based on the camp population). Richard Baer, the last Auschwitz commander, had been working on evacuation plans since autumn 1944. By mid-January 1945, Himmler ordered evacuation of the camps from the Eastern Territories,[116] while Hitler continued to call for fanatical revenge, and, it is believed, ordered the liquidation of all non-evacuated prisoners (Höss recounted that, in April 1945, he was still fuming about the liberation of Buchenwald, claiming that the inmates had destroyed the Weimar because Pohl and Himmler had disobeyed his orders).

Technically, Himmler delegated authority over each camp, at the time of evacuation, to senior local representatives of the SS and the police; Himmler's SS delegate for Silesia was Heinrich Schmauser:[117] on 20 January, he ordered Kraus, a delegate of the RSHA in Auschwitz, to liquidate all inmates unable to walk.[118] However, another contradictory order from the Stutthof/Danzig commander, Hoppe, stipulated that, following orders from above, inmates sick or unable to walk should be left behind in the camp. On the one hand, Himmler,

---

116. Höss, *Kommandant in Auschwitz*, p. 218 n. 1.
117. Ibid., p. 221 n. 1.
118. A preserved document, see Czech, *Kalendarium*, p. 979.

trying to stand in the Führer's place and sign a separate peace agreement, consented *in extremis* that some camps, namely Ravensbrück and Bergen-Belsen, should be delivered to the Allies; on the other hand, orders were given from the hard line of the RSHA (Eichmann, Müller and Kaltenbrunner) to blow up all the camps and unevacuated prisons with their occupants.[119] The delegation of power added to the chaos during the collapse and explains the differences in handling of the crisis.

In some camps in Silesia (including the main camp of Auschwitz), the sick were abandoned; elsewhere, they were liquidated. In the annexed camps of Auschwitz, evacuation took place and, at the same time, mass executions and liquidation of the sick, which in some places cost the lives of half the inmates. For instance, in Gleiwitz IV, an SS and a member of the Todt organisation set fire to the infirmary where 57 sick and exhausted inmates were locked up. Those who tried to jump out of the windows were shot; two survived to testify. In Fürstengrube, 250 inmates who stayed behind were liquidated in two batches: first, those who could still walk, and then the bedridden; 14 survived.

Höss was still chief inspector of the RSHA and moved around the uninvaded part of the Reich. He provided a striking picture of the chaos and lack of preparation for the death marches: the columns evacuated from east Silesia wandered almost randomly towards the west, having received the order to go to Gross-Rosen in German Silesia, but without the means to reach there.[120] Some managed to escape, but many died. According to Broszat, during those death marches, at least one third of the 714,211 evacuees from all the camps under the administration of the WVHA[121] died. In the ensuing chaos, columns of unregistered inmates, who had arrived very late, moved about: Jewish workers from Vienna and Budapest, and Russian prisoners of war.

119. Bauer, 'The Death-Marches, January–May 1945', pp. 494–5.
120. Höss, *Kommandant in Auschwitz*, pp. 218–22.
121. Marrus, *L'Holocauste dans l'Histoire*, p. 268.

The Gross-Rosen Concentration Camp

Gross-Rosen in Silesia[122] was a disciplinarian camp on the eastern boundaries of the First Reich, near the small town of the same name (Rogosnica in Polish), south of the Oder, about 60 kilometres southwest of Breslau/Wroclaw. It was a region populated by Germans in the far reaches of Poland.

A simple outpost of Sachsenhausen in May 1940, Gross-Rosen became an autonomous camp in autumn 1941. Its inmates were mainly Poles, but between 2,000 and 3,000 Frenchmen subject to NN [*Nacht und Nebel*: 'at dead of night'] treatment, Belgians and Dutch ended up there. Built on the slope of a fairly steep hill, its main site was a stone quarry, and commanded some hundred outdoor *kommandos*. The crematorium, built in 1941, was considered insufficient, and was replaced in 1943 by a four-furnace oven from Topf and Sons. The camp had the reputation of being one of the toughest in the concentration camp system, even during the last year of the war. Two hundred thousand inmates passed through the camp, of whom 40,000 died there, in addition to the liquidations in January–February 1945.

The camp was run by criminals: between 1940 and 1943, 90 per cent of the inmate-officials, who were mainly Germans and Poles, wore green triangles; and between 1943 and 1945, the figure was 75 per cent. 'Nowhere else did I see individual murders performed as efficiently as in Gross-Rosen', writes Marc Klein.[123] The *Lagerführer*, Anton Thumann, gave no power to the German political inmates, which is what prevented the camp from evolving like Sachsenhausen or Buchenwald. Those hungry for power tried to outdo each other in their murderous

---

122. For information on Gross-Rosen, a camp not much documented, see Ruby, *Livre de la déportation*, p. 152 ff.; Manson, *Leçon de ténèbres*, p. 176 ff.; K.G. Feig, *Hitler's Death Camps: The Sanity of Madness* (New York/London: Holmes & Meier, 1979), p. 204 ff.; a monograph in Polish by M. Moldawa, *Gross-Rosen: Oboz koncentracyjni na Slasku*; I. Sprenger, '"Der Judenblock bleibt stehen": Jüdische Häftlinge in der ersten Kriegshälfte im Konzentrationslager Gross-Rosen in Schlesien', *Menora*, 5 (1994), pp. 415–33; I. Sprenger, '"Erbarmungsloses Schweigen": Bevölkerung und Konzentrationslager in Gross-Rosen (Niederschlesien)', *Die Alte Stadt*, 20 (1993), pp. 377–80. See also the website of Gross-Rosen Museum: www.region-walbrzych.org.pl/grosrosen.
123. Klein, in Waitz and Klein, *Témoignages strasbourgeois*, p. 506.

activity in order to be noticed by the SS.[124] There was almost no Resistance movement in Gross-Rosen.[125] An active system of denunciation functioned in the camp.[126] The sick were assassinated by lethal injections in the infirmary.[127]

Gross-Rosen was entirely evacuated in February–March 1945 and liberated by the Russians on 5 May.

The Buchenwald Camp

Founded on 19 July 1937, the *Schutzhaftlager* [disciplinarian camp] of Buchenwald[128] first held criminals, German political prisoners and Jehovah's Witnesses [*Bibelforscher*]. The number of inmates didn't go above 10,000 until 1943.

Compelled to work as forced labour in the neighbouring quarry, the prisoners were subjected to extortion, arbitrary abuse, cold, and scarcity of water. When the war broke out, the arms manufacturers, Deutsche Ausrüstungs-Werke (DAW) and Gustloff, set themselves up nearby to exploit the imprisoned labour force. Starting in 1943, the camp contained and commanded over 70 camps and outdoor *kommandos*, including the underground factory of Dora in Nordhausen, where V2 rockets were manufactured. In some of these sub-camps, the inmates' survival rate was almost zero.

In 1941, Hermann Pister succeeded Karl-Otto Koch, a corrupt tyrant, as SS commander of Buchenwald. About 250,000 prisoners were interned between 1937 and 1945, of whom 56,000 died (34,375 registered deaths, others were randomly executed or died during transport). 'Special' political prisoners, notably the former Council President Léon Blum, were detained in a villa of the SS quarters.

At the end of 1941, internal power was taken over entirely by the political prisoners, dominated by the German

---

124. Langbein, *Résistance*, pp. 59 and 102–3.
125. See the testimony of the Belgian philologist, Léon Halkin, cited in Langbein, ibid., p. 206.
126. Ibid., p. 262.
127. Klein, in Waitz and Klein, *Témoignages strasbourgeois*.
128. For the story of Buchenwald, see Kogon, *L'État SS*.

communists; the Resistance organization was strong and struc-
tured.[129] It exercised its power particularly in the hospital and in
the *Arbeitsstatistik* [labour office]. It had the power to assign
inmates to good, bad or deplorable *kommandos*. The role of
some of the leaders of that organization was re-examined after
the war: on the French side, essentially the communist Marcel
Paul,[130] on the German side, the powerful *kapos* of the Revier,
Ernst Busse and Walter Bartel.[131] The Resistance never denied
that it had done its utmost to preserve the most important
political inmates, which automatically involved sacrificing
others. However, important witnesses – themselves Resistance
fighters like Kogon or Langbein – refuted these accusations,
saying that the Resistance had never aimed at anything other
than the good of the whole community of camp inmates,
whenever possible.[132]

The Unknown Musician of Buchenwald

The work of Joza Karas, *La Musique à Terezin*, gives us a good
idea of the intense musical life and the flamboyant culture that
flourished, against all odds, in the camp-ghetto of
Theresienstadt (where 17,000 Jews survived out of 140,000
inmates).

After the incidence of 'family camps' at Birkenau, where
some 1,000 Jews of Theresienstadt were detained in atypical
conditions and then almost all of them gassed (the last ones on
11 July 1944), a large extermination operation sent 18,402
Jewish men, women and children in 11 convoys to Auschwitz-
Birkenau from Theresienstadt between 28 September and 28
October 1944.[133] The proportion of those who had been selected
for work and sent to external camps, like Golleschau, Gleiwitz
I and Fürstengrube, is estimated at 15 per cent; the others were

129. See Langbein, *Résistance*, pp. 98, 107–14 and 209–10.
130. Wieviorka, *Déportation et génocide*, pp. 216–17.
131. Overesch, *Buchenwald und die DDR*, pp. 215 ff. and 220–5.
132. Langbein, *Résistance*, p. 255.
133. Czech, *Kalendarium*, p. 889 ff.

gassed on arrival. According to H.G. Adler, from those 11 convoys, 1,259 survived.[134]

Who could the unknown man who died next to Willy on the night of 10 February 1945 in Buchenwald have been? Among the musician-composers interned in Theresienstadt and never seen again after their deportation to Auschwitz in October 1944, the following should be mentioned: Pavel Haas (born in 1899, student of Janacek); Hans Krása (born in 1899, author of the opera for children, *Brundibar*, created in Theresienstadt); Bernard Kaff (born in 1905, a pianist); Egon Ledec (born in 1899, a violinist in the Czech Philharmonic); Rafaël Schächter (born in 1905, orchestra and choir conductor, active organiser of operas in Theresienstadt); Carlo S. Taube (born in 1897, pianist, composer, interpreter of light music); and Viktor Ullman (born in 1898, student of Schönberg, already a celebrity at the time). These men were all more than 39 years old in 1944, and Taube and Ullman were over 45, so their chances of passing the selection at the ramp were slim. According to the few surviving witnesses, Haas, Krása, Ledec, Schächter and Ullman disappeared immediately after they got off the trains. One other possible hypothesis exists: the unknown musician could have been Gideon Klein (native of Prague, however, and not of Vienna). He was 'the soul of the musical life in Terezin',[135] born in 1919 and thus aged only 26, a virtuoso pianist and talented composer, interned in Theresienstadt in December 1941, probably deported to Auschwitz in the convoy of 18 October 1944, and probably sent to Fürstengrube on 21 October with a number between B 13,307 and B 13,479, and recorded as dead there on 27 January 1945. However, Fürstengrube was evacuated on 19 January for Gleiwitz II, where the survivors joined the evacuees from Monowitz. It is possible that Gideon Klein did not die in Fürstengrube, that he survived the evacuation of Gleiwitz II and found himself in Buchenwald, in a convoy on

---

134. See H.G. Adler, *Theresienstadt, 1941–1945: Das Antlitz einer Zwangsgemeinschaft*, 2nd edn (Tübingen: Mohr, 1960).
135. See J. Karas, *La Musique à Terezin, 1941–1945* (Paris: Gallimard, 1993), pp. 60 and 82–6.

26 January, which regrouped 3,987 inmates, mainly from Monowitz, one of which was registered on 10 February.

We sincerely wish, with this note, to pay final homage to the musician who died on that night, no matter what his name.

The Jews in Buchenwald

The history of the Jews in Buchenwald cannot be written in one chapter. The first Jews arrived in June 1938 and were lodged in a separate corner of the camp in inhuman conditions. Most of them died, some were released, and about 20 survived until 1945.

In September 1938, 2,000 Jews arrived from Dachau, mainly Austrians apprehended after the *Anschluss*, including active anti-fascists. After 9 November 1938 (*Kristallnacht*), German Jews were interned *en masse* in Buchenwald as part of 'Operation Rath': between 9,845 and 12,000 people, according to available sources. They were incredibly ill-treated: beaten and abused, crowded into barracks without latrines or mattresses. Sixty-eight of them went crazy and were locked up in a cage, then strangled in the *Bunker* by SS Sommer; over 600 died. However, most of them – among them, Bruno Bettelheim – were released after a few weeks, on condition that their goods be confiscated; fortunes were seized by the Nazis. The corruption was so bad that Commander Koch gave in and handed the camp's internal administration over to the political prisoners.

After the invasion of Poland, in September 1939, 2,500 Viennese, stateless and Polish Jews arrived, the majority old people and students, who were left to die in the first of the 'Small Camps' made up of tents next to the *Appell* square. Those who didn't die from abuse in the quarry were shot. On 9 November 1939, the day after the attack planned against Hitler at the Bürgerbraü pub in Munich, the seven Blocks of Jews in Buchenwald paid a heavy price: execution of prisoners and deprival of food.

In February 1941, 400 young Dutch Jews arrived. They were then transported to Mauthausen where all except one died.

Buchenwald then became a more secure place for inmates, and the horrors more difficult to perpetrate; Mauthausen took over. In spring 1942, in carrying out the '14f13 programme', an offshoot of the euthanasia programme, 468 Jewish invalids were taken to Bernburg to be gassed on the orders of the SS doctor Waldemar Hoven. Other Jews were the first victims of typhus experiments performed in Block 46, before racial doctrines forbade the manufacture of serum from Jewish blood.

From October 1942 to the summer of 1943, all the Jews of Buchenwald, except 200, were taken to Auschwitz. Then the transports were reversed. From May 1944 onwards, after the invasion of Hungary, over 10,000 Hungarian Jews, selected at Auschwitz for work, flocked to Buchenwald[136] and were thrown into external camps and *kommandos*. Invalids were often transported back to Auschwitz to be exterminated. Finally, in January 1945, inmates from Silesia who had survived the death marches began flowing in. Buchenwald registered 24,955 entries between Christmas 1944 and 30 March 1945, 11,000 to 15,000 of them Jews.[137] The mortality rate among the Jews was terrifying. On 11 April 1945, after the last evacuations of Buchenwald, 6,000 Jews remained in the camp.[138] On the foundations of Block 22, a monument was erected in their memory.

The Small Camp

There were two successive 'Small Camps' in Buchenwald.[139] The first one existed from 1939 to mid-January 1940. The second one, a quarantine or transit camp for deportees from all the conquered countries, was set up in 1942 below the last row of Blocks of the 'Large Camp'. From 1944 until liberation, 10,000 prisoners passed through that camp, many of them in transit. From the end of 1944, some 20,000 prisoners remained there

---

136. Hilberg, *La Destruction*, p. 851.
137. Hackett, *The Buchenwald Report*, p. 245.
138. Kogon, *L'État SS*, pp. 224–34.
139. Ibid., pp. 203–5.

permanently. There was constant hunger, although this was not the case in the Large Camp. Overpopulation, the inmates' appalling sanitary conditions and excrement turned the camp into an indescribable hell and a real death trap within the labour camp. The inmates' organization performed some sanitary work (drainage, whitewashing) without interference from the SS, who didn't care what they did. The Small Camp comprised 17 Blocks (numbers 51–67), which were, like in Birkenau, *Wehrmacht* stables without windows or sanitary equipment, with a collective latrine at the centre. The barracks, built for 400 people, housed 1,500 at a time. A report compiled by the American Commission for War and Displaced Persons gives all the details: 16 inmates shared one bunk of 3.6 metres by 3.9 metres; 60 centimetres separated one level of bunks from the next; the cubage per inmate was one eighteenth of the sanitary minimum in the American Army.[140] Jakob Rüdniger, who became *Lagerältester* of Block 53, on 11 March 1944, confirmed that the number of men in his Block jumped from 450 to 1,800, with no running water or sewerage available (inmates would steal the necessary items from the DAW to set up a rudimentary water station), no benches, no tables, no blankets, no towels, no soap; clothes were insufficient, under-wear and socks non-existent.[141]

The Small Camp was a 'place for natural selection where an enormous percentage of newcomers succumbed to the abuses during their first month',[142] an 'enterprise of voluntary pauperi-zation',[143] 'a world apart, carefully isolated where you ate less and died more, and you were Jewish, but you didn't work there'.[144] Rebels and 'worthless' inmates, such as Jews, were locked up there. It was a place of 'musulmanization': a cesspool where exhausted transports were brought, and a reserve of

---

140. Overesch, *Buchenwald und die DDR*, p. 101.
141. Hackett, *The Buchenwald Report*, p. 318.
142. G. Straka, in Waitz and Klein, *Témoignages strasbourgeois*, p. 91.
143. W. Sofosky, *L'Organisation de la terreur: Les camps de concentration* (Paris: Calmann-Lévy, 1995), p. 73.
144. Steinberg, *Chroniques*, p. 75.

manpower sacrificed to the bad transports.[145] The inmates were kicked out of their Block four times a day, once for the Appell.[146] Block 56 housed many invalids: the French sociologist Maurice Halbwachs died there in March 1945.[147] Paul Steinberg and Georges Wellers stayed in Block 57, Marc Klein in 58. Blocks 62 and 63 were known as Quarantine Blocks for the Jews and the gypsies who arrived from the horrendous outdoor *kommandos*. Blocks 65, 66 and 67 were built after January 1945, at the initiative, according to Kogon, of the political organization and not the SS, who were totally indifferent. This other world was so separate that it didn't even share in the liberation of Buchenwald, nor in the first roll call of the liberated men that took place the next day; its exits remained closed and guarded.

The Final Evacuations from Buchenwald

The evacuation of Buchenwald, from 5 to 10 April 1945, emptied the camp of 26,000 inmates.[148] On 3 April, in the movie theatre, *Kommandant* Pister declared that he had been given the assignment of handing the camp over to the Allies in good condition and without trouble. On 4 April at 4 a.m., the Jews were called to gather at the *Appell* square. Nobody came. The Resistance organization had called for disobedience. At 6 a.m., the SS tried, Block by Block, to sort the Jews from the non-Jews. They were not very successful, because files of the Jews had been destroyed (according to Heymann, by the Resistance organization, according to Kogon, by the bombings), and the *Blockälteste* resisted. Pister then asked the *Lagerältester*, Hans Eiden, why the Jews were hiding; Eiden answered that they

---

145. Report from American officers Fleck and Tenenbaum, in Overesch, *Buchenwald und die DDR*, p. 175. They warn the Allies: the communist organization favours this inhuman discrimination, and even the liberators may be tempted to follow in their footsteps.
146. Wellers, *Un Juif sous Vichy*, p. 261.
147. See the moving story of his death in Semprun, *L'Écriture ou la vie*, p. 52.
148. Bauer, 'The Death-Marches, January–May 1945', p. 505. The reconstruction that we are attempting here is based on Kogon (*L'État SS* and *The Buchenwald Report*), on the long-time inmate-officials Stefan Heymann and Jakob Rüdniger (*The Buchenwald Report*), and on Overesch (ibid.).

were afraid of being killed. The commander then claimed that they were going to be sent safely to Theresienstadt and handed over to the Red Cross.[149]

On 5 April, at the morning *Appell*, the SS tried to separate the Jews from the other inmates; some obeyed and were taken to the ruined site of the DAW. The Resistance organization wondered what it was all about. The order was to remain inside the camp no matter what, and to resist by armed force if necessary; they had a few weapons. Would they have to comply with the evacuation orders? And when? Which inmates would have to be sacrificed and be the first to leave? Heymann admitted that the International Committee had decided, then and there, to evacuate those who would have no role to play in the final rebellion, 'and in particular those who could turn against us': a very ambiguous sentence.[150] Finally, the inmates of the Large Camp were held back and the inmates from the Small Camp – nearly all of them Jews – were selected for the transports.

Commander Pister acted with indolence: he had been encouraged by the inmates' administration to be more lax about regulations in exchange for possible favourable testimonies. Heavily armed and helped by bloodthirsty *kapos*, the SS rounded up 1,500 Jews. Other Jews were added, mainly Hungarians, who had come from the annexed camp of Ohrdruf. (That camp numbered 12,000 inmates and a bloody evacuation took place there on 2 April: over 1,500 political prisoners and common criminals were massacred, but not the Jews, because Himmler had given the order to spare them.) On 6 April, 3,105 Jews of those gathered the night before left on foot for Weimar; the weaker ones were shot almost immediately. At the same time, 1,500 prisoners of the Ohrdruf convoy left for Leitmerice in Bohemia. The *Lagerschutz* managed to bring some of the Jews, still parked at the DAW, back inside the camp. Although the Resistance had planned over 10,000 departures for 7 April, only 4,500 left. The Resistance decided then to

---

149. At that time, Himmler really tried to 'sell' a few Jews; see Bauer, *Juifs à vendre?*, pp. 147 ff. and 327 ff.
150. *The Buchenwald Report*, p. 327.

smuggle out an agent (Kogon was the agent chosen, camouflaged in a box of hospital supplies), with the assignment of
sending Commander Pister a missive, falsely signed by an
Allied officer, urging him to immediately stop the evacuation of
Buchenwald to avoid repeating the Ohrdruf tragedy. On 8
April, after the *Appells* remained ineffectual – the *Lagerältester*
arguing that the inmates had to eat before leaving – the SS
emptied the Blocks of the Large Camp and forced 4,880
inmates to leave for Dachau. The letter from pseudo-comman-
der McLeod arrived in the meantime and further weakened
Pister's resolve, giving the inmates precious time. On 9 April,
4,800 inmates left for Flossenbürg, accompanied by an SS dog-
patrol. On 10 April, under ever-nearing Allied air raids (one
American plane had dropped a parcel in the camp), the
commander tried desperately to evacuate the whole camp, and
sent out a transport of Russian, Czech and Polish prisoners
totalling about 5,000 men. Possessing a few hidden weapons,
they managed to join the American troops quickly enough. On
the night of 10/11 April, the SS prepared to run away, requisitioning civilian clothing from their victims.

The 21,400 inmates who were left in the camp, 900 of them
children and adolescents, including Elie Wiesel, were liberated
the next day. However, the fate of those who had been evacuated was terrible. Some who had left on foot managed to
escape. But those who had been boarded into locked wagons
got lost, without food, water or care, in the chaos of defeat. A
train of 4,000 prisoners was found in Dachau with 2,000 dead.
The convoys on their way to Flossenbürg, a total of 9,000
inmates (some of whom escaped), arrived at their destination
with only 2,000 prisoners alive.[151]

---

151. Bauer, 'The Death-Marches, January–May 1945', p. 505.

The Liberation of Buchenwald

On 11 April 1945,[152] towards 10:15 a.m. during a full air raid alert, Commander Pister invited the *Lagerältester*, Eiden, to formally hand the camp over to him, while at the same time swearing him to secrecy until the arrival of the Americans. At 11:45 a.m., the siren sounded a special tune, announcing the imminent arrival of the enemy. The camp could no longer be evacuated, but the remaining inmates didn't know whether they would be liquidated or liberated. Pister had ordered the air commander of the area, Staupendahl, to bomb the camp, but the man in charge of the military airfield of Nohra ignored the order. At noon, the *Rapportführer* sent the SS an order to retreat. Towards 2 p.m., as battles raged around the camp, the SS guards abandoned their watchtowers and ran away. The Resistance organization then sent its armed 'troops' to take over the entrance tower and the other watchtowers and to cut the barbed wire. At 3 p.m., the white flag was flying over the tower. According to *The Buchenwald Report* (D.A. Hackett), about 70 SS were taken prisoner; according to Olga Wormser-Migot, there were over 600 and they were locked up in Block 17; there was almost no retaliation.[153] At 3:40 p.m., tanks of the 3rd American division reached the entrance to the camp, apparently guided by Russian escapees.[154] The American Army was preparing a move southwards to encircle Nazi Bavaria, which constituted a kind of 'hideout'.[155] The Americans actually found the first camps of Thuringe by chance: Ohrdruf on 5 April and Dora-Nordhausen on the morning of 11 April; their division had no special detachment for liberating the concentration camps.[156] The first two American officers – believed to be

---

152. For the schedule on liberation day, see C. Bernadac, *La libération des camps: Le dernier jour de notre mort* (Paris: Michel Lafon, 1995), p. 242 ff.; *The Buchenwald Report*, pp. 331–4; C. Hauter, 'La libération du camp de Buchenwald', in Waitz and Klein, *Témoignages strasbourgeois*, p. 125 ff.; Overesch, *Buchenwald und die DDR*, pp. 60–85; and R.H. Abzug, *Inside the Vicious Heart: Americans and the Liberation of Nazi Concentration Camps* (New York/Oxford: Oxford University Press, 1985).
153. Wormser-Migot, *Quand les alliés ouvrirent les portes*, p. 184.
154. Wieviorka, *Déportation et génocide*, p. 79.
155. For the military details, see Abzug, *Inside the Vicious Heart*.
156. Wieviorka, *Déportation et génocide*, p. 78.

Edward E. Tenenbaum and Egon W. Fleck – entered free Buchenwald at 5:30 p.m. The Resistance committee organized itself to administer the camp.

An Event with International Repercussions

Following the impetus of General Eisenhower – supreme commander of the Allied forces, and the senior American official – and alerted by stories of atrocities that were uncovered in Ohrdruf and in Buchenwald, others arrived quickly at Thuringe. Generals Patton, Bradley and Eisenhower arrived in Buchenwald on 13 April, only 48 hours after the camp's liberation. Important visitors and journalists followed in the next month. Urgently notified by Eisenhower, the British Prime Minister, Churchill, sent a multiparty commission of ten parliamentary delegates who arrived on 12 April. On 24 April, a bipartisan committee of the American Congress, six senators and six congressmen, arrived, followed by delegations of journalists, religious leaders and American trade union leaders. On 26 April, the United Nations Commission for War Crimes sent a 13-member delegation of different nationalities. France had already sent a special delegation, for which Marcel Paul and Colonel Manhès, former inmates and Resistance fighters of Buchenwald, served as guides.

On 16 April, the American Army forced some local middle-class Germans from Weimar to go to the site. The tour of the camp included the crematorium, its basement (where torture and hangings had been carried out), Block 46 (where typhus trials on human guinea pigs were conducted), and the objects made from tattooed, tanned human skin (a speciality from the time of *Kommandant* Koch and his wife, Ilse). At that date, corpses were still piled up in the camp's alleys.[157]

General Eisenhower thought it would be a good idea for as many soldiers as possible to visit the liberated camps, and told Bradley, in words that have since become famous: 'If the

---

157. 'Journal d'Ernst Thape', in Overesch, *Buchenwald und die DDR*, p. 108.

American soldier does not know what he fights for, he will at least now know what he fights against.'[158] Later, in officer training in the USA, he made the work of psychologist Bruno Bettelheim, *Survivre* [To Survive], compulsory reading. The 'camp tourism' degenerated very quickly into voyeurism, and while inmates were subject to strict quarantine and others were still dying, some visitors behaved as if they were in a zoo. On 9 May 1945, General Bradley ordered an end to the visits. The dead were buried; the survivors repatriated or hospitalized. There was nothing left to see.

---

158. Wieviorka, *Déportation et génocide*, p. 78.

Bibliography

Abadi, Odette, *Terre de détresse: Birkenau–Bergen-Belsen* (Paris: L'Harmattan, 1995).

Abzug, Robert H., *Inside the Vicious Heart: Americans and the Liberation of the Nazi Concentration Camps* (New York/Oxford: Oxford University Press, 1985).

Adler, H.G., *Theresienstadt, 1941–1945: Das Antlitz einer Zwangsgemeinschaft*, 2nd edn (Tübingen: Mohr, 1960).

Adler, H.G., Langbein, Hermann and Lingens-Reiner, Ella (eds), *Auschwitz, Zeugnisse und Berichte* (Hamburg: Europäische Verlagsanstalt, 1962).

Alcan, Louise, *Sans armes et sans bagages* (Limoges: Les imprimés d'art, 1947).

Améry, Jean [Hans Meyer], *Par-delà le crime et le châtimen: Essai pour surmonter l'insurmontable* (Paris: Actes Sud, 1995).

Amicale des Déportés d'Auschwitz et des Camps de Haute-Silésie (eds), *Marseilles, Vichy et les nazis. Le temps des rafles. La déportation des juifs* (Marseilles: Amicale des Déportés d'Auschwitz et des Camps de Haute-Silésie, 1993).

Antelme, Robert, *L'espèce humaine*, 2nd edn (Paris: Gallimard, Tel, 1978).

Apitz, Bruno, *Nackt unter Wölfen* (Roman: Halle/MDV, 1958).

Auschwitz in den Augen der SS: Rudolf Höss, Perry Broad, Johann Paul Kremer (Auschwitz: Staatliches Museum Auschwitz/Interpress, 1992).

Barnavi, Elie, *Une histoire moderne d'Israël*, 2nd edn (Paris: Flammarion/Champs, 1988).

Bauer, Yehuda, *Juifs à vendre?* (Paris: Liana Levi, 1996).

——, 'The Death-Marches, January–May 1945', in *The Nazi Holocaust*, Vol. 9 (Westport, CT/London: Meckler, 1989).

Beller, Steven, *Vienna and the Jews 1867–1939: A Cultural History* (Cambridge: Camabridge University Press, 1990).

Benoist-Méchin, Jacques, *Soixante jours qui ébranlèrent l'Occident (10 mai–10 juillet 1940)*, 2nd edn (Paris: Laffont/'Bouquins', 1981).

Bernadac, Christian, *Le Médecins de l'impossible* (Paris: France-Empire, 1968).

——, *Les Médecins maudits*, 2nd edn (Paris: France-Empire, 1985).

——, *La libération des camps: Le dernier jour de notre mort* (Paris: Michel Lafon, 1995).

Bettelheim, Bruno, *Survivre* (Paris: Laffont, 1979).

Billig, Joseph, *Les Camps de concentration dans l'économie du Reich hitlérien* (Paris: CDJC/PUF, 1973).

Borkin, Joseph, *L'I.G. Farben, ou la puissance, les crimes et la chute d'une entreprise multinationale et nationaliste* (Paris: Alta, 1979).

Borwicz, Michel, *Écrits des condamnés à mort sous l'occupation nazie (1939–1945)*, 2nd edn (Paris: Gallimard/Folio, 1996).

Braun, Helmut, *Rose Ausländer: Materialien zu Leben und Werk* (Frankfurt-am Main: Fischer, 1992).

Bulawko, Henry, *Les Jeux de la mort et de l'espoir: Auschwitz-Jaworzno. Auschwitz 50 ans après* (Paris: Montogueil, 1993).

Burrin, Philip, *Hitler et les Juifs: Genèse d'un génocide* (Paris: Seuil, 1989).

Catalogue of Camps and Prisons in Germany and German-Occupied Territories, September 1939–May 1945 (Arolsen: International Tracing Service, 1949).

Cayrol, Jean, *Nuit et Brouillard* (Paris: Rayard, 1997).

Celan, Paul, *Mohn und Gedächtnis* (Stuttgart: Deutsche Verlags Anstalt, 1952).

Cohen, Robert S. and Schnelle (eds), *Cognition and Fact: Materials on Ludwik Fleck* (Boston: D. Reidel Publishing Company, 1986).

Contribution à l'histoire du KL Auschwitz, 2 Vols (Oswiecim: Éditions du Musée d'État à Oswiecim, 1978).

Czech, Danuba, *Kalendarium der Ereignisse im Konzentrationslager Auschwitz-Birkenau 1939–1945* (Hamburg: Rowohlt, 1989).

Dawidowicz, Lucy S., *The War against the Jews, 1933–1945* (New York: Bantam, 1986).

Delbo, Charlotte, *Auschwitz et après*, 3 Vols (Paris: Minuit, 1970–71).

Duras, Margaret, *La Douleur* (Paris: POL, 1985).

Feig, Konnilyn G., *Hitler's Death Camps: The Sanity of Madness* (New York/London: Holmes & Meier, 1979).

Felstiner, John, *Paul Celan: Poet, Survivor, Jew* (London: Yale University Press, 1995).

Fénelon, Fania, *Sursis pour l'orchestre* (Paris: Stock, 1976).

Fischer, Frans, *L'Enfer de Breendonck* (Brussels: Labor, n.d.)

Fontaine, André, *Le Camp d'étrangers des Milles* (Aix-en-Provence: Edisud, 1989).

Francès-Rousseau, Pierre, *Intact aux yeux du monde* (Paris: Hachette, 1987).

Frankl, Viktor E., *Ein Psychologe erlebt das Konzentrationslager: Trotzdem ja zum Leben sagen*, 2nd edn (Munich: dtv, 1996).

Geve, Thomas, *Es gibt hier keine Kinder: Auschwitz, Gross-Rosen, Buchenwald* (Göttingen: Wallstein, 1997).

Gilbert, Martin, *Auschwitz and the Allies*, 2nd edn (London: Mandarin, 1991).

——, *The Dent Atlas of Jewish History* (London: Dent, 1993).

——, *Endlösung: Die Vertreibung und Vernichtung der Juden. Ein Atlas*, 2nd edn (Hamburg: Rowohlt, 1995).

Gold, Hugo (ed.), *Geschichte der Juden in der Bukowina*, 2 Vols (Tel Aviv: Olamenu, 1958).

Graffard, Sylvie and Tristan, Léon, *Les Bibelforscher et le nazisme, 1933–1945* (Paris: Tirésias, 1990).

Greif, Gideon, *Wir weinten tränenlos: Augenzeugenberichte der jüdischen 'Sonderkommandos' in Auschwitz* (Kö/Weimar/Wien, Böhlau, 1995).

Grynberg, Anne, *Les Camps de la honte: Les internés juifs dans les camps français, 1939–1944* (Paris: La Découverte, 1991).

Guillet, Marcel, 'Gross-Rosen', unedited ms of testimonies, Paris: Centre de Documentation Juive Contemporaine.

Hackett, David A. (trans./ed.) *The Buchenwald Report [Bericht über das Konzentrationslager Buchenwald bei Weimar, April–May 1945]* (Boulder, CA/San Francisco, CA/Oxford, Westview Press, 1995).

Haffner, Désiré, *Aspects pathologiques du camp de concentration d'Auschwitz-Birkenau* (Tours: Imprimerie Union coopérative, 1946).

Hamburger Institut für Sozialforschung (eds), *Die Auschwitz-Hefte: Texte der polnischen Zeitschrift* Przeglad Lekarski *über historische, psychische und medizinische Aspekte des Lebens und Sterbens in Auschwitz* (Hamburg: Rogner u. Bernhard, 1995).

Hautval, Adélaïde, *Médecine et crimes contre l'Humanité: Témoignage* (Paris: Actes Sud, 1991).

Heinemann, Jean, *Auschwitz: Mein Bericht* (Berlin: Das Neue Berlin, 1995).

Hilberg, Raul, *La Destruction des Juifs d'Europe* (Paris: Fayard, 1988).

——, *Perpertrators, Victims, Bystanders: The Jewish Catastrophe, 1933–1945* (New York: Harper Collins, 1992).

Höss, Rudolf, *Kommandant in Auschwitz: Autobiographische Aufzeichnungen*, 2nd edn, Martin Broszat (ed.) (Munich: dtv, 1963).

Israel, A., *Le passage du témoin: Portraits et témoignages de rescapés des camps de concentration et d'extermination nazis* (Brussels: La Lettre volée/Fondation Auschwitz, 1995).

Karas, Joza, *La Musique à Terezin, 1941–1945* (Paris: Gallimard, 1993).

Kershaw, Ian, *Hitler: Essai sur le charisme en politique* (Paris: Gallimard, 1995).

Kielar, Wielsaw, *Anus Mundi: Fünf Jahre in Auschwitz*, 2nd edn (Frankfurt-am-Main: Fischer, 1994).

Klarsfeld, Serge and Steinberg, Maxime, *Mémorial de la déportation de juifs de Belgique* (Brussels: Union des déportés juifs en Belgique et filles et fils de la déportation/New York: Beate Klarsfeld Foundation, 1982).

Kleiger, Bernard, *Le chemin que nous avons fait (Reportages surhumains)* (Brussels: Beka, n.d.).

Kogon, Eugen, *L'État SS: Le système des camps de concentration allemands*, 2nd edn (Paris: Seuil/Points Histoire, 1993).

——, Langbein, Hermann and Rückerl, Adalbert, *Les chambres à gaz: secret d'État* (Paris: Seuil/Points Histoire, 1987).

Laks, Simon, *Mélodies d'Auschwitz* (Paris: Cerf, 1991).

Laks, Simon and Coudy, René, *Musiques d'un autre monde* (Paris: Mercure de France, 1948).

Langbein, Hermann, *Menschen in Auschwitz* (Wien: Europa-Verlag, 1972).

——, *La Résistance dans les camps de concentration natio-naux-socialistes, 1928–1945* (Paris: Fayard, 1981).

——, *Der Auschwitz-Prozess: Eine Dokumentation*, 2 Vols, 2nd edn (Frankfurt: Neue Kritik, 1995).

Laska, Vera, *Nazism, Resistance and Holocaust in World War II: A Bibliography* (Metuchen/London: Scarecrow, 1985).

Lettich, André A.D., *Trente-quatre mois dans les camps de concentration* (Tours: Imprimerie Union coopérative, 1946).

Levi, Primo, *Se questo è un uomo* (Torino: Einaudi, 1958).

——, *I sommersi e i salvati*, 3rd edn (Torino: Einaudi, 1994).

Liddell, Hart, *Histoire de la seconde guerre modiale*, 2nd edn (Brussels: Marabout, 1985).

Lifton, Robert J., *Les Médecins nazis: Le meurtre médical et la psychologie du génocide* (Paris: Laffont, 1989).

Lumans, Valdis O., *Himmler's Auxiliaries: The* Volksdeutsche Mittelstelle *and the German National Minorities in Europe, 1933–1945* (Chapel Hill, NC: University of North Carolina Press, 1993).

Mannarino, Damien, 'La Mémoire déportée: Témoignages des déportés des camps nazis dans l'édition en langue française, 1944–1993', unedited ms of testimonies, Paris: Centre de Documentation Juive Contemporaine.

Manson, Jean (ed.), *FNDIR/UNADIF: Leçon de Ténèbras. Résistants et déportées* (Paris: Plon, 1995).

Marrus, Michael, *L'Holocauste dans l'Histoire*, 2nd edn (Paris: Flammarion/Champs, 1994).

Moldawa, Mieczyslow, *Gross-Rosen: Oboz koncentraji na Slasku.*

Müller, Filip, *Trois ans dans une chambre à gaz d'Auschwitz* (Paris: Pygmalion, 1980).

Münch, Hans, *Hunger und Lebenserwartung in Auschwitz* (1947).

[Nivromont, Pierre] and Epelbaum, Didier, *Matricule 186140: Histoire d'un combat* (Paris: Hagège, 1997).

Nyiszli, Miklos, *Auschwitz: A Doctor's Eyewitness Account* (New York: Arcade, 1993).

Overesch, Manfred, *Buchenwald und die DDR, oder die Suche nach Selbstlegitimation* (Göttingen: Vandenhoeck & Ruprecht, 1995).

Peiffert, Sabine and Jouin, Laurent, 'Le camp d'internement de Compiègne', *Revue Historique*, 598 (1996).

Piper, Franciszek, *Arbeitseinsatz der Häftlinge aus dem KL Auschwitz* (Oswiecim: Éditions du Musèe d'État à Oswiecim, 1995).

Poliakov, Léon, *Auschwitz* (Paris: Julliard/Archives, 1964).

Pozner, Vladimir, *Descente aux Enfers: Récits de déportés et de SS d'Auschwitz* (Paris: Juillard, 1980).

Pressac, Jean-Claude, *Les Crématoires d'Auschwitz: La machinerie du meurtre de masse* (Paris: CNRS-Éditions, 1993).

——, 'Enquête sur les chambres à gaz', in *Auschwitz: la solution finale : Les collections de l'Histoire* (Paris: Les collections de l'Histoire, 1998), pp. 34–9.

Reifer, Manfred, 'Geschichte der Juden in der Bukowina, 1919–1944', in Hugo Gold (ed.), *Geschichte der Juden in der Bukowina*, 2 Vols (Te Aviv: Olamenu Publishers, 1958/1962), pp. 1–26.

Reitlinger, Gerald, *Die Endlösung: Hitlers Versuch der Ausrottung der Juden Europas, 1939–1945* (Berlin: Colloquium, 1992).

Rousset, David, *Les Jours de notre mort*, 2nd edn (Paris: Hachette/Pluriel, 1993).

——, *L'Univers concentrationnaire*, 2nd edn (Paris: Hachette/Pluriel, 1993).

Ruby, Marcel, *Le Livre de la déportation* (Paris: Laffont, 1995).

Schnitzler, Arthur, *Der Weg ins Freie* (Frankfurt-am-Main: Fischer Taschenbuch Verlag, 1978).

Sehn, Jan, *Konzentrationslager Oswiecim-Brzezinka* (Varsovie: Wydawnictwo Prawnicze, 1957).

Semprun, Jorge, *Le Grand Voyage* (Paris: Gallimard, 1963).

——, *Quel beau dimanche!* (Paris: Grasset, 1980).

——, *L'Écriture ou la vie* (Paris: Gallimard, 1994).

Semprun, Jorge and Wiesel, Elie, *Se taire est impossible* (Paris: Arte/Mille et une nuit, 1995).

Shirer, William L., *Le Troisième Reiche: des origines à la chute* (Paris: Livre de Poche, 1966).

Sofsky, Wolfgang, *L'Organisation de la terreur: Les camps de concentration* (Paris: Calmann-Lévy, 1995).

Sprenger, Isabelle, '"Erabrmungloses Schweigen": Bevölkerung und Konzentrationslager in Gross-Rosen (Niederschlesien)', *Die Alte Stadt*, 20 (1993), pp. 377–80.

——, '"Der Judenblock bleibt stehen": Jüdische Häftlinge in der ersten Kriegshälfte im Konzentrationslager Gross-Rosen in Schleisen', *Menora*, 5 (1994), pp. 415–33.

Steinberg, Hermann, *Zur Geschichte der Juden in Czernowitz* (Tel Aviv: Olamenu, n.d.).

Steinberg, Lucien, *La Révolte des Justes: Les Juifs contre Hitler 1933–1945* (Paris: Fayard, 1970).

Steinberg, Maxime, *L'Étoile et le Fusil*, Vol. 1, *La Question juive (1940–1942)*, (Brussels: Vie ouvrière, 1983).

——, *L'Étoile et le Fusil*, Vol. 2, *1942: Les cent jours de la déportation des Juifs de Belgique* (Brussels: Vie ouvrière, 1984).

——, *L'Étoile et le Fusil*, Vol. 3, *La Traque de Juifs 1942–1944*, 2 Vols (Brussels: Vie ouvrière, 1986).

——, 'La *Shoah* en Belgique', *Les Cahiers de la Shoah*, 3 (1996).

Steinberg, Maxime and Verhamme, A., 'Assemblé de la Commission communautaire française', in M. Steinberg and A. Verhamme (eds), *Le fort de Breendonk: Le camp de terreur nazie en Belgique pendant la deuxième guerre mondiale* (Brussels: DOB, 1997).

Steinberg, Paul, *Chroniques d'ailleurs: Récit* (Paris: Ramsay, 1996).

Uris, Leon, *QB VII* (New York: Ballantine Books, 1959).

Vallet, Guillaume, 'Étude de témoignages oraux d'anciens déportés du camp de Buna-Monowitz', unedited ms, Paris: Centre de Documentation Juive Contemporaine.

Vrba, Rudolf and Bestic, Alan, *Je me suis évadé d'Auschwitz* (Paris: Ramsay, 1988).

Waitz, Robert and Klein, Marc (eds), *De l'Université aux camps de concentration: Témoignages strasbourgeois*, 2nd edn (Strasbourg: Presses Universitaires, 1989).

Weissmann Klein, Gerda, *All But My Life*, 2nd edn (New York: Hill & Wang, 1987).

Wellers, Georges, *Un Juif sous Vichy*, 2nd edn (Paris: Tirélas, 1991).

Wiesel, Élie, *La Nuit*, 2nd edn (Paris: Minuit, 1988).

Wieviorka, Annette, *Déportation et génocide: Entre la mémoire et l'oubli* (Paris: Plon, 1992).

Wormser, Olga and Michel, Henri (eds), *Tragédie de la Déportation 1940–1945: Témoignages de survivants des camps de concentration allemands* (Paris: Hachette, 1955).

Wormser-Migot, Olga, *Quand les alliés ouvrirent les portes: Le dernier acte de la tragédie de la déportation* (Paris: Laffont, 1965).

Wyman, David S., *L'Abandon des Juifs: Les Américains et la solution finale* (Paris: Flammarion, 1987).

Yahil, Leni, *The Holocaust: The Fate of European Jewry, 1932–1945* (New York: Oxford University Press, 1991).

Zywulska, Krystina, *Tanz, Mädchen...Vom Warschauer Getto nach Auschwitz: Ein Überlebensbericht* (Munich: dtv, 1988).